REVOLUTIONS
IN
RUSSIA AND CHINA
Revised Second Edition

REVOLUTIONS IN RUSSIA AND CHINA

Revised Second Edition

Edited by

June Grasso

Michael Kort

William Tilchin

John Zawacki

College of General Studies
Boston University

McGraw-Hill, Inc.
College Custom Series

New York St. Louis San Francisco Auckland Bogotá
Caracas Lisbon London Madrid Mexico Milan Montreal
New Delhi Paris San Juan Singapore Sydney Tokyo Toronto

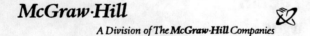

McGraw·Hill
A Division of The McGraw·Hill Companies

REVOLUTIONS IN RUSSIA & CHINA

2 3 4 5 6 7 8 9 0 HAM HAM 9 0 9 8 7

ISBN 0-07-021776-9

Cover photographs of Vladimir I. Lenin and Mao Tse-tung courtesy of Bettmann.
Editor: M. A. Hollander
Cover Design: Jeff Boyd
Printer/Binder: HAMCO/NETPUB Corporation

Contents

Preface

This book focuses on the varieties of modernization and revolution in Russia and China. Both revolutions were inspired by Marxist ideas and each has had a significant effect on the world's population. In addition to their importance and magnitude, there are many reasons to examine the Russian and Chinese revolutionary experience. One key reason is to seek to understand the nature, the origins, the historical and socio-economic context, the meaning and the consequences of these particular revolutions. Another is to comprehend how Marxism, a theory of economic and social change, was translated into concrete political programs. Therefore, the book will trace how the Russian leaders from Lenin to Gorbachev altered Marx's ideas to fit conditions in Russia and how, in turn, the Chinese leader Mao Zedong changed Lenin's and Stalin's ideas to suit the Chinese historical context.

The means by which the editors hope to achieve their goals are primarily of two kinds: (1) speeches and reports by leaders of revolutions and other important participants and (2) critiques by scholars of Russian and Chinese revolutionary tradition. The book is interdisciplinary in nature, and it draws considerably from such fields as history, sociology, political science, and biography.

The editors would like to acknowledge the editorial assistance, advice and key contributions of Jay Corrin and Dennis Fischman. Special thanks to Margaret Hollander.

June Grasso
Michael Kort
William Tilchin
John Zawacki

RUSSIA, USSR
AND THE
COMMONWEALTH OF
INDEPENDENT STATES (CIS)

1. Konstantin Pobedonostsev

REFLECTIONS OF A RUSSIAN STATESMAN

The New Democracy

What is this freedom by which so many minds are agitated, which inspires so many insensate actions, so many wild speeches, which leads the people so often to misfortune? In the democratic sense of the word, freedom is the right of political power, or, to express it otherwise, the right to participate in the government of the State. This universal aspiration for a share in government has no constant limitations, and seeks no definite issue, but incessantly extends... For ever extending its base, the new Democracy now aspires to universal suffrage—a fatal error, and one of the most remarkable in the history of mankind. By this means, the political power so passionately demanded by Democracy would be shattered into a number of infinitesimal bits, of which each citizen acquires a single one. What will he do with it, then? How will he employ it? In the result it has undoubtedly been shown that in the attainment of this aim Democracy violates its sacred formula of "Freedom indissolubly joined with Equality." It is shown that this apparently equal distribution of "freedom" among all involves the total destruction of equality. Each vote, representing an inconsiderable fragment of power, by itself signifies nothing; an aggregation of votes alone has a relative value. The result may be likened to the general meeting of shareholders in public companies. By themselves individuals are ineffective, but he who controls a number of these fragmentary forces is master of all power, and directs all decisions and dispositions. We may well ask in what consists the superiority of Democracy. Everywhere the strongest man becomes master of the State; sometimes a fortunate and resolute general, sometimes a monarch or administrator with knowledge, dexterity, a clear plan of action, and a determined will. In a Democracy, the real rulers are the dexterous manipulators of votes, with their placemen, the mechanics who so skillfully operate the hidden springs which move the puppets in the arena of democratic elections. Men of this kind are ever ready with loud speeches lauding equality; in reality, they rule the people as any despot or military dictator might rule it. The extension of the right to participate in elections is regarded as progress and as the conquest of freedom by democratic theorists, who hold that the more numerous the participants in political rights, the greater is the probability that all will employ this right in the interests of the public welfare, and for the increase of the freedom of the people. Experience proves a very different thing. The history of mankind bears witness that the most necessary and fruitful reforms—the most durable measures—emanated from the supreme will of statesmen, or from a minority enlightened by lofty ideas and deep knowledge, and that, on the contrary, the extension of the representative principle is accompanied by an abasement of political ideas and the vulgarisation of opinions in the mass of the electors. It shows also that this extension—in great States—was inspired by secret aims to

Translated by Robert C. Long, published in London by The Richards Press (John Baker Publishing, Ltd.). US edition published by the University of Michigan Press in 1965.

the centralisation of power, or led directly to dictatorship. In France, universal suffrage was suppressed with the end of the Terror, and was re-established twice merely to affirm the autocracy of the two Napoleons. In Germany, the establishment of universal suffrage served merely to strengthen the high authority of a famous statesman who had acquired popularity by the success of his policy. What its ultimate consequences will be, Heaven only knows....

Organisation and bribery—these are the two mighty instruments which are employed with such-success for the manipulation of the mass of electors....

The Great Falsehood of Our Time

That which is founded on falsehood cannot be right. Institutions founded on false principles cannot be other than false themselves. This truth has been demonstrated by the bitter experience of ages and generations.

Among the falsest of political principles is the principle of the sovereignty of the people, the principle that all power issues from the people, and is based upon the national will—a principle which has unhappily become more firmly established since the time of the French Revolution. Thence proceeds the theory of Parliamentarism, which, up to the present day, has deluded much of the so-called "intelligence," and unhappily infatuated certain foolish Russians. It continues to maintain its hold on many minds with the obstinacy of a narrow fanaticism, although every day its falsehood is exposed more clearly to the world.

In what does the theory of Parliamentarism consist? It is supposed that the people in its assemblies makes its own laws, and elects responsible officers to execute its will. Such is the ideal conception....

Let us look at the practice. Even in the classic countries of Parliamentarism it would satisfy not one of the conditions enumerated. The elections in no way express the will of the electors. The popular representatives are in no way restricted by the opinions of their constituents, but are guided by their own views and considerations, modified by the tactics of their opponents. In reality, ministers are autocratic, and they rule, rather than are ruled by, Parliament. They attain power, and lose power, not by virtue of the will of the people, but through immense personal influence, or the influence of a strong party which places them in power, or drives them from it. They dispose of the force and resources of the nation at will, they grant immunities and favours, they maintain a multitude of idlers at the expense of the people, and they fear no censure while they enjoy the support in Parliament of a majority which they maintain by the distribution of bounties from the rich tables which the State has put at their disposal. In reality, the ministers are as irresponsible as the representatives of the people. Mistakes, abuse of power, and arbitrary acts, are of daily occurrence, yet how often do we hear of the grave responsibility of a minister? It may be once in fifty years a minister is tried for his crimes, with a result contemptible when compared with the celebrity gained by the solemn procedure.

Were we to attempt a true definition of Parliament, we should say that Parliament is an institution serving for the satisfaction of the personal ambition, vanity, and self-interest of its members. The institution of Parliament is indeed one of the greatest illustrations of human delusion....

On the pediment of this edifice is inscribed: "All for the Public Good." This is no more than a lying formula: Parliamentarism is the triumph of egoism—its highest expression. All here is calculated to the service of the ego. In the Parliamentary fiction, the representative, as such, surrenders his personality, and serves as the embodiment of the will and opinions of his constituents; in reality, the constituents in the very act of election surrender all their rights in favour of their representative. In his addresses and speeches the candidate for election lays constant emphasis upon this fiction; he reiterates his phrases about the public welfare; his is nothing but a servant of the people; he will forget himself and his interests for its sake. But these are words, words, words alone—temporary steps of the staircase by which he climbs to the height he aspires to, and which he casts away when he needs them no longer. Then, so far from beginning to work for society, society becomes the instrument of his aims. To him his constituents are a herd, an aggregation of votes, and he, as their possessor, resembles those rich nomads whose flocks constitute their whole capital—the foundation of their power and eminence in society. Thus is developed to perfection the art of playing on the instincts and passions of the mass, in order to attain the personal ends of ambition and power. The people loses all importance for its representative, until the time arrives when it is to be played upon again; then false and flattering and lying phrases are lavished as before; some are suborned by bribery, others terrified by threats—the long chain of maneuvers spun which forms an invariable factor of Parliamentarism. Yet this electoral farce continues to deceive humanity, and to be regarded as an institution which crowns the edifice of State. Poor humanity!...

On the day of polling few give their votes intelligently: these are the individual, influential electors whom it has been worth while to convince in private. The mass of the electors, after the practice of the herd, votes for one of the candidates nominated by the committees. Not one exactly knows the man, or considers his character, his capacity, his convictions; all vote merely because they have heard his name so often. It would be vain to struggle against this herd. If a level-headed elector wished to act intelligently in such a grave affair, and not to give way to the violence of the committee, he would have to abstain altogether, or to give his vote for his candidate according to his conviction. However he might act, he could not prevent the election of the candidate favoured by the mass of frivolous, indifferent, and prejudiced electors.

In theory, the elected candidate must be the favourite of the majority; in fact, he is the favourite of a minority, sometimes very small, but representing an organised force, while the majority, like sand, has no coherence, and is therefore incapable of resisting the clique and the faction. In theory, the election favours the intelligent and capable; in reality, it favours the pushing and impudent. It might be thought that education, experience, conscientiousness in work, and wisdom in affairs, would be essential requirements in the candidate; in reality, whether these qualities exist or not, they are in no way needed in the struggle of the election, where the essential qualities are audacity, a combination of impudence and oratory, and even some vulgarity, which invariably acts on the masses; modesty, in union with delicacy of feeling and thought, is worth nothing....

Such is the complicated mechanism of the Parliamentary farce; such is the great political lie which dominates our age. By the theory of Parliamentarism, the rational majority must rule; in practice, the party is ruled by five or six of its leaders who exercise all power. In theory, decisions are controlled by clear arguments in the course of Parliamentary debates; in practice, they in no wise depend from debates, but are determined by the wills of the leaders and the promptings of personal interest. In theory, the representatives of the people consider only the public welfare; in practice, their first consideration is their own advancement, and the interests of their friends. In theory, they must be the best citizens; in practice, they are the most ambitious and impudent. In theory, the elector gives his vote for his candidate because he knows him and trusts him; in practice, the elector gives his vote for a man whom he seldom knows, but who has been forced on him by the speeches of an interested party. In theory, Parliamentary business is directed by experience, good sense, and unselfishness; in practice, the chief motive powers are a firm will, egoism, and eloquence....

Trial By Jury...

After tests extending over many years, in every country where trial by jury modelled upon the English system has been established, the question has arisen by what it is to be replaced to avoid the inconsequence of the judgments of which it has been the cause. Such difficulties multiply daily, and have permeated even those States where there is a strong judicial system, the product of centuries of experience and of rigorous discipline in science and practice.

It is not hard to understand the consequences of popular justice in those younger States which lack these saving elements—where, instead, we find an innumerable host of advocates who, impelled by ambition and selfishness, quickly attain that remarkable skill in the arts of casuistry and verbal subtlety needed to influence a jury of incongruous constitution, chosen at random, or with ulterior design, by whom the elements of justice are inaccessible, and the necessity for subjecting to analysis the mass of facts requiring consideration ignored. Behind these comes the motley crowd, attracted as to a play, to dissipate the monotony begotten of idleness—the mob, in the phraseology of idealists, denominated "the people." It is not to be wondered at that with such conditions the consequence so often corresponds with the judgment which I have taken from Sir Henry Maine, that "the modern jury, in the majority of cases, surrenders its verdict to the persuasiveness of one or other of the counsel who have been retained to address it."...

The Press

From the day that man first fell falsehood has ruled the world—ruled it in human speech, in the practical business of life, in all its relations and institutions. But never did the Father of Lies spin such webs of falsehood of every kind, as in this restless age when we hear so many falsehoods uttered everywhere on Truth. With the growing complexity of social problems increases the number of relations and institutions pervaded with falsehood through and through. At every step appears some splendid edifice bearing the legend, "Here is Truth." Do you enter— you tread on falsehoods at every step. Would you expose the falsehoods which have angered you, the world will turn on you with anger greater still, and bid you trust and preach that this is truth, and truth unassailable.

Thus we are bidden to believe that the judgments of newspapers and periodicals, the judgments of the so-called Press, are the expression of public opinion. This, too, is a falsehood. The Press is one of the falsest institutions of our time....

In our age the judgment of others has assumed an organised form, and calls itself Public Opinion. Its organ and representative is the Press. In truth, the importance of the Press is immense, and may be regarded as the most characteristic fact of our time—more characteristic even than our remarkable discoveries and inventions in the realm of technical science. No government, no law, no custom can withstand its destructive activity when, from day to day, through the course of years, the Press repeats and disseminates among the people its condemnations of institutions or of men.

What is the secret of this strength? Certainly not the novelties and sensations with which the newspaper is filled, but its declared policy—the political and philosophical ideas propagated in its articles, the selection and classification of its news and rumours, and the peculiar illumination which it casts upon them. The newspaper has usurped the position of judicial observer of the events of the day; it judges not only the actions and words of men, but affects a knowledge of their unexpressed opinions, their intentions, and their enterprises; it praises and condemns at discretion; it incites some, threatens others; drags to the pillory one, and others exalts as idols to be adored and examples worthy of the emulation of all. In the name of Public Opinion it bestows rewards on some, and punishes others with the severity of excommunication. The question naturally occurs: Who are these representatives of this terrible power, Public Opinion? Whence is derived their right and authority to rule in the name of the community, to demolish existing institutions, and to proclaim new ideas of ethics and legislation?...

Any vagabond babbler or unacknowledged genius, any enterprising tradesman, with his own money or with the money of others, may found a newspaper, even a great newspaper.... . Experience proves that the most contemptible persons—retired money-lenders, Jewish factors, newsvendors, and bankrupt gamblers—may found newspapers, secure the services of talented writers, and place their editions on the market as organs of public opinion. The healthy taste of the public is not to be relied upon. The great mass of readers, idlers for the most part, is ruled less by a few healthy instincts than by a base and despicable hankering for idle amusement; and the support of the people may be secured by any editor who provides for the satisfaction of these hankerings, for the love of scandal, and for intellectual pruriency of the basest kinds.... .

How often have superficial and unscrupulous journalists paved the way for revolution, fomented irritation into enmity, and brought about desolating wars! For conduct such as this a monarch would lose his throne, a minister would be disgraced, impeached, and punished; but the journalist stands dry above the waters he has disturbed, from the ruin he has caused he rises triumphant, and briskly continues his destructive work.

This is by no means the worst. When a judge has power to dishonour us, to deprive us of our property and of our freedom, he receives his power from the hands of the State only after such prolonged labour and experience as qualify him for his calling. His power is restricted by rigorous laws, his judgments are subject to revision by higher powers, and his sentence may be altered or commuted. The journalist has the fullest power to defame and dishonour me, to injure my material interests, even to restrict my liberty by attacks which force me to leave my place of abode. These judicial powers he has usurped; no higher authority has conferred them upon him; he has never proven by examination his fitness to exercise them; he has in no way shown his trustworthiness or his impartiality; his court is ruled by no formal procedure; and from his judgment there lies no appeal....

It is hard to imagine a despotism more irresponsible and violent than the despotism of printed words. Is it not strange and irrational, then, that those who struggle most for the preservation of this despotism are the impassioned champions of freedom, the ferocious enemies of legal restrictions and of all interference by the established authority....

Public Instruction...

Seduced by the fantasy of universal enlightenment, we misname education a certain sum of knowledge acquired by completing the courses of schools, skilfully elaborated in the studies of pedagogues. Having organised our school thus, we isolate it from life, and secure by force the attendance of children whom we subject to a process of intellectual training in accordance with our programme. But we ignore or forget that the mass of the children whom we educate must earn their daily bread, a labour for which the abstract notions on which our programmes are constructed will be in vain; while in the interests of some imaginary knowledge we withhold that training in productive labour which alone will bear fruit. Such are the results of our complex educational system, and such are the causes of the aversion with which the masses regard our schools, for which they can find no use.

The vulgar conception of education is true enough, but unhappily it is disregarded in the organisation of the modern school. In the popular mind the function of a school is to teach the elements of reading, writing, and arithmetic, and, in union with these, the duty of knowing, loving, and fearing God, of loving our native land, and of honouring our parents. These are the elements of knowledge, and the sentiments which together form the basis of conscience in man, and give to him the moral strength needed for the preservation of his equilibrium in life, for the maintenance of struggle with the evil impulses of his nature and with the evil sentiments and temptations of the mind. It is an unhappy day when education tears the child from the surroundings in which he first acquired the elements of his future calling, those exercises of his early years through which he acquires, almost unconsciously, the taste and capacity for work. The boy who wishes to become a bachelor or a master or arts must begin his studies at a certain age, and in due time pass through a given course of knowledge; but the vast majority of children must learn to live by the work of their hands. For such work physical training is needed from the earliest age. To close the door to such preparation, that time may be saved for the teaching of schools, is to place a burden upon the lives of the masses who have to struggle for their daily bread, and to shackle in the family the natural development of those economic forces which together constitute the capital of the commonwealth. The sailor qualifies for his calling by spending his boyhood on the sea; the miner prepares for his work by early years spent in the subterranean passages of mines. To the agriculturist it is even more essential that he shall become accustomed to his future work, that he may learn to love it in childhood, in the presence of nature, beside his herds and his plough, in the midst of his fields and his meadows.

Yet we waste our time discussing courses for elementary schools and obligatory programmes which are to be the bases of a finished education....

But few reflect that by tearing the child from the domestic hearth for such a lofty destiny, they deprive his parents of a productive force which is essential to the maintenance of the home, while by raising before his eyes the mirage of illusory learning they corrupt his mind, and subject it to the temptations of vanity and conceit.

2. Sergei Witte

PROGRAM FOR A COMMERCIAL AND INDUSTRIAL POLICY

Russia remains even at the present essentially an agricultural country. It pays for all its obligations to foreigners by exporting raw materials, chiefly of an agricultural nature, principally grain. It meets its demand for finished goods by imports from abroad. The economic relations of Russia with western Europe are fully comparable to the relations of colonial countries with their metropolises. The latter consider their colonies as advantageous markets in which they can freely sell the products of their labor and of their industry and from which they can draw with a powerful hand the raw materials necessary for them. This is the basis of the economic power of the governments of western Europe, and chiefly for that end do they guard their existing colonies or acquire new ones. Russia was, and to a considerable extent still is, such a hospitable colony for all industrially developed states, generously providing them with the cheap products of her soil and buying dearly the products of their labor. But there is a radical difference between Russia and a colony: Russia is an independent and strong power. She has the right and the strength not to want to be the eternal handmaiden of states which are more developed economically. She should know the price of her raw materials and of the natural riches hidden in the womb of her abundant territories, and she is conscious of the great, not yet fully displayed, capacity for work among her people. She is proud of her great might, by which she jealously guards not only the political but also the economic independence of her empire. She wants to be a metropolis herself. On the basis of the people's labor, liberated from the bonds of serfdom, there began to grow our own national economy, which bids fair to become a reliable counterweight to the domination of foreign industry.

The creation of our own national industry—that is the profound task, both economic and political, from which our protectionist system arises.

From T.H. Von Lave, "Sergei Witte on the Industrialization of Imperial Russia," *Journal of Modern History*, XXVI, pp.61-74. Reprinted with permission of The University of Chicago Press.

3. Father Gapon

PETITION AND LETTER TO THE CZAR

The Petition – January 22, 1905

We, working men and inhabitants of St. Petersburg of various classes, our wives and our children and our helpless old parents, come to Thee, Sire, to seek for truth and defense.

…Destroy the wall between Thyself and Thy people, and let them rule the country together with Thyself. Art Thou not placed there for the happiness of Thy people? But this happiness the officials snatch from our hands. It does not come to us. We get only distress and humiliation. Look without anger, attentively upon our requests. They are directed, not to evil, but to good for us as well as for Thee.

The Letter – after Bloody Sunday.

With naive belief in thee as father of thy people, I was going peacefully to thee with the children of these very people. Thou must have known, thou didst know, this. The innocent blood of workers, their wives and children, lies forever between thee, O soul destroyer and the Russian people. Moral connection between thee and them may never be any more.

From James Mavour, *An Economic History of Russia,* published by E.P. Dutton, 1914, pp. 469, 471, 473.

4. Vladimir I. Lenin

WHAT IS TO BE DONE?

I. Dogmatism and "Freedom of Criticism"....

The case of the Russian Social-Democrats strikingly illustrates the fact observed in the whole of Europe (and long ago observed in German Marxism) that the notorious freedom of criticism implies, not the substitution of one theory by another, but freedom from every complete and thought-out theory; it implies eclecticism and absence of principle. Those who are in the least acquainted with the actual state of our movement cannot but see that the spread of Marxism was accompanied by a certain deterioration of theoretical standards....

Without a revolutionary theory there can be no revolutionary movement. This cannot be insisted upon too strongly at a time when the fashionable preaching of opportunism is combined with absorption in the narrowest forms of practical activity....

II. The Spontaneity of the Masses and Class-Consciousness of Social Democracy....

We said that there *could not yet be* Social-Democratic consciousness among the workers. This consciousness could only be brought to them from without. The history of all countries shows that the working class, exclusively by its own effort, is able to develop only trade-union consciousness, i.e., it may itself realise the necessity for combining in unions, to fight against the employers and to strive to compel the government to pass necessary labour legislation, etc.

The theory of Socialism, however, grew out of the philosophic, historical and economic theories that were elaborated by the educated representatives of the propertied classes, the intellectuals. The founders of modern scientific Socialism, Marx and Engels, themselves belonged to the bourgeois intelligentsia. Similarly, in Russia, the theoretical doctrine of Social-Democracy arose quite independently of the spontaneous growth of the labour movement; it arose as a natural and inevitable outcome of the development of ideas among the revolutionary Socialist intelligentsia. At the time of which we are speaking, i.e., the middle of the nineties, this doctrine not only represented the completely formulated programme of the Emancipation of Labour group but had already won the adhesion of the majority of the revolutionary youth in Russia....

...subservience to the spontaneity of the labour movement, the belittling of the role of "the conscious element," of the role of Social-Democracy, *means, whether one likes it or not, growth of influence of bourgeois ideology among the workers*. All those who talk about "exaggerating the importance of ideology," about exaggerating the role of the conscious elements, etc., imagine that the pure and simple labour movement can work out an independent ideology for

From Vladimir I Lenin: *Collected Works*, 4th edition (Moscow: Progress Publishers, (1964) Vol.5, pp. 14-24, 352-355, 369-370. Reprinted with permission of International Publishers Co., Inc.

itself, if only the workers "take their fate out of the hands of the leaders." But in this they are profoundly mistaken....

IV. The Primitiveness of the Economists and the Organization of Revolutionists....

C. Organisation of Workers, and Organisation of Revolutionists

It is only natural that a Social-Democrat who conceives the political struggle as being identical with the "economic struggle against the employers and the government," should conceive "organisation of revolutionists" as being more or less identical with "organisation of workers." And this, in fact, is what actually happens; so that when we talk about organisation, we literally talk in different tongues....

The political struggle carried on by the Social-Democrats is far more extensive and complex than the economic struggle the workers carry on against the employers and the government. Similarly (and indeed for that reason), the organisation of revolutionary Social-Democrats must inevitably *differ* from the organisations of the workers designed for the latter struggle. The workers' organisations must in the first place be trade organisations; secondly, they must be as wide as possible; and thirdly, they must be as public as conditions will allow (here, of course, I have only autocratic Russia in mind). On the other hand, the organisations of revolutionists must be comprised first and foremost of people whose profession is that of revolutionists (that is why I speak of organisations of *revolutionists*, meaning revolutionary Social-Democrats). As this is the common feature of the members of such an organisation, *all distinctions as between workers and intellectuals*, and certainly distinctions of trade and profession, must be dropped. Such an organisation must of necessity be not too extensive and as secret as possible. Let us examine this threefold distinction.

In countries where political liberty exists the distinction between a labour union and a political organisation is clear, as is the distinction between trade unions and Social-Democracy. The relation of the latter to the former will naturally vary in each country according to historical, legal and other conditions—it may be more or less close or more or less complex (in our opinion it should be as close and simple as possible); but trade-union organisations are certainly not in the least identical with the Social-Democratic party organisations in those countries. In Russia, however, the yoke of autocracy appears at first glance to obliterate *all* distinctions between a Social-Democratic organisation and trade unions, because *all* trade unions and all circles are prohibited, and because the principal manifestation and weapon of the workers' economic struggle— the strike—is regarded as a crime (and sometimes even as a political crime!). Conditions in our country, therefore, strongly "impel" the workers who are conducting the economic struggle to concern themselves with political questions. They also "impel" the Social-Democrats to confuse trade unionism with Social-Democracy....

But the conclusion that should be drawn from this is that we must have a committee of professional *revolutionists* and it does not matter whether a student or a worker is capable of qualifying himself as a professional revolutionist. The conclusion you draw, however, is that the working-class movement must not be pushed on from outside! In your political innocence you fail to observe that you are playing into the hands of our Economists and furthering our primitiveness. I would like to ask, what is meant by the students "pushing on" the workers? *All* it means is that the students bring to the worker the fragments of political knowledge they possess, the crumbs of Socialist ideas they have managed to acquire (for the principal intellectual diet of the present-day student, legal Marxism, can furnish only the A. B. C., only the crumbs of knowledge). *Such* "pushing on from outside" can never be too excessive; on the contrary, so far there has been too little, all too little of it in our movement; we have been stewing in our own juice far too long; we have bowed far too slavishly before the spontaneous "economic struggle of the workers against the employers and the government." We professional revolutionists must continue, and will continue, *this kind* of "pushing," and a hundred times more forcibly than we have done hitherto. The very fact that you select so despicable a phrase as "pushing on from outside"—a phrase which cannot but rouse in the workers (at least in the workers who are as ignorant as you are yourselves) a sense of distrust towards *all* who bring them political knowledge and revolutionary experience from outside, and rouse in them an instinctive hostility to such people—proves that you are demagogues—and a *demagogue* is the worst enemy of the working class....

You began by talking, and continued to talk, of catching a "committee," of catching an "organisation," and now you skip to the question of getting hold of the "roots" of the movement in the "depths." The fact is, of course, that our movement cannot be caught precisely because it has hundreds and hundreds of thousands of roots deep down among the masses, but that is not the point we are discussing. As far as "roots in the depths" are concerned, we cannot be "caught" even now, in spite of all our primitiveness; but, we all complain, and cannot but complain, of the ease with which the organisations can be caught, with the result that it is impossible to maintain continuity in the movement....

As I have already said, by "wise men," in connection with organisations, I mean *professional revolutionists*, irrespective of whether they are students or working men. I assert:
1. That no movement can be durable without a stable organisation of leaders to maintain continuity;
2. that the more widely the masses are drawn into the struggle and form the basis of the movement, the more necessary is it to have such an organisation and the more stable must it be (for it is much easier then for demagogues to side-track the more backward sections of the masses);
3. that the organisation must consist chiefly of persons engaged in revolution as a profession;
4. that in a country with a despotic government, the more we restrict the membership of this organisation to persons who are engaged in revolution as a profession and who have been professionally trained in the art of combating the political police, the more difficult will it be to catch the organisation; and
5. the wider will be the circle of men and women of the working class or of other classes of society able to join the movement and perform active work in it....

We can never give a mass organisation that degree of secrecy which is essential for the persistent and continuous struggle against the government. But to concentrate all secret functions in the hands of as small a number of professional revolutionists as possible, does not mean that the latter will "do the thinking for all" and that the crowd will not take an active part in the movement.... The active and widespread participation of the masses will not suffer; on the contrary, it will benefit by the fact that a "dozen" experienced revolutionists, no less professionally trained than the police, will concentrate all the secret side of the work in their hands—prepare leaflets, work out approximate plans and appoint bodies of leaders for each town district, for each factory district, and for each educational institution (I know that exception will be taken to my "undemocratic" views, but I shall reply to this altogether unintelligent objection later on). The centralisation of the more secret functions in an organisation of revolutionists will not diminish, but rather increase the extent and the quality of the activity of a large number of other organisations intended for wide membership and which, therefore, can be as loose and as public as possible, for example, trade unions, workers' circles for self-education, and the reading of illegal literature, and Socialist, and also democratic, circles for *all other sections of the population*, etc., etc. We must have *as large a number as possible* of such organisations having the widest possible variety of functions, but it is absurd and dangerous to *confuse these with organisations of revolutionists*, to erase the line of demarcation between them, to dim still more the already incredibly hazy appreciation by the masses that to "serve" the mass movement we must have people who will devote themselves exclusively to Social-Democratic activities, and that such people must train themselves patiently and steadfastly to be professional revolutionists.

Aye, this consciousness has become incredibly dim. The most grievous sin we have committed in regard to organisation is that by our primitiveness we have lowered the prestige of revolutionists in Russia. A man who is weak and vacillating on theoretical questions, who has a narrow outlook, who makes excuses for his own slackness on the ground that the masses are awakening spontaneously, who resembles a trade-union secretary more than a people's tribune, who is unable to conceive a broad and bold plan, who is incapable of inspiring even his enemies with respect for himself, and who is inexperienced and clumsy in his own professional art—the art of combating the political police—such a man is not a revolutionist but a hopeless amateur!

Let no active worker take offence at these frank remarks, for as far as insufficient training is concerned, I apply them first and foremost to myself. I used to work in a circle that set itself a great and all-embracing task: and every member of that circle suffered to the point of torture from the realisation that we were proving ourselves to be amateurs at a moment in history when we might have been able to say—paraphrasing a well-known epigram: "Give us an organisation of revolutionists, and we shall overturn the whole of Russia!" And the more I recall the burning sense of shame I then experienced, the more bitter are my feelings towards those pseudo-Social-Democrats whose teachings bring disgrace on the calling of a revolutionist, who fail to understand that our task is not to degrade the revolutionist to the level of an amateur, but to *exalt* the amateur to the level of a revolutionist....

E. "Conspirative" Organisation and "Democracy"

There are many people among us who are so sensitive to the "voice of life" that they fear that voice more than anything in the world, and accuse those, who adhere to the views here expounded, of Narodovolism, of failing to understand "democracy," etc....

The *form* a strong revolutionary organisation... takes in an autocratic country may be described as a "conspirative" organisation, because the French word *"conspiration"* means in Russian "conspiracy," and we must have the utmost conspiracy for an organisation like that. Secrecy is such a necessary condition for such an organisation that all the other conditions (number and selection of members, functions, etc.) must all be subordinated to it....

Against us it is argued: Such a powerful and strictly secret organisation, which concentrates in its hands all the threads of secret activities, an organisation which of necessity must be a centralised organisation may too easily throw itself into a premature attack, may thoughtlessly intensify the movement before political discontent, the ferment and anger of the working class, etc., are sufficiently ripe for it. To this we reply: Speaking abstractly, it cannot be denied, of course, that a militant organisation may thoughtlessly commence a battle, which *may* end in defeat, which might have been avoided under other circumstances. But we cannot confine ourselves to abstract reasoning on such a question, because every battle bears within itself the abstract possibility of defeat, and there is no other way of *reducing this possibility to a minimum* than by organised preparation for battle. If, however, we base our argument on the concrete conditions prevailing in Russia at the present time, we must come to the positive conclusion that a strong revolutionary organisation is absolutely necessary precisely for the purpose of giving firmness to the movement, and of *safeguarding* it against the possibility of its making premature attacks....

It is further argued against us that the views on organisation here expounded contradict the "principles of democracy." ...

Every one will probably agree that "broad principles of democracy" presupposes the two following conditions: first, full publicity and second, election to all functions. It would be absurd to speak about democracy without publicity, that is a publicity that extends beyond the circle of the membership of the organisation. We call the German Socialist Party a democratic organisation because all it does is done publicly; even its party congresses are held in public. But no one would call an organisation that is hidden from every one but its members by a veil of secrecy, a democratic organisation. What is the use of advancing *"broad principles of democracy"* when the fundamental condition for this principle *cannot be fulfilled* by a secret organisation. "Broad principles" turns out to be a resonant, but hollow phrase. More than that, this phrase proves that the urgent tasks in regard to organisation are totally misunderstood. Every one knows how great is the lack of secrecy among the "broad" masses of revolutionists. We have heard the bitter complaints of B-v on this score, and his absolutely just demand for a "strict selection of members" [*Rabocheye Dyelo*, No. 6, p. 42]. And yet people who boast about their "sensitiveness to life" come forward in a situation like this and *urge* that strict secrecy and a strict (and therefore more restricted) selection of members is unnecessary, and that what is necessary are— *"broad* principles of democracy"! This is what we call being absolutely wide of the mark.

Nor is the situation with regard to the second attribute of democracy, namely, the principle of election, any better. In politically free countries, this condition is taken for granted. "Membership of the party is open to those who accept the principles of the party programme, and render all the support they can to the party"—says paragraph 1 of the rules of the German Social-Democratic Party. And as the political arena is as open to the public view as is the stage in a theatre, this acceptance or non-acceptance, support or opposition is announced to all in the press and at public meetings. Every one knows that a certain political worker commenced in a certain way, passed through a certain evolution, behaved in difficult periods in a certain way; every one knows all his qualities, and consequently, knowing all the facts of the case, *every party member can decide for himself whether or not to elect this person for a certain party office.* The general control (in the literal sense of the term) that the party exercises over every act this person commits on the political field brings into being an automatically operating mechanism which brings about what in biology is called "survival of the fittest." "Natural selection," full publicity, the principle of election and general control provide the guarantee that, in the last analysis, every political worker will be "in his proper place," will do the work for which he is best fitted, will feel the effects of his mistakes on himself, and prove before all the world his ability to recognise mistakes and to avoid them.

Try to put this picture in the frame of our autocracy! Is it possible in Russia for all those "who accept the principles of the party programme and render it all the support they can," to control every action of the revolutionist working in secret? Is it possible for all the revolutionists to elect one of their number to any particular office when, in the very interests of the work, he *must conceal his identity* from nine out of ten of these "all?" Ponder a little over the real meaning of the high-sounding phrases ... and you will realise that "broad democracy" in party organisation, amidst the gloom of autocracy and the domination of the gendarmes, is nothing more than a *useless and harmful toy*. It is a useless toy, because as a matter of fact, no revolutionary organisation has ever practiced *broad* democracy, nor could it, however much it desired to do so. It is a harmful toy, because any attempt to practice the "broad principles of democracy" will simply facilitate the work of the police in making big raids, it will perpetuate the prevailing primitiveness, divert the thoughts of the practical workers from the serious and imperative task of training themselves to become professional revolutionists to that of drawing up detailed "paper" rules for election systems. Only abroad, where very often people who have no opportunity of doing real live work gather together, can the "game of democracy" be played here and there, especially in small groups.

5. Vladimir I. Lenin

THE STATE AND REVOLUTION

In the first place, at the very outset of his argument, Engels says that, in seizing state power, the proletariat thereby "abolishes the state as state." As a matter of fact, Engels speaks here of the proletarian revolution "abolishing" the bourgeois state, while the words about the state withering away refer to the remnants of the proletarian state after the socialist revolution. According to Engels, the bourgeois state does not "wither away", but is "abolished" by the proletariat in the course of the revolution. What withers away after this revolution is the proletarian state or semi-state.

Secondly, the state is a "special coercive force." Engels gives this splendid and extremely profound definition here with the utmost lucidity. And from it follows that the "special coercive force" for the suppression of the proletariat by the bourgeoisie, of millions of working people by handful of the rich, must be replaced by a "special coercive force" for the suppression of the bourgeoisie by the proletariat (the dictatorship of the proletariat). This is precisely the "act" of taking possession of the means of production in the name of society. And it is self-evident that such a replacement of one (bourgeois) "special force" by another (proletarian) "special force" cannot possibly take place in the form of "withering away."

The Economic Basis of the Withering Away of the State

The whole theory of Marx is the application of the theory of development—in its most consistent, complete, considered and pithy form—to modern capitalism. Naturally, Marx was faced with the problem of applying this theory both to the forthcoming collapse of capitalism and to the future development of future communism.

On the basis of what facts, then, can the question of the future development of future communism be dealt with?

On the basis of the fact that it has its origin in capitalism, that it develops historically from capitalism, that it is the result of the action of a social force to which capitalism gave birth. There is no trace of an attempt on Marx's part to make up a utopia, to indulge in idle guess work about what cannot be known. Marx treated the question of the development of, say, a new biological variety, once he knew that it had originated in such and such a way and was changing in such and such a definite direction....

The first fact that has been established most accurately by the whole theory of development, by science as a whole—a fact that was ignored by the utopians, and is ignored by the present-day opportunists, who are afraid of the socialist revolution—is that, historically, there must undoubtedly be a special stage, or a special phase, of transition from capitalism to communism.

The Transition from Capitalism to Communism

Marx continued:

> Between capitalist and communist society lies the period of the revolutionary transformation of the one into the other. Corresponding to this is also a political transition period in which the state can be nothing but the revolutionary dictatorship of the proletariat.

Marx bases this conclusion on an analysis of the role played by the proletarian modern society, on the data concerning the development of this society, and on the irreconcilability of the antagonistic interests of the proletariat and the bourgeoisie.

Previously the question was put as follows: to achieve its emancipation, the proletariat must overthrow the bourgeoisie, win political power and establish its revolutionary dictatorship.

Now the question is put somewhat differently: the transition from capitalist society—which is developing towards communism— to communist society is impossible without a "political transition period", and the state in this period can only be the revolutionary dictatorship of the proletariat.

In capitalist society, providing it develops under the most favorable conditions, we have a more or less complete democracy in the democratic republic. But this democracy is always hemmed in by the narrow limits set by capitalist exploitation, and consequently always remains, in effect, a democracy for the minority, only for the propertied classes, only for the rich. Freedom in capitalist society always remains about the same as it was in the ancient Greek republics: freedom for the slave-owners. Owing to the conditions of capitalist exploitation, the modern wage slaves are so crushed by want and poverty that "they cannot be bothered with democracy," "cannot be bothered with politics"; in the ordinary, peaceful course of events, the majority of the population is debarred from participation in the public and political life....

But from this capitalist democracy—that is inevitably narrow and stealthily pushes aside the poor, and is therefore hypocritical and false through and through—forward development does not proceed simply, directly and smoothly, towards "greater and greater democracy", as the liberal professors and petty-bourgeois opportunists would have us believe. No, forward development, i.e., development towards communism, proceeds through the dictatorship of the proletariat, and cannot do otherwise, for the resistance of the capitalist exploiters cannot be broken by anyone or else in any other way.

And the dictatorship of the proletariat, i.e., the organization of the vanguard of the oppressed as the ruling class for the purpose of suppressing the oppressors, cannot result merely in an expansion of democracy. Simultaneously with an immense expansion of democracy, which for the first time becomes democracy for the poor, democracy for the people, and not democracy for the moneybags, the dictatorship of the proletariat imposes a series of restrictions on the freedom of the oppressors, the exploiters, the capitalists. We must suppress them in order to free humanity from wage slavery, their resistance must be crushed by force; it is clear that there is no freedom and no democracy where there is suppression and where there is violence.

Democracy for the vast majority of the people, and suppression by force, i.e., exclusion from democracy, of the exploiters and oppressors of the people—that is the change democracy undergoes during the transition from capitalism to communism.

Only in communist society, when the resistance of the capitalists has been completely crushed, when the capitalists have disappeared, when there are no classes (i.e., when there is no distinction between the members of society as regards their relation to the social means of production), only then the state ceases to exist, and it becomes possible to speak of freedom. Only then will a truly complete democracy become possible and be realized, a democracy without any exceptions whatever. And only then will democracy begin to wither away, owing to the simple fact that, freed from capitalist slavery, from the untold horrors, savagery, absurdities and infamies of capitalist exploitation, people will gradually become accustomed to observing the elementary rules of social intercourse that have been known for centuries and repeated for thousands of years in all copy-book maxim. They will become accustomed to observing them without force, without coercion, without subordination, without the special apparatus for coercion called the state.

Furthermore, during the transition from capitalism to communism suppression is still necessary, but it is now the suppression of the exploiting minority by the exploited majority. A special apparatus, a special machine for suppression, the "state", is still necessary, but this is now a transitional state. It is no longer a state in the proper sense of the word; for the suppression of the minority of exploiters by the majority of the wage slaves of yesterday is comparatively so easy, simple and natural a task that it will entail far less bloodshed than the suppression of the risings of slaves, serfs or wage-laborers, and it will cost mankind far less. And it is compatible with the extension of democracy to such an overwhelming majority of the population that the need for a special machine of suppression will begin to disappear. Naturally, the exploiters are unable to suppress the people without a highly complex machine for performing this task, but the people can suppress the exploiters even with a very simple "machine", almost without a "machine", without a special apparatus, by the simple organization of the armed people (such as the Soviets of Workers' and Soldiers' Deputies, we would remark, running ahead).

Lastly, only communism makes the state absolutely unnecessary, for there is nobody to be suppressed—"nobody" in the sense of a class, of a systematic struggle against a definite section of the population. We are not utopians, and do not in the least deny the possibility and inevitability of excesses on the part of individual persons, or the need to stop such excesses. !n the first place, however, no special machine, no special apparatus of suppression, is needed for this; this will be done by the armed people themselves, as simply and as readily as any crowd of civilized people, even in modern society, interferes to put a stop to a scuffle or to prevent a woman from being assaulted. And, secondly, we know that the fundamental social cause of excesses, which consist in the violation of the rules of social intercourse, is the exploitation of the people, their want and their poverty. With the removal of this chief cause, excesses will inevitably begin to "wither away". We do not know how quickly and in what succession, but we do know they will wither away. With their withering away the state will also wither away.

The First Phase of Communist Society....

It is this communist society, which has just emerged into the light of day out of the womb of capitalism and which is in every respect stamped with the birthmarks of the old society, that Marx terms the "first" or lower, phase of communist society.

The means of production are no longer the private property of individuals. The means of production belong to the whole of society. Every member of society, performing a certain part of the socially-necessary work, receives a certificate from society to the effect that he has done a certain amount of work. And with this certificate he receives from the public store of consumer goods a corresponding quantity of products. After a deduction is made of the amount of labor which goes to the public fund, every worker, therefore, receives from society as much as he has given to it.

The first phase of communism, therefore, cannot yet provide justice and equality; differences, and unjust differences, in wealth will still persist, but the exploitation of man by man will have become impossible because it will be impossible to seize the means of production—the factories, machines, land, etc.—and make them private property. Marx shows the course of development of communist society, which is compelled to abolish at first only the "injustice" of the means of production seized by individuals, and which is unable at once to eliminate the other injustice, which consists in the distribution of consumer goods "according to the amount of labor performed" (and not according to needs)....

Marx not only most scrupulously takes account of the inevitable inequality of men, but he also takes into account the fact that the mere conversion of the means of production into the common property of the whole of society (commonly called socialism) does not remove the defects of distribution and the inequality of "bourgeois right" which continues to prevail so long as products are divided "according to the amount of labor performed". Continuing, Marx says:

> But these defects are inevitable in the first phase of communist society as it is
> when it has just emerged, after prolonged birth pangs, from capitalist society.
> Right can never be higher than the economic structure of society and its cultural
> development conditioned thereby.

And so, in the first phase of communist society (usually called socialism) "bourgeois right" is not abolished in its entirety, but only in part, only in proportion to the economic revolution so far attained, i.e., only in respect of the means of production. "Bourgeois right" recognizes them as the private property of individuals. Socialism converts them into common property. To that extent—and to that extent alone—"bourgeois right" disappears.

However, it persists as far as its other part is concerned: it persists in the capacity of regulator (determining factor) in the distribution of products and the allotment of labor among the members of society. The socialist principle, " He who does not work shall not eat", is already realized; the other socialist principle, "An equal amount of products for an equal amount of labor," is also already realized. But this is not yet communism, and it does not yet abolish "bourgeois right", which gives unequal individuals, in return for unequal (really unequal) amounts of labor, equal amounts of products.

The state withers away insofar as there are no longer any capitalists, any classes, and, consequently, no class can be suppressed.

But the state has not yet completely withered away, since there still remains the safe-guarding of "bourgeois right", which sanctifies actual inequality. For the state to wither away completely, complete communism is necessary.

The Higher Phase of Communist Society

Only now can we fully appreciate the correctness of Engels's remarks mercilessly ridicul-ing the absurdity of combining the words "freedom" and "state". So long as the state exists there is no freedom. Where there is freedom, there will be no state.

The economic basis for the complete withering away of the state is such a high stage of development of communism at which the antithesis between mental and physical labor disap-pears, at which there consequently disappears one of the principal sources of modern social inequality—a source, moreover, which cannot on any account be removed immediately by the mere conversion of the means of production into public property, by the mere expropriation of the capitalists.

The state will be able to wither away completely when society adopts the rule: "From each according to his ability, to each according to his needs", i.e., when people have become so accustomed to observing the fundamental rules of social intercourse and when their labor has become so productive that they will voluntarily work according to their ability. "The narrow horizon of bourgeois right", which compels one to calculate with the the heartlessness of a Shylock whether one has not worked half an hour more than somebody else, whether one is not getting less pay than somebody else—this narrow horizon will then be crossed. There will then be no need for society, in distributing products, to regulate the quantity to be received by each; each will take freely "according to his needs".

From the bourgeois point of view, it is easy to declare that such a social order is "sheer utopia" and to sneer at the socialists for promising everyone the right to receive from society, without any control over the labor of the individual citizen, any quantity of truffles, cars, pianos, etc. Even to this day, most bourgeois "savants" confine themselves to sneering in this way, there-by betraying both their ignorance and their selfish defence of capitalism.

Ignorance—for it has never entered the head of any socialist to "promise" that the higher phase of the development of communism will arrive; as for the great socialists' forecast that it will arrive, it presupposes not the present productivity of labor and not the present ordinary run of people, who, like the seminary students in Pomyalovsky's stories, are capable of damaging the stocks of public wealth "just for fun", and of demanding the impossible.

Until the higher phase of communism arrives, the socialists demand the strictest control by society and by the state over the measure of labor and the measure of consumption; but this control must start with the expropriation of the capitalists, and must be exercised not by a state of bureaucrats, but by a state of armed workers....

Democracy is of enormous importance to the working class in its struggle against the cap-italists for its emancipation. But democracy is by no means a boundary not to be overstepped; it is only one of the stages on the road from feudalism to capitalism, and from capitalism to com-munism.

Democracy means equality. The great significance of the proletariat's struggle for equality and of equality as a slogan will be clear if we correctly interpret it as meaning the abolition of classes. But democracy means only formal equality. And as soon as equality is achieved for all members of society in relation to ownership of the means of production, that is, equality of labor and wages, humanity will inevitably be confronted with the question of advancing further, i.e., to the operation of the rule "from each according to his ability, to each according to his needs". By what stages, by means of what practical measures humanity will proceed to this supreme aim we do not and cannot know. But it is important to realize how infinitely mendacious is the ordinary bourgeois conception of socialism as something lifeless, rigid, fixed once and for all whereas in reality only socialism will be the beginning of a rapid, genuine, truly mass forward movement, embracing first the majority and then the whole of the population, in all spheres of public and private life....

Given these economic preconditions, it is quite possible, after the overthrow of the capitalists and the bureaucrats, to proceed immediately, overnight, to replace them in the control over production and distribution, in the work of keeping account of labor and products, by the armed workers, by the whole of the armed population. (The question of control and accounting should not be confused with the question of the scientifically trained staff of engineers, agronomists and so on. These gentlemen are working today in obedience to the wishes of the capitalists, and will work even better tomorrow in obedience to the wishes of the armed workers).

Accounting and control—that is mainly what is needed for the "smooth working", for the proper functioning, of the first phase of communist society. All citizens are transformed into hired employees of the state, which consists of the armed workers. All citizens become employees and workers of a single countrywide state "syndicate". All that is required is that they should work equally, do their proper share of work, and get equal pay. The accounting and control necessary for this have been simplified by capitalism to the utmost and reduced to the extraordinarily simple operations—which any literate person can perform—of supervising and recording, knowledge of the four rules of arithmetic, and issuing appropriate receipts.

When the majority of the people beginning dependently and everywhere to keep such accounts and exercise such control over the capitalists (now converted into employees) and over the intellectual gentry who preserve their capitalist habits, this control will really become universal, general and popular; and there will be no getting away from it, there will be "nowhere to go".

The whole society will have become a single office and a single factory, with equality of labor and pay.

But this "factory" discipline, which the proletariat, after defeating the capitalists, after overthrowing the exploiters, will extend to the whole of society, is by no means our idea, or our ultimate goal. It is only a necessary step for thoroughly cleaning society of all the infamies and abominations of capitalist exploitation, and for further progress.

From the moment all members of society, or at least the vast majority, have learned to administer the state themselves, have taken this work into their own hands, have organized control over the insignificant capitalist minority, over the gentry who wish to preserve their capitalist habits and over the workers who have been thoroughly corrupted by capitalism—from this moment the need for government of any kind begins to disappear altogether. The more complete the democracy, the nearer the moment when it becomes unnecessary. The more democratic the "state" which consists of the armed workers, and which is "no longer a state in the proper sense of the word", the more rapidly every form of state begins to wither away.

From when all have learned to administer and actually do independently administer social production, independently keep accounts and exercise control over the parasites, the sons of the wealthy, the swindlers and other "guardians of capitalist traditions", the escape from this popular accounting and control will inevitably become so incredibly difficult, such a rare exception, and will probably be accompanied by such swift and severe punishment (for the armed workers are practical men and not sentimental intellectuals, and they will scarcely allow anyone to trifle with them), that the necessity of observing the simple, fundamental rules of the community will very soon become a habit.

Then the door will be thrown wide open for the transition from the first phase of communist society to its higher phase, and with it to the complete withering away of the state.

6. Petrograd Soviet

ORDER NO. 1, MARCH 14, 1917

[handwritten: military is subordinated to Soviet & cannot listen to Duma.]

To the garrison of the Petrograd District, to all the soldiers of the guard, army, artillery, and navy, for immediate and strict execution, and to the workers of Petrograd for their information:

The Soviet of Workers' and Soldiers' Deputies has resolved:

1. In all companies, battalions, regiments, parks, batteries, squadrons, in the special services of the various military administrations, and on the vessels of the navy, committees from the elected representatives of the lower ranks of the above-mentioned military units shall be chosen immediately.

2. In all those military units which have not yet chosen their representatives to the Soviet of Workers' Deputies, one representative from each company shall be selected, to report with written credentials at the building of the State Duma by ten o'clock on the morning of the fifteenth of this March.

3. In all its political actions, the military branch is subordinated to the Soviet of Workers' and Soldiers' Deputies and to its own committees.

4. The orders of the military commission of the State Duma shall be executed only in such cases as do not conflict with the orders and resolutions of the Soviet of Workers' and Soldiers' Deputies.

5. All kinds of arms, such as rifles, machine guns, armored automobiles, and others, must be kept at the disposal and under the control of the company and battalion committees, and in no case be turned over to officers, even at their demand.

6. In the ranks and during their performance of the duties of the service, soldiers must observe the strictest military discipline, but outside the service and the ranks, in their political, general civic, and private life, soldiers cannot in any way be deprived of those rights which all citizens enjoy. In particular, standing at attention and compulsory saluting, when not on duty, is abolished.

7. Also, the addressing of the officers with the title, "Your Excellency," "Your Honor," etc., is abolished, and these titles are replaced by the address of "Mister General," "Mister Colonel," etc. Rudeness towards soldiers of any rank, and, especially, addressing them as "Thou," is prohibited, and soldiers are required to

From Frank Alfred Golder (ed.): *Documents of Russian History, 1914-1917*, translated by Emanuel Aronsberg (New York: The Century Co., 1927) pp. 386-387.

bring to the attention of the company committees every infraction of this rule, as well as all misunderstandings occurring between officers and privates.

The present order is to be read to all companies, battalions, regiments, ships' crews, batteries, and other combatant and non-combatant commands.

bolsheviks and mensheviks have similar views

7. Vladimir I. Lenin

→ *rev. not radical enough*

→ *view of a new phase of development is put forth.*

APRIL THESES

1917

1. In our attitude towards the war, which under the new government of Lvov and Co. unquestionably remains on Russia's part a predatory imperialist war owing to the capitalist nature of that government, not the slightest concession to "revolutionary defencism" is permissible.

shouldn't defend the few

territory Russia had conquered

The class-conscious proletariat can give its consent to a revolutionary war, which would really justify revolutionary defencism, only on condition:

   (a) that the power pass to the proletariat and the poorest sections of the peasants aligned with the proletariat;
   (b) that all annexations be renounced in deed and not in word;
   (c) that a complete break be effected in actual fact with all capitalist interests.

In view of the undoubted honesty of those broad sections of the mass believers in revolutionary defencism who accept the war only as a necessity, and not as a means of conquest, in view of the fact that they are being deceived by the bourgeoisie, it is necessary with particular thoroughness, persistence and patience to explain their error to them, to explain the inseparable connection existing between capital and the imperialist war, and to prove that without overthrowing capital it is impossible to end the war by a truly democratic peace, a peace not imposed by violence.

The most widespread campaign for this view must be organised in the army at the front.

Fraternization.

2. The specific feature of the present situation in Russia is that the country is passing from the first stage of the revolution—which, owing to the insufficient class-consciousness and organisation of the proletariat, placed power in the hands of the bourgeoisie—to its second stage, which must place power in the hands of the proletariat and the poorest sections of the peasants.

This transition is characterised, on the one hand, by a maximum of legally recognised rights (Russia is now the freest of all the belligerent countries in the world); on the other, by the absence of violence towards the masses, and, finally, by their unreasoning trust in the government of capitalists, those worst enemies of peace and socialism.

This peculiar situation demands of us an ability to adapt ourselves to the special condi-

From Vladimir I. Lenin: *Collected Works*, 4th edition (Moscow: Progress Publishers, 1964), xxiv, pp. 21-24. Reprinted with permission of International Publishers Co., Inc.

tions of Party work among unprecedentedly large masses of proletarians who have just awakened to political life.

3. No support for the Provisional Government; the utter falsity of all its promises should be made clear, particularly of those relating to the renunciation of annexations. Exposure in place of the impermissible, illusion-breeding "demand" that this government, a government of capitalists, should cease to be an imperialist government.

4. Recognition of the fact that in most of the Soviets of Workers' Deputies our Party is in a minority, so far a small minority, as against a bloc of all the petty-bourgeois opportunist elements, from the Popular Socialists and the Socialist-Revolutionaries down to the Organising Committee (Chkheidze, Tsereteli, etc.), Steklov, etc., etc., who have yielded to the influence of the bourgeoisie and spread that influence among the proletariat.

The masses must be made to see that the Soviets of Workers' Deputies are the only possible form of revolutionary government, and that therefore our task is, as long as this government yields to the influence of the bourgeoisie, to present a patient, systematic and persistent explanation of the errors of their tactics, an explanation especially adapted to the practical needs of the masses.

As long as we are in the minority we carry on the work of criticising and exposing errors and at the same time we preach the necessity of transferring the entire state power to the Soviets of Workers' Deputies, so that the people may overcome their mistakes by experience.

5. Not a parliamentary republic—to return to a parliamentary republic from the Soviets of Workers' Deputies would be a retrograde step—but a republic of Soviets of Workers', Agricultural Labourers' and Peasants' Deputies throughout the country, from top to bottom.

Abolition of the police, the army and the bureaucracy. (The standing army to be replaced by the arming of the whole people.)

The salaries of all officials, all of whom are elective and displaceable at any time, not to exceed the average wage of a competent worker.

6. The weight of emphasis in the agrarian programme to be shifted to the Soviets of Agricultural Labourers' Deputies. Confiscation of all landed estates. Nationalisation of *all* lands in the country, the land to be disposed of by the local Soviets of Agricultural Labourers' and Peasants' Deputies. The organisation of separate Soviets of Deputies of Poor Peasants. The setting up of a model farm on each of the large estates (ranging in size from 100 to 300 dissiatines, according to local and other conditions, and to the decisions of the local bodies) under the control of the Soviets of Agricultural Labourers' Deputies and for the public account.

7. The immediate amalgamation of all banks in the country into a single national bank, and the institution of control over it by the Soviet of Workers' Deputies.

8. It is not our immediate task to "introduce" socialism, but only to bring social production and the distribution of products at once under the control of the Soviets of Workers' Deputies.

9. Party tasks:
   a) Immediate convocation of a Party congress;
   b) Alteration of the Party Programme, mainly:
      1) On the question of imperialism and the imperialist war;
      2) On our attitude towards the state and our demand for a "commune state";
      3) Amendment of our out-of-date minimum programme.
   c) Change of the party's name. Instead of "Social Democracy," whose official leaders throughout the world have betrayed socialism and deserted to the bourgeoisie (the "defencists" and the vacillating "Kautskyites"), we must call ourselves the Communist Party.
10. A new International

   We must take the initiative in creating a revolutionary International, an International against the social-chauvinists and against the "Centre."

8. Alexander Rabinowitch

TROTSKY-MARTOV DEBATE—October, 1917

Martov's Resolution: Before All-Russian Congress of Soviets

Taking into consideration that this coup d'état threatens to bring about bloodshed, civil war, and the triumph of a counterrevolution . . . [and] that the only way out of this situation which could still prevent the development of a civil war might be an agreement between insurgent elements and the rest of the democratic organizations on the formation of a democratic government which is recognized by the entire revolutionary democracy and to which the Provisional Government could painlessly surrender its power, the Menshevik [Internationalist] faction proposes that the congress pass a resolution on the necessity of a peaceful settlement of the present crisis by the formation of an all-democratic government . . . that the congress appoint a delegation for the purpose of entering into negotiations with other democratic organs and all the socialist parties . . . [and] that it discontinue its work pending the disclosure of the results of this delegation's efforts.

Trotsky's Reply

A rising of the masses of the people requires no justification. What has happened is an insurrection, and not a conspiracy. We hardened the revolutionary energy of the Petersburg workers and soldiers. We openly forged the will of the masses for an insurrection, and not a conspiracy. The masses of the people followed our banner and our insurrection was victorious. And now we are told: Renounce your victory, make concessions, compromise. With whom? I ask: With whom ought we to compromise? With those wretched groups who have left us or who are making this proposal? But after all we've had a full view of them. No one in Russia is with them any longer. A compromise is supposed to be made, as between two equal sides, by the millions of workers and peasants represented in this congress, whom they are ready, not for the first time or the last, to barter away as the bourgeoisie sees fit. No, here no compromise is possible. To those who have left and to those who tell us to do this we must say: You are miserable bankrupts, your role is played out; go where you ought to go: into the dustbin of history!

From Alexander Rabinowich: *The Bolsheviks Come to Power*, © 1976 by W. W. Norton, and Company, Inc., pp. 295-6. Reprinted with permission of the publisher.

9. LENIN ORDERS DEPORTATIONS

At the time he wrote this letter in 1922, Lenin was the unquestioned leader of the ruling Communist Party and Stalin was his right-hand man, serving as party Secretary General. The excerpt indicates Lenin's desire to rid the country of any potential political opponents.

July 17, 1922

Comrade Stalin!

On the matter of deporting Mensheviks, National Socialists, Kadets, etc. from Russia I would like to ask a few questions, since this operation, which was started before my leave, still has not been completed.

Has the decision been made to "eradicate" all the NS's? Peshekhonov, Myakotin, Gornfeld, Petrishchev, et al.?

As far as I'm concerned, deport them all. [They are] more harmful than any SR [Socialist Revolutionary]—because [they are] more clever.

Also A. N. Potresov, Izgoyev and all the "Ekonomist" contributors (Ozerov and many, many others). The Mensheviks, Rozanov (a physician, cunning), Vigdorchik, (Migulov or something like that) Liubov, Nikolayevna Radchenko and her young daughter (rumor has it they're the vilest enemies of Bolshevism), N. A. Rozhkov (he has to be deported; incorrigible); S. A. Frank (author of "Metodologiya"). The commission supervised by Mantsev, Messing, et al. should present lists and several hundred such ladies and gentlemen must be deported without mercy. Let's purge Russia for a long while!

This must be done at once. Before the end of the SR's trial, no later. Arrest a few hundred and without a declaration of motives—get out, ladies and gentlemen! . . .

With a communist greeting,

LENIN

10. Alexandra Kollontai

THE TRADE UNION CONTROVERSY AND THE WORKERS' OPPOSITION

...the Workers' Opposition is composed of the most advanced part of our class-organized proletarian-Communists. The opposition consists almost exclusively of members of the trade unions, and this face is attested by the signatures of those who side with the opposition under the theses of the role of industrial unions. Who are these members of the trade unions? Workers - that part of the advanced guard of the Russian proletariat which has borne on its shoulders all of the difficulties of the revolutionary struggle, and did not dissolve itself into the soviet institutions by losing contact with the laboring masses, but on the contrary, remained closely connected with them....

Through their class instinct, these comrades standing at the head of the Workers' Opposition became conscious of the fact that there was something wrong: they understood that even though during these three years we have created the soviet institutions and reaffirmed the principles of the workers' republic, yet the working class, *as a class*, as a self-contained social unit with identical class aspirations, tasks, interests, and hence, *with a uniform, consistent, clear-cut policy*, becomes an ever less important factor in the affairs of the soviet republic....

Why was it that none but the unions stubbornly defended the principle of collective management, even without being able to adduce scientific arguments in favor of it; and why was it that the specialists' supporters at the same time defended the "one-man management" which is a product of the individualist conception of the bourgeois class. The "one-man management" is in principle an unrestricted, isolated, free will of one man, disconnected from the collective.

This idea finds its reflection in all spheres of human endeavor-beginning with the appointment of a sovereign for the state and ending with a sovereign director of the factory. This is the supreme wisdom of bourgeois thought. The bourgeoisie do not believe in the power of a collective body. They like only to whip the masses into an obedient flock, and drive them wherever their unrestricted will desires....

Rejection of a principle—the principle of collective management in the control of industry—was a tactical compromise on behalf of our party, an act of adaption; it was, moreover, an act of deviation from that class policy which we so zealously cultivated and defended during the first phase of the revolution.

Why did this happen? How did it happen that our party, matured and tempered in the struggle of the revolution, was permitted to be carried away from the direct road in order to journey along the round-about path of adaptation formerly condemned severely and branded as

From Alexander Kollontai, *The Workers' Opposition* (1921; English translation, Chicago, Industrial Workers of the World), pp. 3-4, 7, 11, 20, 22-23, 32-33, 37-41, 44.

"opportunism"?...

Beside peasant-owners in the villages and burgher elements in the cities, our party in its soviet state policy is forced to reckon with the influence exerted by the representatives of wealthy bourgeoisie now appearing in the form of specialists, technicians, engineers, and former managers of financial and industrial affairs, who by all their past experiences are bound to the capitalist system of production. They can not even imagine any other mode of production but only that one which lies *within the traditional bounds of capitalist economics.*

The more Soviet Russia finds itself in need of specialists in the sphere of technique and management of production, the stronger becomes the influence of these elements, foreign to the working class elements, on the development of our economy. Having been thrown aside during the first period of the revolution, and being compelled to take up an attitude of watchful waiting or sometimes even open hostility toward the soviet authorities, particularly during the most trying months (the historical sabotage by the intellectuals), this social group of brains in capitalist production, of servile, hired, well-paid servants of capital, acquire more and more influence and importance in politics with every day that passes....

The basis of the controversy is namely this: whether we shall realize communism through workers or over their heads, by the hands of soviet officials. And let us, comrades, ponder whether it is possible to attain and build a communist economy by the hands and creative abilities of the scions from the other class, who are imbued with their *routine of the past*? If we begin to think as Marxians, as men of science, we shall answer categorically and explicitly—no....

The solution of this problem as it is proposed by the industrial unions, consists in giving complete freedom to the workers as regards experimenting, class training, adjusting and feeling out the new forms of production, as well as expression and development of their creative abilities, that is, to that class which alone can be the creator of communism. This is the way the Workers' Opposition handles the solution of this difficult problem from which follows the most essential point of their theses. "Organization of control over the social economy is a prerogative of the All-Russian Congress of Producers, who are united in the trade and industrial unions which elect the central body directing the whole economic life of the republic" (Theses of the Workers' Opposition). This point secures freedom for the manifestation of class creative abilities, not restricted and crippled by the bureaucratic machine which is saturated with the spirit of routine of the bourgeois capitalist system of production and control. The Workers' Opposition relies on the creative powers of its own class - the workers. From this premise is deduced the rest of the program.

But right at this point there begins the deviation of the Workers' Opposition from the line that is followed by the party leaders. Distrust toward the working class (not in the sphere of politics, but in the sphere of economic creative abilities) is the whole essence of the theses signed by our party leaders. They do not believe that by the rough hands of workers, untrained technically, can be created those basic outlines of the economic forms from which in the course of time shall develop a harmonious system of communist production....

There can be no self-activity without freedom of thought and opinion, for self-activity manifests itself not only in initiative, action, and work, but in *independent thought as well.* We are afraid of mass-activity. We are afraid to give freedom to the class activity, we are afraid of criticism, we have ceased to rely on the masses, hence, *we have bureaucracy with us.* That is why the Workers' Opposition considers that bureaucracy is our enemy, our scourge, and the greatest danger for the future existence of the Communist Party iself.

In order to do away with the bureaucracy that is finding its shelter in the soviet institutions, *we must first of all get rid of all bureaucracy in the party itself....*

The Workers' Opposition, together with a group of responsible workers in Moscow, in the name of party regeneration and elimination of bureaucracy from the soviet institutions, demands complete realization of all democratic principles, not only for the present period of respite, but also for times of internal and external tension. This is the first and basic condition of the party regeneration, of its return to the principles of the program, from which in practice it is more and more deviating under the pressure of elements that are foreign to it.

The second condition, fulfillment of which with all determination is insisted upon by the Workers' Opposition, is the *expulsion from the party* of all non-proletarian elements....

The third decisive step toward democratization of the party is the elimination of all non-workers' elements from all the administrative positions; in other words, the central, provincial, and county committees of the party must be composed so that workers closely connected with the working masses would have the preponderant majority therein....

The fourth basic demand of the Workers' Opposition is this: *the party must reverse its policy to the elective principle.*

Appointments must be permissible only as exceptions, but lately they began to prevail as a rule. Appointments are very characteristic of bureaucracy, and yet at present they are a general, legalized and well recognized daily occurrence. The procedure of appointments produces a very unhealthy atmosphere in the party, and disrupts the relationship of equality among the members by rewarding friends and punishing enemies as well as by other no less harmful practices in our party and soviet life....

Wide publicity, freedom of opinion and discussion, right to criticize within the party and among the members of the trade unions - such is the decisive step that can put an end to the prevailing system of bureaucracy. Freedom of criticism, right of different factions to freely present their views at party meetings, freedom of discussion - are no longer the demands of the Workers' Opposition alone. Under the growing pressure from the masses a whole series of measures that were demanded by the rank and file long before the All-Russian conference[1] was held, are recognized and promulgated officially at present.... however, we must not overestimate this "leftism," for it is only a declaration of principles to the congress. It may happen, as it has happened many a time with the decisions of our party leaders during these years, that this radical declaration will be forgotten for, as a rule, they are accepted by our party centres only just as the mass impetus is felt, and as soon as life again swings into normal channels the decisions are forgotten....

The Workers' Opposition has said what has long ago been printed in "The Communist Manifesto" by Marx and Engels, viz.: "Creation of communism can and will be the work of the toiling masses themselves. Creation of communism belongs to the workers."....

NOTES

1. The Ninth Party Conference, September, 1920.

11. What Are We Fighting For?

THE KRONSTADT REBELLION

...After carrying out the October Revolution, the working class hoped to achieve emancipation. The result has been to create even greater enslavement of the individual man.

The power of the police-gendarme monarchy has gone into the hands of the Communist-usurpers, who instead of freedom offer the toilers the constant fear of falling into the torture-chambers of the Cheka, which in their horrors surpass many times the gendarme administration of the czarist regime.

Bayonets, bullets, and the harsh shouts of the *oprichniki*[1] of the Cheka, are what the working man of Soviet Russia has got after a multitude of struggles and sufferings. The glorious arms of labor's state - the sickle and hammer - have actually been replaced by the Communist authorities with the bayonet and the barred window, for the sake of preserving the calm, carefree life of the new bureaucracy of Communist commissars and officials.

But the most hateful and criminal thing which the Communists have created is moral servitude: they laid their hands even on the inner life of the toilers and compelled them to think only in the Communist way.

With the aid of militarized trade unions they have bound the workers to their benches, and have made labor not into a joy but into a new slavery. To the protests of the peasants, expressed in spontaneous uprisings, and of the workers, who are compelled to strike by the circumstances of their life, they answer with mass executions and bloodthirstiness, in which they are not surpassed by the czarist generals.

Labor's Russia, the first country to raise the banner of the liberation of labor, has been continuously covered with the blood of the people who have been tortured for the glory of Communist domination. In this sea of blood the Communists are drowning all the great and glowing pledges and slogans of labor's revolution.

It has been sketched out more and more sharply, and now has become obvious, that the Russian Communist Party is not the defender of the toilers which it represents itself to be; the interests of the working nation are alien to it; having attained power, it is afraid only of losing it, and therefore all means are allowed: slander, violence, deceit, murder, vengeance on the families of rebels.

The enduring patience of the toilers has reached its end.

Here and there the glow of insurrection has illuminated the country in its struggle against oppression and violence. Strikes by the workers have flared up.

But the Bolshevik *okhrana*[2] has not slept and has taken every measure to forestall and

---

From "What Are We Fighting For," *News* of the Kronstadt Temporary Revolutionary Committee, March 8, 1921 (reprinted in *The Truth About Kronstadt*, Prague, Volia, Rossi, 1921, pp. 82-83.

suppress the unavoidable third revolution....

There can be no middle ground. Victory or death!

Red Kronstadt gives this example, threatening the counterrevolutionaries of the right and of the left.

The new revolutionary upheaval has been accomplished here. Here the banner of insurrection has been raised for liberation from the three-year violence and oppression of Communist domination, which has overshadowed the three-century yoke of monarchism. Here at Kronstadt the first stone of the third revolution has been laid, to break off the last fetters on the toiling masses and open a new broad road for socialist creativity.

This new revolution will rouse the laboring masses of the East and of the West, since it shows an example of the new socialist construction as opposed to the Communists' backroom "creativity" and directly convinces the laboring masses abroad that everything created here up to now by the will of the workers and peasants was not socialism.

The first step has been completed without a single shot, without a drop of blood. The toilers do not need blood. They will shed it only at a moment of self-defense. Firmness is enough for us, in spite of the outrageous actions of the Communists, to confine ourselves to isolating them from social life, so that their evil false agitation will not interfere with revolutionary work.

The workers and peasants unreservedly go forward, abandoning behind them the Constituent Assembly with its bourgeois stratum and the dictatorship of the party of the Communists with its Cheka men, its state capitalism, its hangman's noose encircling the neck of the masses and threatening to strangle them for good.

The present overturn at last makes it possible for the toilers to have their freely elected soviets, working without any violent party pressure, and remake the state trade unions into free associations of workers, peasants and the laboring intelligentsia. At last the policeman's club of the Communist autocracy has been broken.

NOTES

1. "Oprichniki": originally, members of the sixteenth-century police force of Czar Ivan the Terrible.
2. "Okhrana": originally, the Czarist secret police.

12. Vladimir I. Lenin

BETTER FEWER, BUT BETTER

At the end of his life, Lenin recognized a terrible danger that threatened the future of Bolshevism: the "bureaucratism" of the government and party. "Bureaucratism," to Lenin, meant the growth of a corrupt and self-perpetuating elite that cared for its own power and privilege. The chief source of "bureaucratism" was the ambitions of Joseph Stalin.

Lenin had proposed the creation of a new watchdog agency, the Workers' and Peasants' Inspection, to let the average member of the party inform the operations of the party and the government (what he calls "the state apparatus"). In the following article, Lenin describes how the Inspection should work. A complete revolution in culture will be necessary in order for the workers to overcome "bureaucratism," he writes. "In order to renovate our state apparatus we must at all costs set out, first, to learn, secondly, to learn, and thirdly, to learn . . . ."

In the matter of improving our state apparatus, the Workers' and Peasants' Inspection should not, in my opinion, either strive after quantity or hurry. We have so far been able to devote so little thought and attention to the efficiency of our state apparatus that it would now be quite legitimate if we took special care to secure its thorough organisation, and concentrated in the Workers' and Peasants' Inspection a staff of workers really abreast of the times, i.e., not inferior to the best West-European standards. For a socialist republic this condition is, of course, too modest. But our experience of the first five years has fairly crammed our heads with mistrust and scepticism. These qualities assert themselves involuntarily when, for example, we hear people dilating at too great length and too flippantly on "proletarian" culture. For a start, we should be satisfied with real bourgeois culture; for a start, we should be glad to dispense with the cruder types of pre-bourgeois culture, i.e., bureaucratic culture or serf culture, etc. In matters of culture, haste and sweeping measures are most harmful. Many of our young writers and Communists should get this well into their heads.

Thus, in the matter of our state apparatus we should now draw the conclusion from our past experience that it would be better to proceed more slowly.

Our state apparatus is so deplorable, not to say wretched, that we must first think very carefully how to combat its defects, bearing in mind that these defects are rooted in the past,

From V.I. Lenin, *Selected Works* (New York: International Publishers, 1967), Vol. 3, pp. 774-6, 778-9. Reprinted with permission of International Publishers Co., Inc., New York.

which, although it has been overthrown, has not yet been overcome, has not yet reached the stage of a culture that has receded into the distant past. I say culture deliberately, because in these matters we can only regard as achieved what has become part and parcel of our culture, of our social life, our habits. We might say that the good in our social system has not been properly studied, understood, and taken to heart; it has been hastily grasped at; it has not been verified or tested, corroborated by experience, and not made durable, etc. Of course, it could not be otherwise in a revolutionary epoch, when development proceeded at such breakneck speed that in a matter of five years we passed from tsarism to the Soviet system.

It is time we did something about it. We must show sound scepticism for too rapid progress, for boastfulness, etc. We must give thought to testing the steps forward we proclaim every hour, take every minute and then prove every second that they are flimsy, superficial and misunderstood. The most harmful thing here would be haste. The most harmful thing would be to rely on the assumption that we know at least something, or that we have any considerable number of elements necessary for the building of a really new state apparatus, one really worthy to be called socialist, Soviet, etc.

No, we are ridiculously deficient of such an apparatus, and even of the elements of it, and we must remember that we should not stint time on building it, and that it will take many, many years.

What elements have we for building this apparatus? Only two. First, the workers who are absorbed in the struggle for socialism. These elements are not sufficiently educated. They would like to build a better apparatus for us, but they do not know how. They cannot build one. They have not yet developed the culture required for this; and it is culture that is required. Nothing will be achieved in this by doing things in a rush, by assault, by vim or vigour, or in general, by any of the best human qualities. Secondly, we have elements of knowledge, education and training, but they are ridiculously inadequate compared with all other countries.

Here we must not forget that we are too prone to compensate (or imagine that we can compensate) our lack of knowledge by zeal, haste, etc.

In order to renovate our state apparatus we must at all costs set out, first, to learn, secondly, to learn, and thirdly, to learn, and then see to it that learning shall not remain a dead letter, or a fashionable catch-phrase (and we should admit in all frankness that this happens very often with us), that learning shall really become part of our very being, that it shall actually and fully become a constituent element of our social life. In short, we must not make the demands that are made by bourgeois Western Europe, but demands that are fit and proper for a country which has set out to develop into a socialist country.

The conclusions to be drawn from the above are the following: we must make the Workers' and Peasants' Inspection a really exemplary institution, an instrument to improve our state apparatus.

In order that it may attain the desired high level, we must follow the rule: "Measure your cloth seven times before you cut."

For this purpose, we must utilise the very best of what there is in our social system, and utilise it with the greatest caution, thoughtfulness and knowledge, to build up the new People's Commissariat.

For this purpose, the best elements that we have in our social system— such as, first, the advanced workers, and second, the really enlightened elements for whom we can vouch that they will not take the word for the deed, and will not utter a single word that goes against their conscience— should not shrink from admitting any difficulty and should not shrink from any struggle in order to achieve the object they have seriously set themselves.

We have been bustling for five years trying to improve our state apparatus, but it has been mere bustle, which has proved useless in these five years, or even futile, or even harmful. This bustle created the impression that we were doing something, but in effect it was only clogging up our institutions and our brains.

It is high time things were changed.

We must follow the rule: Better fewer, but better. We must follow the rule: Better get good human material in two or even three years than work in haste without hope of getting any at all.

I know that it will be hard to keep to this rule and apply it under our conditions. I know that the opposite rule will force its way through a thousand loopholes. I know that enormous resistance will have to be put up, that devilish persistence will be required, that in the first few years at least work in this field will be hellishly hard. Nevertheless, I am convinced that only by such effort shall we be able to achieve our aim; and that only by achieving this aim shall we create a republic that is really worthy of the name of Soviet, socialist, and so on, and so forth. . . .

In substance, the matter is as follows:

Either we prove now that we have really learned something about state organisation (we ought to have learned something in five years), or we prove that we are not sufficiently mature for it. If the latter is the case, we had better not tackle the task.

I think that with the available human material it will not be immodest to assume that we have learned enough to be able systematically to rebuild at least one People's Commissariat. True, this one People's Commissariat will have to be the model for our entire state apparatus.

We ought at once to announce a contest in the compilation of two or more textbooks on the organisation of labour in general, and on management in particular. We can take as a basis the book already published by Yermansky, although it should be said in parentheses that he obviously sympathises with Menshevism and is unfit to compile textbooks for the Soviet system. We can also take as a basis the recent book by Kerzhentsev, and some of the other partial textbooks available may be useful too.

We ought to send several qualified and conscientious people to Germany, or to Britain, to collect literature and to study this question. I mention Britain in case it is found impossible to send people to the U.S.A. or Canada.

We ought to appoint a commission to draw up the preliminary programme of examinations for prospective employees of the Workers' and Peasants' Inspection; ditto for candidates to the Central Control Commission.

These and similar measures will not, of course, cause any difficulties for the People's Commissar or the collegium of the Workers' and Peasants' Inspection, or for the Presidium of the Central Control Commission.

Simultaneously, a preparatory commission should be appointed to select candidates for membership of the Central Control Commission. I hope that we shall now be able to find more than enough candidates for this post among the experienced workers in all departments, as well as among the students of our Soviet higher schools. It would hardly be right to exclude one or another category beforehand. Probably preference will have to be given to a mixed composition for this institution, which should combine many qualities, and dissimilar merits. Consequently, the task of drawing up the list of candidates will entail a considerable amount of work. For example, it would be at least desirable for the staff of the new People's Commissariat to consist of people of one type, only of officials, say, or for it to exclude people of the propagandist type, or people whose principal quality is sociability or the ability to penetrate into circles that are not altogether customary for officials in this field, etc.

13. Vladimir I. Lenin

TESTAMENT

DECEMBER 24, 1922

By stability of the Central Committee, of which I spoke above, I mean measures against a split, as far as such measures can at all be taken. For, of course, the white guard in *Russkaya Mysl* (it seems to have been S. S. Oldenburg) was right when, first, in the white guards' game against Soviet Russia he banked on a split in our Party, and when, secondly, he banked on grave differences in our Party to cause that split.

Our Party relies on two classes and therefore its instability would be possible and its downfall inevitable if there were no agreement between those two classes. In that event this or that measure, and generally all talk about the stability of our C.C., would be futile. No measures of any kind could prevent a split in such a case. But I hope that this is too remote a future and too improbable an event to talk about.

I have in mind stability as a guarantee against a split in the immediate future, and I intend to deal here with a few ideas concerning personal qualities.

I think that from this standpoint the prime factors in the question of stability are such members of the C.C. as Stalin and Trotsky. I think relations between them make up the greater part of the danger of a split, which could be avoided, and this purpose, in my opinion, would be served, among other things, by increasing the number of C.C. members to 50 or 100.

Comrade Stalin, having become Secretary-General, has unlimited authority concentrated in his hands, and I am not sure whether he will always be capable of using that authority with sufficient caution. Comrade Trotsky, on the other hand, as his struggle against the C.C. on the question of the People's Commissariat for Communications has already proved, is distinguished not only by outstanding ability. He is personally perhaps the most capable man in the present C.C., but he has displayed excessive self-assurance and shown excessive preoccupation with the purely administrative side of the work.

These two qualities of the two outstanding leaders of the present C.C. can inadvertently lead to a split, and if our Party does not take steps to avert this, the split may come unexpectedly.

I shall not give any further appraisals of the personal qualities of other members of the C.C. I shall just recall that the October episode with Zinoviev and Kamenev was, of course, no accident, but neither can the blame for it be laid upon them personally, any more than non-Bolshevism can upon Trotsky.

Speaking of the young C.C. members, I wish to say a few words about Bukharin and Pyatakov. They are, in my opinion, the most outstanding figures (among the youngest ones), and the following must be borne in mind about them: Bukharin is not only a most valuable and major

From Vladimir I. Lenin: *Collected Works* (Moscow: Progress Publishers, 1966), xxvi, pp. 594-596. Reprinted with permission of International Publishers Co., Inc.

theorist of the Party; he is also rightly considered the favourite of the whole Party, but his theoretical views can be classified as fully Marxist only with great reserve, for there is something scholastic about him (he has never made a study of dialectics, and, I think, never fully understood it).

As for Pyatakov, he is unquestionably a man of outstanding will and outstanding ability, but shows too much zeal for administrating and the administrative side of the work to be relied upon in a serious political matter.

Both of these remarks, of course, are made only for the present, on the assumption that both these outstanding and devoted Party workers fail to find an occasion to enhance their knowledge and amend their one-sidedness.

Lenin
December 25, 1922
Taken down by M.V.

Postscript

Stalin is too rude and this defect, although quite tolerable in our midst and in dealings among us Communists, becomes intolerable in a Secretary-General. That is why I suggest that the comrades think about a way of removing Stalin from that post and appointing another man in his stead who in all other respects differs from Comrade Stalin in having only one advantage, namely, that of being more tolerant, more loyal, more polite and more considerate to the comrades, less capricious, etc. This circumstance may appear to be a negligible detail. But I think that from the standpoint of safeguards against a split and from the standpoint of what I wrote above about the relationship between Stalin and Trotsky it is not a detail, or it is a detail which can assume decisive importance.

Lenin
January 4, 1923
Taken down by L.F.

14. Joseph V. Stalin

DIZZY WITH SUCCESS

March 2, 1930

The Soviet government's successes in the sphere of the collective-farm movement are now being spoken of by everyone. Even our enemies are forced to admit that the successes are substantial. And they really are very great.

It is a fact that by February 20 of this year 50 per cent of the peasant farms throughout the U.S.S.R. had been collectivised. That means that by February 20, 1930, 23 had *overfulfilled* the five-year plan of collectivisation by more than 100 per cent.

It is a fact that on February 28 of this year the collective farms had *already succeeded* in stocking upwards of 36,000,000 centners, i.e., about 220,000,000 poods, of seed for the spring sowing, which is more than 90 per cent of the plan. It must be admitted that the accumulation of 220,000,000 poods of seed by the collective farms along—after the successful fulfillment of the grain-procurement plan—is a tremendous achievement.

What does all this show?

That a *radical turn of the countryside towards socialism may be considered as already achieved.*

There is no need to prove that these successes are of supreme importance for the fate of our country, for the whole working class, which is the directing force of our country, and, lastly, for the Party itself. To say nothing of the direct practical results, these successes are of immense value for the internal life of the Party, for the education of our Party. They imbue our Party with a spirit of cheerfulness and confidence in its strength. They arm the working class with confidence in the victory of our cause. They bring forward additional millions of reserves for our Party.

Hence the Party's task is: to *consolidate* the successes achieved and to *utilise* them systematically for our further advancement.

But successes have their seamy side, especially when they are attained with comparative "ease"—"unexpectedly," so to speak. Such successes sometimes induce a spirit of vanity and conceit: "We can achieve anything." "There's nothing we can't do!" People not infrequently become intoxicated by such successes; they become dizzy with success, lose all sense of proportion and the capacity to understand realities; they show a tendency to overrate their own strength and to underrate the strength of the enemy; adventurist attempts are made to solve all questions of socialist construction "in a trice." In such a case, there is no room for concern to consolidate the successes achieved and to *utilise* them systematically for further advancement. Why should we consolidate the successes achieved when, as it is, we can dash to the full victory of socialism

From J.V. Stalin: *Works* (Moscow: Foreign Language Publishing House, 1955) XII, pp.197-205. Reprinted with permission of International Publishers Co., Inc.

"in a trice": We can achieve anything!" "There's nothing we can't do!"

Hence the Party's task is: to wage a determined struggle against these sentiments, which are dangerous and harmful to our cause, and to drive them out of the Party.

It cannot be said that these dangerous and harmful sentiments are at all widespread in the ranks of our Party. But they do exist in our Party, and there are no grounds for asserting that they will not become stronger And if they should be allowed free scope, then there can be no doubt that the collective-farm movement will be considerably weakened and the danger of its breaking down may become a reality.

Hence the task of our press is: systematically to denounce these and similar anti-Leninist sentiments.

A few facts.

1. The successes of our collective-farm policy are due, among other things, to the fact that it rests on the *voluntary character* of the collective-farm movement and on *taking into account the diversity of conditions* in the various regions of the U.S.S.R. Collective farms must not be established by force. That would be foolish and reactionary. The collective-farm movement must rest on the active support of the main mass of the peasantry. Examples of the formation of collective farms in the developed areas must not be mechanically transplanted to underdeveloped areas. That would be foolish and reactionary. Such a "policy" would discredit the collectivisation idea at one stroke. In determining the speed and methods of collective-farm development, careful consideration must be given to the diversity of conditions in the various regions of the U.S.S.R.

Our grain-growing areas are ahead of all others in the collective-farm movement. Why is this?

Firstly, because in these areas we have the largest number of already firmly-established state farms and collective farms, thanks to which the peasants have had the opportunity to convince themselves of the power and importance of the new technical equipment, of the power and importance of the new, collective organisation of farming.

Secondly, because these areas have had a two-years' schooling in the fight against the kulaks during the grain-procurement campaigns, and this could not but facilitate the development of the collective-farm movement.

Lastly, because these areas in recent years have been extensively supplied with the best cadres from the industrial centres.

Can it be said that these especially favourable conditions also exist in other areas, the consuming areas, for example, such as our northern regions, or in areas where there are still backward nationalities, such as Turkestan, say?

No, it cannot be said.

Clearly, the principle of taking into account the diversity of conditions in the various regions of the U.S.S.R. is, together with the voluntary principle, one of the most important prerequisites for a sound collective-farm movement.

But what actually happens sometimes? Can it be said that the voluntary principle and the principle of taking local peculiarities into account are not violated in a number of areas? No, that cannot be said, unfortunately. We know, for example, that in a number of the northern areas of the consuming zone, where conditions for the immediate organisation of collective farms are comparatively less favourable than in the grain-growing areas, attempts are not infrequently made to replace preparatory work for the organisation of collective farms by bureaucratic decreeing of the collective-farm movement, paper resolutions on the growth of collective farms, organisation of collective farms on paper—collective farms which have as yet no reality, but whose "existence' is proclaimed in a heap of boastful resolutions.

Or take certain areas of Turkestan, where conditions for the immediate organisation or collective farms are even less favourable than in the northern regions of the consuming zone. We know that in a number of areas of Turkestan there have already been attempts to "overtake and outstrip" the advanced areas of the U.S.S.R. by threatening to use armed force, by threatening that peasants who are not yet ready to join the collective farms will be deprived of irrigation water and manufactured goods.

What can there be in common between this Sergeant Prishibeyev "policy" and the Party's policy of relying on the voluntary principle and of taking local peculiarities into account in collective-farm development? Clearly, there is not and cannot be anything in common between them.

Who benefits by these distortions, this bureaucratic decreeing of the collective-farm movement, these unworthy threats against the peasants? Nobody, except our enemies!

What may these distortions lead to? To strengthening our enemies and to discrediting the idea of the collective-farm movement.

Is it not clear that the authors of these distortions, who imagine themselves to be "Lefts," are in reality bringing grist to the mill of Right opportunism?

2. One of the greatest merits of our Party's political strategy is that it is able at any given moment to pick out the *main link* in the movement, by grasping which the Party draws the whole chain towards one common goal in order to achieve the solution of the problem. Can it be said that the Party has already picked out the main link of the collective-farm movement in the system of collective-farm development? Yes, this can and should be said.

What is this chief link?

Is it, perhaps, *association for joint cultivation* of the land? No, it is not that. Associations for joint cultivation of the land, in which the means of production are not yet socialised, are already a past stage of the collective-farm movement.

Is it, perhaps, the *agricultural commune*? No, it is not that. Communes are still of isolated occurrence in the collective-farm movement. The conditions are not yet ripe for agricultural communes—in which not only production, but also distribution is socialised—to be the *predominant* form.

The main link of the collective-farm movement, its *predominant* form at the present moment, the link which has to be grasped now, is the *agricultural artel*.

In the *agricultural artel*, the basic means of production, primarily for grain-farming—labour, use of the land, machines and other implements, draught animals and farm buildings—are socialised. In the artel, the household plots (small vegetable gardens, small orchards), the dwelling houses, a part of the dairy cattle, small livestock, poultry, etc., are *not socialised.*

The artel is the *main link of the collective-farm movement* because it is the form best adapted for solving the grain problem. And the grain problem is the *main link in the whole system of agriculture* because, if it is not solved, it will be impossible to solve either the problem of stock-breeding (small and large), or the problem of the industrial and special crops that provide the principal raw materials for industry. That is why the agricultural artel is the main link in the system of the collective-farm movement at the present moment.

That is the point of departure of the "Model Rules" for collective farms, the final text of which is published today.

And that should be the point of departure of our Party and Soviet workers, one of whose duties it is to make a thorough study of these Rules and to carry them out down to the last detail.

Such is the line of the Party at the present moment.

Can it be said that this line of the Party is being carried out without violation or distortion? No, it cannot, unfortunately. We know that in a number of areas of the U.S.S.R., where the struggle for the existence of the collective farms is still far from over, and where artels are not yet consolidated, attempts are being made to skip the artel framework and to leap straight away into the agricultural commune. The artel is still not consolidated, but they are already "socialising" dwelling houses, small livestock and poultry; moreover, this "socialisation" is degenerating into bureaucratic decreeing on paper, because the conditions which would make such socialisation necessary do not yet exist. One might think that the grain problem has already been solved in the collective farms, that it is already a past stage, that the principal task at the present moment is not solution of the grain problem, but solution of the problem of livestock and poultry-breeding. Who, we may ask, benefits from this blockheaded "work" of lumping together different form of the collective-farm movement? Who benefits from this running too far ahead, which is stupid and harmful to our cause? Irritating the collective-farm peasant by "socialising" dwelling houses, all dairy cattle, all small livestock and poultry, when the grain problem is still *unsolved*, when the artel form of collective farming is not yet *consolidated*—is it not obvious that such a "policy" can be to the satisfaction and advantage only of our sworn enemies?

One such overzealous "socialiser" even goes so far as to issue an order to an artel containing the following instructions: "within three days, register all the poultry of every household," establish posts of special "commanders" for registration and supervision; "occupy the key positions in the artel"; "command the socialist battle without quitting your posts" and—of course—get a tight grip on the whole life of the artel.

What is this—a policy of directing the collective farms, or a policy of *disrupting* and *discrediting* them?

I say nothing of those "revolutionaries"—save the mark!—who begin the work of organising artels by removing the bells from the churches. Just imagine, removing the church bells—how r-r-revolutionary!

How could there have arisen in our midst such blockheaded exercises in "socialisation," such ludicrous attempts to overleap oneself, attempts which aim at bypassing classes and the class struggle, and which in fact bring grist to the mill of our class enemies?

They could have arisen only in the atmosphere of our "easy" and "unexpected" successes on the front of collective-farm development.

They could have arisen only as a result of the blockheaded belief of a section of our Party: "We can achieve anything!" "There's nothing we can't do!"

They could have arisen only because some of our comrades have become dizzy with success and for the moment have lost clearness of mind and sobriety of vision.

To correct the line of our work in the sphere of collective-farm development, *we must put an end to these sentiments.*

That is now one of the immediate tasks of the Party.

The art of leadership is a serious matter. One must not lag behind the movement, because to do so is to lose contact with the masses. But neither must one run too far ahead, because to run too far ahead is to lose the masses and to isolate oneself. He who wants to lead a movement and at the same time keep in touch with the vast masses must wage a fight on two fronts—against those who lag behind and against those who run too far ahead.

Our Party is strong and invincible because, when leading a movement, it is able to preserve and multiply its contacts with the vast masses of the workers and peasants.

15. OFFICIAL VERDICT AGAINST Y. L. PYATAKOV AND ASSOCIATES IN THE PURGE TRIAL, JANUARY 30, 1937

[The Military Collegium of the Supreme Court of the U.S.S.R.] in an open Court session, in the city of Moscow, on January 23-30, 1937, heard the case against:

1. *Pyatakov*, Yuri (Georgi) Leonidovich, born 1890, employee;
2. *Sokolnikov*, Grigori Yakovlevich, born 1888, employee;
3. *Radek*, Karl Berngardovich, born 1885, journalist;
4. *Serebryakov*, Leonid Petrovich. born 1888, employee;
5. *Livshitz*, Yakov Abramovich, born 1896, employee;
6. *Muralov*, Nikolai Ivanovich, born 1877, employee;
7. *Drobnis*, Yakov Naumovich, born 1891, employee;
8. *Boguslavsky*, Mikhail Solomonovich, born 1886, employee;
9. *Knyazev*, Ivan Alexandrovich, born 1893, employee;
10. *Rataichak*, Stanislav Antonovicy, born 1894, employee;
11. *Norkin*, Boris Osipovich, born 1895, employee;
12. *Shestov*, Alexei Alexandrovich, born 1896, employee;
13. *Stroilov*, Mikhail Stepanovich, born 1899, employee;
14. *Turok*, Yosif Dmitrievich, born 1900, employee;
15. *Hrasche*, Ivan Yosifovich, born 1886, employee;
16. *Pushin*, Gavriil Yefremovich, born 1896, employee;
17. *Arnold*, Valentin Volfridovich, alias Vasilyev Valentin Vasilyevich, born 1894, employee;

all being charged with having committed crimes covered by Articles 581a, 588, 589 and 5811 of the Criminal Code of the R.S.F.S.R.

The preliminary and Court investigations have established that:

In 1933, in accordance with direct instructions given by the enemy of the people, L. Trotsky, who was deported from the U.S.S.R. in 1929, there was formed in Moscow, apart from the so-called "united Trotskyite-Zinovievite terrorist centre," consisting of Zinoviev, Kamenev, Smirnov and others, an underground parallel anti-Soviet, Trotskyite centre, members of which were the accused in the present case, Y.L. Pyatakov, K.B. Radek, G.Y. Sokolnikov and L.P. Serebryakov.

In accordance with instructions received from the enemy of the people, L. Trotsky, the principal aim of the parallel anti-Soviet Trotskyite centre was to overthrow the Soviet power in

Report of Court Proceedings in the Case of Anti-Soviet Trotskyite Center. (Moscow, 1937), pp. 574-580.

the U.S.S.R. and to restore capitalism and the power of the bourgeoisie by means of wrecking, diversive, espionage and terrorist activities designed to undermine the economic and military power of the Soviet Union, to expedite the armed attack on the U.S.S.R., to assist foreign aggressors and to bring about the defeat of the U.S.S.R.

In full conformity with this principal aim, the enemy of the people L. Trotsky, abroad, and the parallel anti-Soviet Trotskyite centre, represented by Radek and Sokolnikov, in Moscow, entered into negotiations with certain representatives of Germany and Japan. During the course of negotiation with one of the leaders of the National-Socialist Party of Germany, Rudolph Hess, the enemy of the people, L. Trotsky, promised in the event of a Trotskyite government coming to power as a result of the defeat of the Soviet Union, to make a number of political, economic and territorial concessions to Germany and Japan at the expense of the U.S.S.R., including the cession of the Ukraine to Germany and of the Maritime Provinces and the Amur region to Japan. At the same time, the enemy of the people, L. Trotsky, undertook in the event of seizing power to liquidate the state farms, to dissolve the collective farms, to renounce the policy of industrialization of the country and to restore on the territory of the Soviet Union social relations of capitalist society. Furthermore, the enemy of the people L. Trotsky undertook to render all possible help to aggressors by developing defeatist propaganda and wrecking, diversive and espionage activities, both in time of peace and, in particular, in time of an armed attack on the Soviet Union.

In fulfilment of the instructions of the enemy of the people L. Trotsky, several times received by Radek, and also personally by Pyatakov during a meeting with the enemy of the people L. Trotsky, in December 1935 in the neighbourhood of the city of Oslo, members of the anti-Soviet Trotskyite parallel centre, Pyatakov, Radek, Sokolnikov and Serebryakov developed wrecking, diversive, espionage and terrorist activities.

Local Trotskyite centres were set up in certain large cities in the Soviet Union to exercise direct guidance of anti-Soviet activities in the provinces. In, particular, a West-Siberian anti-Soviet Trotskyite centre consisting of N.I. Muralov, M.S. Boguslavsky and Y.N. Drobnis, accused in the present case, was set up in Novosibirsk on the direct instructions of Pyatakov.

Diversive and wrecking work in industry, chiefly in enterprises of importance for defence purposes, and also on the railways, was performed by the accused in the present case at the behest of the enemy of the people Trotsky, and on the instructions and with the direct participation of agents of the German and Japanese intelligence services, and consisted in disrupting plans of production, lowering the quality of product, organizing train wrecks and damaging rolling stock and railway track.

In organizing diversive activities, the accused were guided by the instructions of the enemy of the people Trotsky "to strike palpable blows at the most sensitive places," supplemented by directions from Pyatakov, Livshitz and Drobnis not to shrink before loss of human life, because, "the more victims, the better, since this will rouse the anger of the workers."

In the chemical industry, the accused Rataichak and Pushin, on the instructions of Pyatakov, performed wrecking work with the object of disrupting the State production plan, delaying the construction of new factories and enterprises and spoiling the quality of the construction work on new enterprises.

In addition, in 1934-1935, the accused Rataichak and Pushin organized three diversive acts at the Gorlovka Nitrogen Fertilizer Works, and two of them were accompanied by explosions which caused the death of workers and heavy material loss.

Diversive acts were also organized at the instigation of the accused Rataichak at the

Voskressensk Combined Chemical Works and the Nevsky Plant.

In the coal and chemical industries of the Ruznetsk Basin, the accused Drobnis, Norkin, Shestov and Stroilov, on the instructions of Pyatakov and Muralov, carried on wrecking and diversive works with the object of disrupting the output of coal, delaying the building and development of new mines and chemical works, to create conditions of work harmful and dangerous to the workers by allowing gas to accumulate in the galleries and pits, while on September 23, 1936, on the instructions of Drobnis, members of the local Trotskyite organization caused an explosion at the Tsentralnaya Pit in the Kemerovo mine, as a result of which ten workers lost their lives and 14 workers received grave injuries.

On the railways, the diversive and wrecking activities carried on by the accused Serebryakov, Boguslavsky, Livshitz, Knyazev and Turok in accordance with the stand of the anti-Soviet Trotskyite centre, aimed to disrupt the State plan of freight loading, especially for the most important freight (coal, ore, grain), to damage the rolling stock (cars and locomotives) and the railway track, and to organize the wrecking of trains, especially of troop trains.

At the instructions of Livshitz, and being commissioned therefore by an agent of the Japanese intelligence service, Mr. H————————————, the accused Knyazev in 1935-1936 organized and brought about the wrecking of a number of freight trains, passenger trains and troop trains involving loss of life; as a result of the wreck of a troop train at the Shumikha Station on October 27, 1935, 29 Red Army men were killed and 29 Red Army men injured.

On the direct instructions of the enemy of the people Trotsky, Pyatakov and Serebryakov, members of the anti-Soviet Trotskyite centre, made preparations, in the event of an armed attack on the U.S.S.R., to carry out a number of diversive acts in industries of importance for defense purposes and also on important railway trunk lines.

On the instructions of Pyatakov, the accused Norkin made preparations to set fire to the Kemerovo Chemical Works upon the outbreak of war.

On the instructions of Livshitz, the accused Knyazev proceeded to carry out the commission given him by Mr. H————————————, an agent of the Japanese intelligence service, to organize during war time the blowing up of railway structures, the burning of military stores and army provision bases, the wreck of troop trains, and also the deliberate infection of trains designed for the transportation of troops, provision supply depots and sanitary centres of the Workers' and Peasants' Red Army with highly virulent bacilli.

In addition to diversive and wrecking activities, the accused Livshitz, Knyazev, Turok, Stroilov, Shestov, Rataichak, Pushin and Hrasche, at the orders of the Trotskyite anti-Soviet centre, engaged in securing and handing over secret information of utmost State importance to agents of the German and Japanese intelligence services.

The accused Rataichak, Pushin and Hrasche were connected with agents of the German intelligence service, Meyerowitz and Lenz, to whom, in 1935-1936, they handed over strictly secret material relating to the condition and operation of chemical plants; Pushin in 1935 handed over to Lenz, agent of the German intelligence service, secret information on the output of products by all the chemical plants of the Soviet Union in 1934, the program of work of all the chemical plants in 1935 and the plan for the construction of nitrogen works, while the accused Rataichak handed over to the same Lenz absolutely secret material on the output in 1934 and the program of the work of chemical enterprises supplying the army for 1935.

The accused Shestov and Stroilov were connected with agents of the German intelligence service Schebesto, Flessa, Floren, Sommeregger and others, and handed over to them secret information about the coal and chemical industries of the Kuznetsk Basin.

The accused Livshitz, Knyazev and Turok regularly transmitted to Mr.H————————, agent of the Japanese intelligence service, strictly secret information regarding the technical condition and mobilization capacity of the railways of the U.S.S.R., and also regarding transportation of troops.

At the direct behest of the enemy of the people L. Trotsky, the anti-Soviet Trotskyite centre formed several terrorist groups in Moscow, Leningrad, Kiev, Rostov, Novosibirsk, Sochi and other cities of the U.S.S.R., which engaged in making preparations for terrorist acts against the leaders of the Communist Party of the Soviet Union and the Soviet government, Comrades Stalin, Molotov, Kaganovich, Voroshilov, Orjonikidze, Yezhov, Zhdanov, Kossior, Eiche, Postyshev and Beria; certain terrorist groups (in Moscow, Novosibirsk, in the Ukraine and in Transcaucasia) were under the personal direction of the accused Pyatakov and Serebryakov, members of the anti-Soviet Trotskyite centre.

In organizing terrorist acts, the anti-Soviet Trotskyite centre endeavoured to take advantage of visits paid to the provinces by leaders of the Communist Party of the Soviet Union and the Soviet government.

Thus in the autumn of 1934, Shestov, at the behest of Muralov, endeavoured to carry out a terrorist act against V.M. Molotov, Chairman of the Council of People's Commissars of the U.S.S.R., during his visit to the Kuznetsk Basin, for which purpose a member of the local Trotskyite terrorist group, the accused Arnold, attempted to cause an accident to the automobile in which Comrade V.M. Molotov rode.

Furthermore, on the instructions of Pyatakov and Muralov, the accused Shestov made preparations for a terrorist act against R.I. Eiche, Secretary of the West-Siberian Territory Committee of the C.P.S.U., while the accused Arnold at the instigation of Shestov made preparations for a terrorist act against G.K. Orjonikidze.

Thus the Military Collegium of the Supreme Court of the U.S.S.R. has established that:

I. Pyatakov, Serebryakov, Radek and Sokolnikov were members of the anti-Soviet Trotskyite centre and, at the direct behest of the enemy of the people L. Trotsky, now abroad, with the object of expediting an armed attack on the Soviet Union, assisting foreign aggressors in seizing territory of the Soviet Union, overthrowing the Soviet power and restoring capitalism and the power of the bourgeoisie, directed the treacherous, diversive, wrecking, espionage and terrorist activities or Soviet Trotskyite organization in the Soviet Union—i.e., have committed crimes covered by Articles 581a, 588, 589 and 5811 of the Criminal Code of the R.S.F.S.R.

II. Pyatakov and Serebryakov, mentioned in clause I, as well as Muralov, Drobnis, Livshitz and Boguslavsky, members of an anti-Soviet Trotskyite organization, organized and personally directed the treasonable, espionage, diversive and terrorist activities of the members of the anti-Soviet Trotskyite organization—i.e., have committed crimes covered by Articles 581a , 588 , 589 and 5811 of the Criminal Code of the R.S.F.S.R.

III. Knyazev, Rataichak, Norkin, Shestov, Turok, Pushin and Hrasche, while members of an anti-Soviet Trotskyite organization, carried out the instructions of the anti-Soviet Trotskyite centre concerning treasonable, espionage, undermining, wrecking and terrorist activities—i.e., have committed crimes covered by Articles 581a , 588 , 589 and 5811 of the Criminal Code of the R.S.F.S.R.

IV. Arnold, while a member of an anti-Soviet Trotskyite organization, at the instigation of the accused Muralov and Shestov, attempted to carry out terrorist acts against Comrades Molotov and Orjonikidze—i.e., has committed crimes covered by Articles 19, 588 and 5811 of the Criminal Code of the R.S.F.S.R.

V. Stroilov partially carried out certain individual commissions for espionage and wrecking work—i.e., has committed crimes covered by Articles 586 and 587 of the Criminal Code of the R.S.F.S.R.

On the basis of the above, and guided by Articles 319 and 320 of the Code of Criminal Procedure of the R.S.F.S.R., *The Military Collegium of the Supreme Court of the U.S.S.R.*

SENTENCES

1. *Pyatakov*, Yuri (Georgi) Leonidovich and
2. *Serebryakov*, Leonid Petrovich,

as members of the anti-Soviet Trotskyite centre who organized and directly guided treasonable, espionage, undermining, wrecking and terrorist activities to the supreme penalty—to be shot.

3. *Muralov*, Nikolai Ivanovich,
4. *Drobnis*, Yakov Naumovich,
5. *Livshitz*, Yakov Abramovich,
6. *Boguslavsky*, Mikhail Solomonovich,
7. *Knyazev*, Ivan Alexandrovich,
8. *Rataichak*, Stanislav Antonovich,
9. *Norkin*, Boris Osipovich,
10. *Shestov*, Alexei Alexandrovich,
11. *Turok*, Yosif Dmitrievich,
12. *Pushin*, Gavriil Yefremovich, and
13. *Hrasche*, Ivan Yosifovich,

as organizers and direct executors of the above-mentioned crimes, to the supreme penalty—to be shot.

14. *Sokolnikov*, Grigori Yakovlevich, and
15. *Radek*, Karl Berngardovich,

as members of the anti-Soviet Trotskyite centre, responsible for its criminal activities, but not directly participating in the organization and execution of acts of a diversive, wrecking, espionage and terrorist nature each to imprisonment for a term of ten years.

16. *Arnold*, Valentin Volfridovich, alias Vasilyev, Valentin Vasilyevich, to imprisonment for a term of ten years.

17. *Stroilov*, Mikhail Stepanovich,

in view of the facts mentioned in point V of the defining section of the present verdict—to imprisonment for a term of eight years.

Sokolnikov, Radek, Arnold and Stroilov, who are condemned to imprisonment, shall be deprived of political rights for a period of five years each.

The personal property of all the condemned shall be confiscated.

Enemies of the people, Lev Davidovich Trotsky, and his son, Lev Lvovich Sedov, who were in 1929 deported from the U.S.S.R. and by the decision of the Central Executive

Committee of the U.S.S.R. of February 20, 1932, were deprived of citizenship of the U.S.S.R., having been convicted by the testimony of the accused Y.L. Pyatakov, K.B. Radek, A.A. Shestov and N.I. Muralov, and by the evidence of V.G. Romm and D.P. Bukhartsev, who were examined as witnesses at the trial, as well as by the materials in the present case, of personally directing the treacherous activities of the Trotskyite anti-Soviet centre, in the event of their being discovered on the territory of the U.S.S.R., are liable to immediate arrest and trial by the Military Collegium of the Supreme Court of the U.S.S.R.

16. Osip Mandelstam

WE LIVE, NOT FEELING...[1]

We live, not feeling the country beneath us,
Our speech inaudible ten steps away,
But where they're up to half a conversation—
They'll speak of the Kremlin mountain man.[2]

His thick fingers are fat like worms,
And his words certain as pound weights.
His cockroach whiskers laugh,
And the tops of his boots glisten.

And all around his rabble of thick-skinned leaders,
He plays through services of half-people.
Some whistle, some meow, some snivel,
He alone merely caterwauls and prods.

Like horseshoes he forges decree after decree—
Some get it in the forehead, some in the brow,
 some in the groin, and some in the eye.
Whatever the execution—it's a raspberry[3] to him
And his Georgian[4] chest is broad.

NOTES

1   This poem is believed to be connected to the reason for Mandelstam's arrest and subsequent death in prison.
2   In the first version, which fell into the hands of the secret police, these last two lines read:
> All we hear is the Kremlin mountain man,
> The murderer and peasant-slayer.
3   The Russian word *malina* (raspberry) is often used for that which is pleasant and comfortable, the sweet life. It is also criminal slang for "den of thieves," the "hole-up place for thugs."
4   In the Russian it is Ossetian. Though Stalin was known as a Georgian, there were persistent stories that he was also Ossetian, a people of Iranian stock, different from the Georgians, who are located farther north in the Caucasus.

From Osip Mandelstam [1934 (?)] in *20th Century Russian Poetry*, ed. A.C. Todd & M. Hayward, pp.106-107. Translated by Albert C. Todd. Copyright © 1993 by Doubleday. Used by permission of Doubleday, a division of Bantam Doubleday Dell Publishing Group.

17. Nikolai Bukharin

TO A FUTURE GENERATION OF PARTY LEADERS

I am leaving life. I am lowering my head not before the proletarian ax, which must be merciless but also virginal. I feel my helplessness before a hellish machine, which, probably by the use of medieval methods, has acquired gigantic power, fabricates organized slander, acts boldly and confidently.

Dzerzhinsky is gone; the remarkable traditions of the Cheka have gradually faded into the past, when the revolutionary idea guided all its actions, justified cruelty to enemies, guarded the state against any kind of counterrevolution. That is how the Cheka earned special confidence, special respect, authority and esteem. At present, most of the so-called organs of the NKVD are a degenerate organization of bureaucrats, without ideas, rotten, well-paid, who use the Cheka's bygone authority to cater to Stalin's morbid suspiciousness (I fear to say more) in a scramble for rank and fame, concocting their slimy cases, not realizing that they are at the same time destroying themselves—history does not put up with witnesses of foul deeds.

Any member of the Central Committee, any member of the party can be rubbed out, turned into a traitor, terrorist, diversionist, spy, by these "wonder-working organs." If Stalin should ever get any doubts himself, confirmation would instantly follow.

Storm clouds have risen over the party. My one head, guilty of nothing, will drag down thousands of guiltless heads. For an organization must be created, a Bukharinite organization, which is in reality not only nonexistent now, the seventh year that I have had not a shadow of disagreement with the party, but was also nonexistent then, in the years of the right opposition. About the secret organizations of Ryutin and Uglanov, I knew nothing. I expounded my views, together with Rykov and Tomsky, openly.

I have been in the party since I was eighteen, and the purpose of my life has always been to fight for the interests of the working class, for the victory of socialism. These days the paper with the sacred name Truth (Pravda) prints the filthiest lie, that I, Nikolai Bukharin, has wished to destroy the triumphs of October, to restore capitalism. That is unexampled insolence, in irresponsibility to the people, only by such a lie as this: it has been discovered that Nikolai Romanov devoted his whole life to the struggle against capitalism and monarchy, to the struggle for the achievement of a proletarian revolution. If, more than once, I was mistaken about the methods of building socialism, let posterity judge me no more harshly than Vladimir Ilych did. We were moving toward a single goal for the first time, on a still unblazed trail. Other times, other customs. Pravda used to carry a discussion page; everyone argued, searched for ways and means, quarreled, made up, and moved on together.

From *Let History Judge: The Origins and Consequences of Stalinism* by Roy Medvedev, 1988, © Columbia University Press, New York. Reprinted with the permission of the publisher.

I appeal to you, a future generation of party leaders, whose historical mission will include the obligation to take apart the monstrous cloud of crimes that is growing ever huger in these frightful times, taking fire like a flame suffocating the party.

I appeal to all party members! In these days, perhaps the last of my life, I am confident that sooner or later the filter of history will inevitably sweep the filth from my head. I was never a traitor; without hesitation I would have given my life for Lenin's, I loved Kirov, started nothing against Stalin. I ask a new young and an honest generation of party leaders to read my letter at a party plenum, to exonerate me and reinstate me in the party.

Know, comrades, that on that banner, which you will be carrying in the victorious march to communism, is also my drop of blood.

N. Bukharin.

18. Alec Nove

WAS STALIN REALLY NECESSARY?

Stalin has suffered a dramatic post-mortem demotion, and a monument to his victims is to be erected in Moscow. The present Soviet leadership is thus disassociating itself publicly from many of the highly disagreeable features of Stalin's rule, while claiming for the Party and the Soviet system the credit for making Russia a great economic and military power. Is this a logically consistent standpoint? How far was Stalin, or Stalinism, an integral, unavoidable, "necessary" part of the achievements of the period? How much of the evil associated with the Stalin system is attributable to the peculiar character of the late dictator, and how much was the consequence of the policies adopted by the large majority of the Bolshevik party, or of the effort of a small and dedicated minority to impose very rapid industrialization on a peasant country?

To ask these questions is of interest from several standpoints. Firstly, in trying to answer them we might be able to see a little more clearly the meaning of such misused terms as "determinism", causality, or the role of personality in history, and so continue to explore some of the problems which E. H. Carr presented in so stimulating a way in his Trevelyan lectures. Secondly, an examination of the circumstances which brought Stalin to power and led to (or provided an opportunity for) crimes on a massive scale is surely of very practical interest, since it might help in understanding how to avoid a repetition of these circumstances, particularly in those underdeveloped countries which are being tempted by their very real difficulties to take the totalitarian road.

To some people, the word "necessary" smacks of "historicism," of a belief in inevitability, or suggests that the author wishes to find some historic justification, a whitewash to be applied to Stalin and his system. This is far from being my intention. "Necessity" is used here with no moral strings attached. If I say that to travel to Oxford it is necessary to go to Paddington station, this implies no approval, moral or otherwise, of the service provided by the Western Region of British Railways, still less of the project of making the journey to Oxford. It is simply that if I wish to do A, it involves doing B.

It is true that there may be alternatives. One might, for instance, do not B but C, or D. Thus I could go to Oxford by car, or by bus. However, it could be that these physically possible methods are not in fact open to me; I may not own a car, and shortage of time precludes taking the bus. Thus a judgment on the "necessity" or otherwise of an action in pursuit of a given purpose requires some consideration of what could have been done instead.

The range of choice is not, in practice, limited only by what is *physically* possible. There are also actions which are excluded by religious or ideological principle. Far example, it is not in fact open to a rabbi to eat a ham sandwich or an orthodox Hindu to eat cow meat. Thus if an

Alec Nove: "Was Stalin Really Necessary?" *Encounter*, (April, 1962). Used with permission of the author. Nove's most recent views can be found in *The Stalin Phenomenon* (1993), edited by Alec Nove.

"alternative" happens to involve such acts, it is *for them* not an alternative at all. This is because, were they to act otherwise, they would cease to be what they in fact are. A rabbi does not eat pork; were he to do so, he would not be a rabbi. The fact that he is a rabbi would also affect his outlook, his "freedom" to choose between alternative modes of conduct, where religious law is less strict: for instance, there is nothing in the Talmud or in Deuteronomy about smoking on the Sabbath, but rabbis would tend to be the kind of people who, faced with this "new" problem, would give the answer "no".

Thus, to come nearer our subject, there may have been a number of solutions to the problems posed by Russia of the twenties which the Communists could not have chosen because they were Communists, and in considering the practical alternatives before them we have to bear this in mind. In doing so, we are by no means driven to any generalizations about the "inevitability" of the Russian revolution or of the Bolshevik seizure of power, and *a fortiori* we need not assume that non-Bolsheviks could not have found some other ways of coping with the problems of the period. (Indeed, though the problems would still have been acute, they might in important respects have been different.) Before his assassination in 1911, the last intelligent Tsarist prime minister, Stolypin, expressed the belief that his land reform measures would create in about twenty years a prosperous peasantry which would provide a stable foundation for society and the throne. No one will know if he would have been right, if he had not been murdered, if the Tsar had been wise, if Rasputin had not existed, if the war had not broken out...But of what use is it to indulge in such speculations? A 19th-century Russian blank-verse play provides, if somewhat inaccurately, relevant comment:

> if, if, if grandma had a beard,
> She would be grandpa...

In assessing the choices open to the Bolsheviks in, say, 1926, the events before that date must be taken as given. The real question, surely, is to consider the practical alternatives which Stalin and his colleagues had before them.

In doing so, we should certainly not assume that what happened was inevitable. "Necessity" and "inevitable" are quite distinct concepts, though same critics seem to confuse them. Two simple and probably uncontroversial propositions will illustrate this: it was necessary for 18th-century Poland to make drastic changes in its constitution if she were to survive as an independent state; and for China around 1890 a strong, modernizing government was urgently necessary if many disasters were to be avoided. Yet the "necessary" steps were not taken and the disasters occurred. Unless we believe that whatever was not avoided was for that reason unavoidable, we would wish to examine the actions which men took, their choices between *available* alternatives, and see whether viable alternatives in fact existed.

At this point, many historians (at times one feels E. H. Carr is among them) tend to brush aside impatiently any talk of what might have been; they are concerned, they would claim, with chronicling and explaining what was. Curiously, this line is often taken both by those who believe in strict historical determinism, i.e., that what happened *had* to happen, and by those who consider history to be merely a chronological series of events, i.e., that by implication *anything* could have happened. Both these apparently opposite extremes agree in not examining the actual possibilities as they were seen by the statesmen of the period. Yet how can one speak meaningfully of the reasons for, or causes of, any political act unless one implicitly or explicitly considers what could have been done instead? In other words, we must be concerned with freedom of choice, or its converse, necessity whether we like it or not, unless we hold either that freedom of choice is infinite or that it is non-existent.

There are several more things to be said on the subject of "necessity". One of these concerns what might be called consequences of consequences, or indirect effects. For example, it is difficult to marry a wife without simultaneously acquiring a mother-in-law. Or, moving nearer to our subject, a sergeant is an unavoidable element in an army, and the needs of discipline involve giving him powers over his men which he is likely to abuse. Bullying N.C.O.'s are likely to be found if an army exists, and so, given the necessity for an army, they become an inevitable consequence of its existence, just as the mother-in-law is an unavoidable appendage of a "necessary" wife. Thus, getting still nearer to the point, a situation which requires many bureaucrats, which gives exceptional power to many policemen, may bring into action certain forces, certain behavioral tendencies, which are typical of bureaucrats or policemen and which, though not needed or desired as such, cannot in the circumstances be avoided.

The saying that "you cannot make omelets without breaking eggs" (or its Russian equivalent: "if you chop trees, the chips fly") has been used so often as an excuse for excesses and crimes, that we sometimes forget that you really *cannot* make omelets without breaking eggs.

Now on to Stalin, or rather to Stalinism, since the idea of "necessity" does not of course mean that the leader had to be a Georgian with a long mustache, but rather a tough dictator ruling a totalitarian state of the Stalinist type. What were the practical alternatives before the Bolsheviks in the late twenties, which contributed to the creation of the Stalinist regime, or, if one prefers a different formulation, gave the opportunity to ambitious men to achieve so high a degree of absolutism?

The key problem before the Bolsheviks concerned the linked questions of industrialization and political power. They felt they had to industrialize for several reasons, some of which they shared with non-Bolshevik predecessors. Thus the Tsarist minister, Count Witte, as well as Stalin, believed that to achieve national strength and maintain independence, Russia needed a modern industry, especially a heavy industry. The national defense argument, re-labeled "defense of the revolution", was greatly strengthened by the belief that the Russian revolution was in constant danger from a hostile capitalist environment, militarily and technically far stronger than the U.S.S.R. Then there was the belief that the building of socialism or communism involved industrialization, and, more immediately, that a "proletarian dictatorship" was insecure so long as it ruled in an overwhelmingly petty-bourgeois, peasant, environment. There had to be a large increase in the number and importance of the proletariat, while the rise of a rich "kulak" class in the villages was regarded as a dangerous (or potentially dangerous) resurgence of capitalism. It was clear, by 1927, that it was useless to wait for "world revolution" to solve these problems. These propositions were common to the protagonists of the various platforms of the middle twenties. Thus even the "moderate" Bukharin wrote: "if there were a fall in the relative weight of the working class in its political and its social and class power, ... this would subvert the basis of the proletarian dictatorship, the basis of our government". He too spoke in principle of the "struggle against the kulak, against the capitalist road", and warned of the "kulak danger", He too, even in the context of an attack on Zinoviev and the "left" opposition, argued the need for "changing the production relations of our country".

Until about 1927, a rapid rise in industrial production resulted from (or, "was a result of") the reactivation of pre-revolutionary productive capacity, which fell into disuse and disrepair in the civil war period. However, it now became urgent to find material and financial means to expand the industrial base. This at once brought the peasant problem to the fore. The revolution had distributed land to 25 million families, most of whom were able or willing to provide only small marketable surpluses. Supplies of food to the towns and for export fell, peasant consumption rose. Yet the off-farm surplus must grow rapidly to sustain industrialization, especially where large scale loans from abroad could scarcely be expected. As the "left" opposition vigorously pointed out, the peasants, the bulk of the population, had somehow to be made to contribute produce and money, to provide the bulk of "primitive Socialist accumulation".

The arguments around these problems were inextricably entangled in the political factional struggles of the twenties. The moderate wing, led by Bukharin, believed that it was possible to advance slowly towards industrialization "at the pace of a tortoise", a pace severely limited by what the peasant was willing to do voluntarily. This was sometimes described as "riding towards socialism on a peasant nag". The logic of this policy demanded priority for developing consumers' goods industries, to make more cloth to encourage the peasants to sell more food. At first, Stalin sided with the moderates.

The case against the Bukharin line was several different kinds. Firstly, free trade with the peasants could only provide inadequate surpluses if the better-off peasants (i.e., those known as kulaks) were allowed to expand, since they were the most efficient producers and provided a large part of the marketable produce. Yet all the Bolshevik leaders (including, despite momentary aberrations, Bukharin himself) found this ideologically and politically unacceptable. A strong group of independent, rich peasants was Stolypin's dream as a basis for Tsardom. It was the Bolsheviks' nightmare, as totally inconsistent in the long run with their rule or with a socialist transformation of "petty-bourgeois" Russia. But this made the Bukharin approach of doubtful internal consistency. This was understood at the time by intelligent non-party men. Thus the famous economist Kondratiev, later to perish in the purges, declared in 1927: "if you want a higher rate of accumulation... then the stronger elements of the village must be allowed to exploit (the weaker)," in other words that the "kulaks" must expand their holdings and employ landless laborers. The "peasant nag" could not pull the cart, or it, and the peasant, would pull in the wrong direction.

A second reason concerned the pace of the tortoise. The Bolsheviks were in a hurry. They saw themselves threatened by "imperialist interventionists." Even though some war scares were manufactured for factional reasons, the Party as a whole believed that war against them would come before very long. This argued not merely for speed, but also for priority to *heavy* and not light industry, since it provided a basis for an arms industry. Still another reason was a less tangible but still very real one: the necessity of maintaining political *élan*, of not appearing to accept for an indefinite period a policy of gradualism based on the peasant, which would have demoralized the Party and so gravely weakened the regime. It was widely felt, in and out of Russia, that by 1927 the regime had reached a *cul-de-sac*. I have in front of me a contemporary Menshevik pamphlet published abroad, by P.A. Garvi, which describes its dilemma quite clearly and indeed the political and economic problem was extremely pressing: to justify its existence, to justify the Party dictatorship in the name of the proletariat, a rapid move forward was urgent; but such a move forward would hardly be consistent with the "alliance with the peasants" which was the foundation of the policy of the moderates in the twenties. Stalin at this point swung over towards the left, and his policy of all-out industrialization and collectivization was a means of breaking out of the cul-de-sac, of mobilizing the Party to smash peasant resistance, to make possible the acquisition of farm surplus without having to pay the price which any free peasants or free peasant associations would have demanded. He may well have felt he had little choice. It is worth quoting from the reminiscences of another Menshevik, who in the late twenties was working in the Soviet planning organs: "The financial base of the first five-year plan, *until Stalin found it in levying tribute on the peasants in primitive accumulation by the methods of Tamerlane*, was extremely precarious... (It seemed likely that) everything would go to the devil... No wonder that no one, literally no one, of the well-informed economists, believed or could believe in the fulfillment (of the plan)."

It does not matter in the present context whether Stalin made this shift through personal conviction of its necessity, or because this seemed to him to be a clever power-maneuver. The cleverness in any case largely consisted in knowing that he would thus strengthen his position by becoming the spokesman of the view which was widely popular among Party activists. The "Leftists", destroyed organizationally by Stalin in earlier years, had a considerable following. Stalin's left-turn brought many of them to his support—though this did not save them from being shot in due course on Stalin's orders. It is probably the case he had at this time genuine majority support within the Party for his policy, though many had reservations about certain excesses of which more will be said. But if this be so, the policy as such cannot be attributed to Stalin personally, and therefore the consequences which flowed from its adoption must be a matter of more than personal responsibility.

Let us examine some of these consequences. Collectivization could not be voluntary. Rapid industrialization, especially with priority for heavy industry, meant a reduction in living standards, despite contrary promises in the first five-year plans. This meant a sharp increase in the degree of coercion, in the powers of the police, in the unpopularity of the regime. The aims of the bulk of the people were bound to be in conflict with the aims of the Party. It should be added that this conflict is probably bound to arise in some form wherever the *state* is responsible for financing rapid industrialization; the sacrifices are then imposed by political authority, and the masses of "small" people do not and cannot provide voluntarily the necessary savings, since in the nature of things their present abstinence cannot be linked with a future return which they as individuals can identify. However, this possibly unavoidable unpopularity was greatly increases in the U.S.S.R. by the sheer pace of the advance and by the attack on peasant property, and, as we shall see, both these factors reacted adversely on production of consumers' goods and so led to still further hardships and even greater unpopularity. The strains and priorities involved in a rapid move forward required a high degree of economic centralization, to prevent resources from being diverted to satisfy needs which were urgent but of a nonpriority character. In this situation, the Party was the one body capable of carrying out enormous changes and resisting social and economic pressures in a hostile environment; this was bound to affect its structure. For a number of years it had already been in the process of transformation from a political into a power machine. The problems involved in the "revolution from above" intensified the process of turning it into an obedient instrument for changing, suppressing, controlling.

This, in turn, required hierarchical subordination, in suppression of discussion; therefore, there had to be an unquestioned commander-in-chief. Below him, toughness in executing unpopular orders became the highest qualification for Party office. The emergence of Stalin, and of Stalin-type bullying the officials of the sergeant-major species, was accompanied by the decline in the importance of the cosmopolitan journalist-intellectual type of party leader who had played so prominent a role earlier.

The rise of Stalin to supreme authority was surely connected with the belief among many Party members that he was the kind of man who could cope with this kind of situation. Of course, it could well be that Stalin tended to adopt policies which caused him and his type to be regarded as indispensable, and he promoted men to office in the Party because they were loyal to him. Personal ambition, a desire for power, were important factors in shaping events. But this is so obvious, so clearly visible on the surface, that the underlying problems, policy choices and logical consequences of policies need to be stressed.

Let us recapitulate: the Communists needed dictatorial power if they were to continue to rule; if they were to take effective steps towards industrialization these steps were bound to give rise to problems which would require further tightening of political and economic control. While we cannot say, without much further research, whether a Bukharinite or other moderate policy was impossible, once the decision to move fast was taken this had very radical consequences; the need for a tough, coercive government correspondingly increased. Given the nature of the Party apparatus, the mental and political development of the Russian masses, the logic of police rule, these policies were bound to lead to a conflict with the peasantry and to excesses of various kinds. Thus, given the premises, certain elements of what may be called Stalinism followed, were objective "necessities". In this sense, and to this extent, Stalin was, so to speak, operating within the logical consequences of Leninism.

It is an essential part of Lenin's views that the Party was to seize power and use it to change Russian society. This is what distinguished him from the Mensheviks who believed that conditions for socialism should ripen within society. Lenin also suppressed opposition parties and required stern discipline from his followers. (It is impossible to ban free speech outside the Party without purging the Party of those who express "wrong" views within it). Indeed Lenin promoted Stalin because he knew he was tough, would "prepare peppery dishes", though he had last minute regrets about it. While it would be going too far to describe Stalin as a true Leninist, if only because Lenin was neither personally brutal nor an oriental despot, Stalin undoubtedly carried through some of the logical consequences of Lenin's policies and ideas. This remains true even though Lenin thought that the peasant problem could be solved by voluntary inspiration, and would probably have recoiled at the conditions of forced collectivization.

Is it necessary to stress that this does not make these actions right, or good? Yes, it is, because so many critics assume that to explain is to justify. So it must be said several times that no moral conclusions follow, that even the most vicious acts by politicians and others generally have causes which must be analyzed. We are here only concerned to disentangle the special contribution of Stalin, the extent to which Stalinism was, so to speak, situation-determined. This is relevant, indeed, to one's picture of Stalin's personal responsibility, but in no way absolves him of such responsibility. If in order to do A it proves necessary to do B, we can, after all, refuse to do B, abandon or modify the aim of attaining A, or resign, or, in extreme circumstances—like Stalin's old comrade Ordzhonikidze—commit suicide.

But Stalin's personal responsibility goes far beyond his being the voice and leader of a party majority in a given historical situation. For one cannot possibly argue that all the immense evils of the Stalin era flowed inescapably from the policy decisions of 1928-29. In assessing Stalin's personal role in bringing these evils about, it is useful to approach the facts from two angles. There was, first, the category of evils which sprang from policy choices which Stalin made and which he need not have made; in other words we are here concerned with consequences (perhaps necessary) of unnecessary decisions. The other category consists of evil actions which can reasonably be attributed to Stalin and which are his direct responsibility.

Of course, these categories shade into one another, as do murder and manslaughter. In the first case, the evils were in a sense situation-determined, but Stalin had a large hand in determining the situation. In the second, his guilt is as clear as a politician's guilt can be.

The most obvious examples of the first category are: the brutality of collectivization and the madly excessive pace of industrial development. In each case, we are dealing with *"excessive excesses"*, since we have already noted that collectivization without coercion was impossible, and rapid industrialization was bound to cause stresses and strains.

Take collectivization first. Some over zealous officials were presumably bound to overdo things, especially since the typical Party man was a townsman with no understanding or sympathy for peasants and their problems. But these officials received orders to impose rapid collectivization, to deport *kulaks*, to seize all livestock, and Stalin was surely the source of these orders. The deportation of the kulaks (which in reality meant anyone who voiced opposition to collectivization) removed at one blow the most efficient farmers. There had been no serious preparation of the measures, no clear orders about how a collective farm should be run. Chinese experience, at least before the communes, suggests that milder ways of proceeding are possible. In any event, the attempt to collectivize all private livestock ended in disaster and a retreat. It is worth reproducing the figures from the official handbook of agricultural statistics:

Livestock Population (Million of Head)

	1928	1934
Horses	32.1	15.4
Cattle	60.1	33.5
Pigs	22.0	11.5
Sheep	97.3	32.9

Yet already by 1934 private livestock holdings were again permitted, and in 1938 over three-quarters of all cows, over two-thirds of all pigs, nearly two-thirds of all sheep, were in private hands. This is evidence of a disastrous error.

Its consequences were profound. Peasant hostility and bitterness were greatly intensified. For many years there were in fact no net investments in agriculture, since the new tractors merely went to replace some of the slaughtered horses. Acute food shortage made itself felt—though the state's control over produce ensured that most of those who died in the resulting famine were peasants and not townsmen. But once all this happened, the case for coercion was greatly strengthened, the need for police measures became more urgent than ever as the power of the censorship was increased, freedom of speech had still further to be curtailed, as part of the necessities of remaining in power and continuing the industrial revolution in an environment grown more hostile as a result of such policies. So Stalin's policy decisions led to events which contributed greatly to the further growth of totalitarianism and the police state.

The same is true of the attempt to do the impossible on the industrial front in the years of the first five-year plan. Much of the effort was simply wasted, as when food was taken from hungry peasants and exported to pay for machines which rusted in the open or were wrecked by untrained workmen. At the same time, the closing of many private workshops deprived the people of consumers' goods which the state, intent on building steelworks and machine-shops, was quite unable to provide. Again, living standards suffered, the hatred of many citizens for the regime increased, the N.K.V.D. had to be expanded and the logic of police rule followed. But Stalin had a big role in the initial decisions to jump too far too fast. (It is interesting to note that Mao, who should have learned the lessons of history, repeated many of these mistakes in China's "great leap forward" of 1958-1959, which suggests that *there are certain errors which Communists repeatedly commit*, possibly due to the suppression, in "anti-rightist" campaigns, of the voice of moderation and common sense.)

One of the consequences of these acute hardships was isolation from foreign countries. Economists often speak of the "demonstration effect", i.e., of the effect of the knowledge of higher living standards abroad on the citizens of poor and underdeveloped countries. This knowledge may act as a spur to effort—but it also generates resistance to sacrifice. Stalin and his regime systematically "shielded" Soviet citizens from knowledge of the outside world, by censorship, by cutting off personal contacts, by misinformation. The need to do so, in their eyes, was greatly increased by the extent of the drop in living standards in the early thirties.

But we must now come to Stalin's more direct contribution to the brutality and terrorism of the Stalin era. There was, firstly, his needless cruelty which showed itself already in the methods used to impose collectivization. The great purges were surely not "objectively necessary". To explain them one has to take into account Stalin's thirst for supreme power, his intense pathological suspiciousness, i.e. matters pertaining to Stalin's personal position and character. These led him to massacre the majority of the "Stalinist" central committee elected in 1934, who had supported or at the very least tolerated Stalin's policies up to that date. The facts suggest that they believed that relaxation was possible and desirable; many of them seem to have died for the crime of saying so. Nor was there any "police logic" for the scale and drastic nature of the purges. Indeed, the police chiefs figured prominently among the victims. True, there was a kind of "snow-balling" of arrests which might have got out of control in 1938, but this was due largely to the effect of the terror on the police, who had to show zeal or go under. Nor can any "necessity" explain the post-war repressions, the death of Voznesensky, the so-called "Leningrad affair", the shooting of the Jewish intellectuals, the "doctors' plot". Stalin played so prominently a personal role in establishing a reign of terror in the Party and the country that he must bear direct responsibility even where executions were the result of false information supplied to him by his subordinates for reasons of their own.

The atmosphere of terror had, of course, far-reaching consequences in every sphere of Soviet life. It became particularly grotesque and purposeless in the last years of Stalin, when the social and economic developments, plus victory in war, provided the Soviet regime with a much firmer base among the people, so that a considerable part of the discontent was the result, rather than the cause, of repressive measures. Many obviously overdue reforms had to await his death. As did Tsar Nicholas I, a century earlier, Stalin was able to delay "necessary" changes.

Many other examples can be given of the personal role of Stalin. On the economic front, the miserable state of the peasants in 1953 was due largely to Stalin's obstinate refusal to face the facts and listen to serious advice. He contributed greatly to wasteful and grandiose schemes to "transform nature", and to a wasteful and grandiose style of architecture. In the military field, history will, I think, support Khrushchev's accusation that Stalin's inability to see the signs of a German attack, his unwillingness to allow preparations, his massacre of the best Soviet officers, all made a personal contribution to the Russian disasters of 1941. Stalin personally insisted on his own deification, the rewriting of history, the creation of myths. Some myths were based on lies which he himself publicly uttered. For instance, in 1935 he announced: "We have had no poor for two or three years now"— and this when bread had reached the highest price, in relation to wages, that it had ever attained in Soviet history. Or equally ridiculous was his claim, in 1947, that Moscow "had completely abolished slums". In this personal way he made impossible all serious discussion either of living standards or the housing problem, just as his wildly false assertions about "Bukharin and Trotsky, agents of Hitler and the Mikado", made the writing of Soviet history impossible in Russia. One could argue that the myth about "voluntary collectivization" was an objectively necessary lie, in the sense of transcending Stalin's personality; indeed, this lie figures in the Party program adopted by the 22nd Congress last November. But Stalin's lies went very much beyond this, and beyond the distortions and myths which can be ascribed to other politicians in other countries.

Throughout Russia, officials at all levels modeled themselves on Stalin, and each succeeded in imposing more unnecessary misery on more subordinates, stultifying initiative, penalizing intelligence, discouraging originality. The price of all this is still being paid.

The urgent need to prepare for war has often been advanced as an excuse for Stalin's industrial "tempos" and for the terror. This can hardly be accepted. In the worst years of social coercion and over-ambitious plans, i.e., 1929-33, Hitler was only just climbing to power, and Comintern policy showed that he was not then regarded as the main enemy. It is possible that Stalin was liquidating all potential opponents in the Purges of 1936-38 as a precaution in case war broke out, though this seems doubtful for a variety of reasons. But it is quite false to use the result of the war as ex-post-factum justification of Stalinism. Perhaps with less harsh policies, the greater degree of loyalty in 1941 would have offset a smaller industrial base? In any event the Purges not only led to the slaughter of the best military officers but also halted the growth of heavy industry.

The attentive reader will have noticed that this analysis has some features in common with Khrushchev's. Before 1934, Stalin had been carrying out policies which commanded the assent of a majority of the Party and which, like collectivization, had been accepted as necessary and irreversible by the bulk of Party members, whatever their reservations about particular mistakes and acts of brutality. However, after that date he took more and more personal, arbitrary measures, massacred much of the Party, behaved like an oriental despot. It is true that he was also arbitrary before 1934, and that he took some wise decisions after that date; but there is a case for placing a qualitative change around then.

But this is by no means the end of the matter. It is not only a question of making some obvious remarks concerning Khruschev's own role during the terror. Of much more general significance is the fact that the events prior to 1934, including the building-up of Stalin into an all-powerful and infallible dictator (by men many of whom he afterwards massacred), cannot be disassociated with what followed; at the very least they provided Stalin with his opportunity. This is where the historian must avoid the twin and opposite pitfalls of regarding it as a chapter of "personalized" accidents. At each stage there are choices to be made, though the range of possible choices is generally much narrower than people suppose. In 1928 any practicable Bolshevik program would have been harsh and unpopular. It might not have been so harsh and unpopular but for choices which need not necessarily have been made. If before 1934, i.e., in the very period of maximum social coercion, Stalin truly represented the will of the Party, and Khrushchev argues that he did, some totalitarian consequences logically follow. One of these, as already suggested, is the semi-militarized party led by a Fuehrer, a dictator, because without an unquestioned leader the consequences of the policies adopted could not be faced.

But even if it is true that the triumph of a dictator may be explained by objective circumstances which certainly existed in the Soviet situation, the acts of a dictator once he has "arrived" involve a considerable (though of course not infinite) degree of personal choice. Those who gave him the opportunity to act in an arbitrary and cruel way, who adopted policies which involved arbitrariness and coercion on a big scale, cannot ascribe subsequent events to the wickedness of one man or his immediate associates and claim that their hands are clean, even indeed if they were shot themselves on Stalin's orders. The whole-hog Stalin, in other words, was not "necessary", but the possibility of a Stalin was a necessary consequence of the effort of a minority group to keep power and to carry out a vast social economic revolution in a very short time. And some elements of Stalinism were, in those circumstances, scarcely avoidable.

The serious problem for us is to see how far certain elements of Stalinism, in the sense of purposefully-applied social coercion, imposed by a party in the name of an ideology, are likely or liable to accompany rapid economic development even in non-Communist countries. For it is surely true that many of the problems tackled by Stalin so brutally are present elsewhere, though events in the U.S.S.R. were, of course, deeply affected by peculiar features of Russia and of Bolshevism. The West should indeed emphasize the high cost in human and material terms of a Stalin, and show that the rise of such a man to supreme power in the Soviet Union was, to use the familiar Soviet-Marxist jargon phrase, "not accidental". Indeed, some Western historians who normally write "personalist" and empiricist history will begin to see the virtues of an approach they normally deride as "historicist"; they will analyze Soviet history to establish patterns, regularities, "necessities" which lead to Stalin. By contrast, an embarrassed Khrushchev will be—is being forced to give an un-Marxist emphasis to personal and accidental factors.

But, of course, we must not confine our search for "necessities" in history only to instances which happen to serve a propagandist purpose. This would be a typically Soviet approach to historiography, only in reverse. It is particularly important to think very seriously about the interrelationship of coercion and industrialization, about the nature of the obstacles and vicious circles which drive men to think in totalitarian terms. Unless we realize how complex are the problems which development brings, how irrelevant are many of our ideas to the practical possibilities open to statesmen in these countries, we may unconsciously drive them towards the road which led to Stalin. They cannot be satisfied with "the pace of a tortoise".

19. Nikita Khrushchev

DE-STALINIZATION SPEECH

February 24-25, 1956

Comrades, in the report of the Central Committee of the party at the 20th Congress, in a number of speeches by delegates to the Congress, as also formerly during the plenary CC/CPSU [Central Committee of the Communist Party of the Soviet Union] sessions, quite a lot has been said about the cult of the individual and about its harmful consequences.

After Stalin's death the Central Committee of the party began to implement a policy of explaining concisely and consistently that it is impermissible and foreign to the spirit of Marxism-Leninism to elevate one person, to transform him into superman possessing supernatural characteristics akin to those of a god. Such a man supposedly knows everything, sees everything, thinks for everyone, can do anything, is infallible in his behavior.

Such a belief about a man, and specifically about Stalin, was cultivated among us for many years.

The objective of the present report is not a thorough evaluation of Stalin's life and activity. Concerning Stalin's merits, an entirely sufficient number of books, pamphlets and studies had already been written in his lifetime. The role of Stalin in the preparation and execution of the Socialist revolution, in the civil-war, and in the fight for the construction of socialism in our country is universally known. Everyone knows this well. At present, we are concerned with a question which has immense importance for the party now and for the future—(we are concerned) with how the cult of the person of Stalin has been gradually growing, the cult which became at a certain specific stage the source of a whole series of exceedingly serious and grave perversions of party principles, of party democracy, of revolutionary legality.

Because of the fact that not all as yet realize fully the practical consequences resulting from the cult of the individual, the great harm caused by the violation of the principle of collective direction of the party and because of the accumulation of immense and limitless power in the hands of one person—the Central Committee of the party considers it absolutely necessary to make the material pertaining to this matter available to the 20th Congress of the Communist Party of the Soviet Union.

Allow me first of all to remind you how severely the classics of Marxism-Leninism denounced every manifestation of the cult of the individual....

Sometime later Engels wrote: "Both Marx and I have always been against any public manifestation with regard to individuals, with the exception of cases when it had an important purpose; and we most strongly opposed such manifestations which during our lifetime concerned us personally."

The great modesty of the genius of the Revolution, Vladimir Ilyich Lenin, is known. Lenin had always stressed the role of the people as the creator of history, the directing and organizational role of the party as a living and creative organism, and also the role of the Central Committee.

Marxism does not negate the role of the leaders of the workers' class in directing the revolutionary liberation movement.

While ascribing great importance to the role of the leaders and organizers of the masses, Lenin at the same time mercilessly stigmatized every manifestation of the cult of the individual, inexorably combated the foreign-to-Marxism views about a "hero" and a "crowd," and countered all efforts to oppose a "hero" to the masses and to the people.

Lenin taught that the party's strength depends on its indissoluble unity with the masses, on the fact that behind the party follow the people— workers, peasants and intelligentsia. "Only he will win and retain the power," said Lenin, "who believes in the people, who submerges himself in the fountain of the living creativeness of the people."

Lenin spoke with pride about the Bolshevik Communist Party as the leader and teacher of the people; he called for the presentation of all the most important questions before the opinion of knowledgeable workers, before the opinion of their party; he said: "We believe in it, we see in it the wisdom, the honor, and the conscience of our epoch."

Lenin resolutely stood against every attempt aimed at belittling or weakening the directing role of the party in the structure of the Soviet state. He worked out Bolshevik principles of party direction and norms of party life, stressing that the guiding principle of party leadership is its collegiality. Already during the prerevolutionary years, Lenin called the central committee of the party a collective of leaders and the guardian and interpreter of party principles. "During the period between congresses," pointed out Lenin, "the central committee guards and interprets the principles of the party."

Underlining the role of the central committee of the party and its authority, Vladimir Ilyich pointed out: "Our central committee constituted itself as a closely centralized and highly authoritative group."

During Lenin's life the central committee of the party was a real expression of collective leadership of the party and of the nation. Being a militant Marxist-revolutionist, always unyielding in matters of principle, Lenin never imposed by force his views upon his co-workers. He tried to convince; he patiently explained his opinions to others. Lenin always diligently observed that the norms of party life were realized, that the party statute was enforced, that the party congresses and the plenary sessions of the central committee took place at the proper intervals.

In addition to the great accomplishments of V. I. Lenin for the victory of the working class and of the working peasants, for the victory of our party and for the application of the ideas of scientific communism to life, his acute mind expressed itself also in this that he detected in Stalin in time those negative characteristics which resulted later in grave consequences. Fearing the future fate of the party and of the Soviet nation, V. I. Lenin made a completely correct characterization of Stalin, pointing out that it was necessary to consider the question of transferring Stalin from the position of Secretary General because of the fact that Stalin is excessively rude, that he does not have a proper attitude toward his comrades, that he is capricious and abuses his power.

In December 1922, in a letter to the party congress, Vladimir Ilyich wrote: "After taking over the position of Secretary General, Comrade Stalin accumulated in his hands immeasurable power and I am not certain whether he will be always able to use this power with the required care."

This letter—a political document of tremendous importance, known in the party history as Lenin's testament—was distributed among the delegates to the Thirteenth Party Congress. You have read it and will undoubtedly read it again more than once. You might reflect on Lenin's plain words, in which expression is given to Vladimir Ilyich's anxiety concerning the party, the people, the state, and the future direction of party policy....

This document of Lenin's was made known to the delegates at the 13th Party Congress, who discussed the question of transferring Stalin from the position of Secretary General. The delegates declared themselves in favor of retaining Stalin in this post, hoping that he would heed the critical remarks of Vladimir Ilyich and would be able to overcome the defects which caused Lenin serious anxiety.

Comrades, the party congress should become acquainted with two new documents, which confirm Stalin's character as already outlined by Vladimir Ilyich Lenin in his testament. These documents are a letter from Nadezhda Konstantinovna Krupskaya to [Lev B.] Kamenev, who was at that time head of the Political Bureau, and a personal letter from Vladimir Ilyich Lenin to Stalin.

1. I will now read these documents:

Lev Borisovich:

Because of a short letter which I had written in words dictated to me by Vladimir Ilyich by permission of the doctors, Stalin allowed himself yesterday an unusually rude outburst directed at me. This is not my first day in the party. During all these 30 years I have never heard from any comrade one word of rudeness. The business of the party and of Ilyich are not less dear to me than to Stalin. I need at present the maximum of self-control. What one can and what one cannot discuss with Ilyich—I know better than any doctor, because I know what makes him nervous and what does not, in any case I know better than Stalin. I am turning to you and to Grigory [E. Zinoviev] as much closer comrades of V. I. and I beg you to protect me from rude interference with my private life and from vile invectives and threats. I have no doubt as to what will be the unanimous decision of the Control Commission, with which Stalin sees fit to threaten me; however, I have neither the strength nor the time to waste on this foolish quarrel. And I am a living person and my nerves are strained to the utmost.

N. Krupskaya

Nadezhda Konstantinovna wrote this letter on December 23, 1922. After two and a half months, in March 1923, Vladimir Ilyich Lenin sent Stalin the following letter:

2. The Letter of V. I. Lenin

To Comrade Stalin:
(Copies For : Kamenev and Zinoviev.)
Dear Comrade Stalin:

You permitted yourself a rude summons of my wife to the telephone and a rude reprimand of her. Despite the fact that she told you that she agreed to forget what was said, nevertheless Zinoviev and Kamenev heard about it from her. I have no intention to forget so easily that which is being done against me and I need not stress here that I consider as directed against me that which is being done against my wife. I ask you, therefore, that you weigh carefully whether you are agreeable to retracting your words and apologizing or whether you prefer the severance of relations between us. [Commotion in the hall]

Sincerely,
Lenin
March 5, 1923

Comrades, I will not comment on these documents. They speak eloquently for themselves. Since Stalin could behave in this manner during Lenin's life, could thus behave toward Nadezhda Konstantinovna Krupskaya, whom the party knows well and values highly as a loyal friend of Lenin and as an active fighter for the cause of the party since its creation—we can easily imagine how Stalin treated other people. These negative characteristics of his developed steadily and during the last years acquired an absolutely insufferable character.

As later events have proven, Lenin's anxiety was justified; in the first period after Lenin's death Stalin still paid attention to his (i.e. Lenin's) advice, but, later he began to disregard the serious admonitions of Vladimir Ilyich.

When we analyze the practice of Stalin in regard to the direction of the party and of the country, when we pause to consider everything which Stalin perpetrated, we must be convinced that Lenin's fears were justified. The negative characteristics of Stalin, which, in Lenin's time, were only incipient, transformed themselves during the last years into a grave abuse of power by Stalin which caused untold harm to our party.

We have to consider seriously and analyze correctly this matter in order that we may preclude any possibility of a repetition in any form whatever of what took place during the life of Stalin, who absolutely did not tolerate collegiality in leadership and in work, and who practiced brutal violence, not only toward everything which opposed him, but also toward that which seemed, to his capricious and despotic character, contrary to his concepts.

Stalin acted not through persuasion, explanation, and patient cooperation with people, but by imposing his concepts and demanding absolute submission to his opinion. Whoever opposed this concept or tried to prove his viewpoint, and the correctness of his position was doomed to removal from the leading collective and to subsequent moral and physical annihilation. This was especially true during the period following the 17th party congress, when many prominent party leaders and rank-and-file party workers, honest and dedicated to the cause of communism, fell victim to Stalin's despotism.

We must affirm that the party had fought a serious fight against the Trotskyites, rightists and bourgeois nationalists, and that it disarmed ideologically all the enemies of Leninism. This ideological fight was carried on successfully as a result of which the party became strengthened and tempered. Here Stalin played a positive role.

The party led a great political-ideological struggle against those in its own ranks who proposed anti-Leninist theses, who represented a political line hostile to the party and to the cause of socialism. This was a stubborn and a difficult fight but a necessary one, because the political line of both the Trotskyite-Zinovievite bloc and of the Bukharinites led actually toward the restoration of capitalism and capitulation to the world bourgeoisie. Let us consider for a moment what would have happened if in 1928-1929 the political line of right deviation had prevailed among us, or orientation toward "cotton-dress industrialization," or toward the kulak, etc. We would not now have a powerful heavy industry, we would not have the Kolkhozes, we would find ourselves disarmed and weak in a capitalist encirclement.

It was for this reason that the party led an inexorable ideological fight and explained to all party members and to the non-party masses the harm and the danger of the anti-Leninist proposals of the Trotskyite opposition and the rightist opportunists. And this great work of explaining the party line bore fruit; both Trotskyites and the rightist opportunists were politically isolated; the overwhelming party majority supported the Leninist line and the party was able to awaken and organize the working masses to apply the Leninist party line and to build socialism.

Worth noting is the fact that even during the progress of the furious ideological fight against the Trotskyites, the Zinovievites, the Bukharinites and others, extreme repressive measures were not used against them. The fight was on ideological grounds. But some years later when socialism in our country was fundamentally constructed, when the exploiting classes were generally liquidated, when the Soviet social structure had radically changed, when the social basis for political movements and groups hostile to the party had violently contracted, when the ideological opponents of the party were long since defeated politically—then the repression directed against them began.

It was precisely during this period (1935, 1937, and 1938) that the practice of mass repression through the government apparatus was born, first against the enemies of Leninism—Trotskyites, Zinovievites, Bukharinites, long since politically defeated by the party, and subsequently also against many honest Communists, against those party cadres who had borne the heavy load of the Civil War and the first and most difficult years of industrialization and collectivization, who actively fought against the Trotskyites and the rightists for the Leninist party line.

Stalin originated the concept enemy of the people. This term automatically rendered it unnecessary that the ideological errors of a man or men engaged in a controversy be proven; this term made possible the usage of the most cruel repression, violating all norms of revolutionary legality, against anyone who in any way disagreed with Stalin, against those who were only suspected of hostile intent, against those who had bad reputations. This concept, enemy of the people, actually eliminated the possibility of any kind of ideological fight or the making of one's views known on this or that issue even those of a practical character. In the main, and in actuality, the only proof of guilt used, against all norms of current legal science, was the confession of the accused himself, and, as subsequent probing proved, confessions were acquired through physical pressures against the accused.

This led to glaring violations of revolutionary legality, and to the fact that many entirely innocent persons, who in the past had defended the party line, became victims.

We must assert that in regard to those persons who in their time had opposed the party line, there were often no sufficiently serious reasons for their physical annihilation. The formula "enemy of the people" was specifically introduced for the purpose of physically annihilating such individuals.

It is a fact that many persons who were later annihilated as enemies of the party and people had worked with Lenin during his life. Some of these persons had made errors during Lenin's life, but, despite this, Lenin benefited by their work, he corrected them, and he did everything possible to retain them in the ranks of the party; he induced them to follow him....

Everyone knows how irreconcilable Lenin was with the ideological enemies of Marxism, with those who deviated from the correct party line. At the same time, however, Lenin, as is evident from the given document, in his practice of directing the party demanded the most intimate party contact with people who have shown indecision or temporary nonconformity with the party line, but whom it was possible to return to the party path. Lenin advised that such people should be patiently educated without the application of extreme methods.

Lenin's wisdom in dealing with people was evident in his work with cadres.

An entirely different relationship with people characterized Stalin. Lenin's traits—patient work with people, stubborn and painstaking education of them; the ability to induce people to follow him without using compulsion, but rather through the ideological influence on them of the whole collective—were entirely foreign to Stalin. He (Stalin) discarded the Leninist method of convincing and educating; he abandoned the method of ideological struggle for that of administrative violence, mass repressions, and terror. He acted on an increasingly larger scale and more stubbornly through punitive organs, at the same time often violating all existing norms of morality and of Soviet laws.

Arbitrary behavior by one person encouraged and permitted arbitrariness in others. Mass arrests and deportations of many thousands of people, execution without trial and without normal investigation created conditions of insecurity, fear, and even desperation.

This, of course, did not contribute toward unity of the party ranks and of all strata of working people, but on the contrary brought about annihilation and the expulsion from the party of workers who were loyal but inconvenient to Stalin.

Our party fought for the implementation of Lenin's plans for the construction of socialism. This was an ideological fight. Had Leninist principles been observed during the course of this fight, had the party's devotion to principles been skillfully combined with a keen and solicitous concern for people, had they not been repelled and wasted but rather drawn to our side—we certainly would not have had such a brutal violation of revolutionary legality and many thousands of people would not have fallen victim of the method of terror. Extraordinary methods would then have been resorted to only against those people who had in fact committed criminal acts against the Soviet system.

Let us recall some historical facts.

In the days before the October Revolution, two members of the central committee of the Bolshevik Party—Kamenev and Zinoviev—declared themselves against Lenin's plan for an armed uprising. In addition, on October 18 they published in the Menshevik newspaper, *Novaya Zhizn*, a statement declaring that the Bolsheviks were making preparations for an uprising and that they considered it adventuristic. Kamenev and Zinoviev thus disclosed to the enemy the decision of the central committee to stage the uprising, and that the uprising had been organized to take place within the very near future.

This was treason against the party and against the revolution. In this connection, V. I. Lenin wrote: "Kamenev and Zinoviev revealed the decision of the central committee of their party on the armed uprising to Rodzyanko and Kerensky..." He put before the central committee the question of Zinoviev's and Kamenev's expulsion from the party.

However, after the great Socialist October revolution, as is known, Zinoviev and Kamenev were given leading positions. Lenin put them in positions in which they carried out most responsible party tasks and participated actively in the work of the leading party and Soviet organs. It is known that Zinoviev and Kamenev committed a number of other serious errors during Lenin's life. In his testament Lenin warned that "Zinoviev's and Kamenev's October episode was of course not an accident." But Lenin did not pose the mention of their arrest and certainly not of their shooting.

Or, let us take the example of the Trotskyites. At present, after a sufficiently long historical period, we can speak about the fight with the Trotskyites with complete calm and can analyze this matter with sufficient objectivity. After all, around Trotsky were people whose origin cannot by any means be traced to bourgeois society. Part of them belonged to the party intelligentsia and a certain part were recruited from among the workers. We can name many individuals who in their time joined the Trotskyites; however, these same individuals took an active part in the workers' movement before the Revolution, during the Socialist October revolution itself, and also in the consolidation of the victory of this greatest of revolutions. Many of them broke with Trotskyism and returned to Leninist positions. Was it necessary to annihilate such people? We are deeply convinced that had Lenin lived such an extreme method would not have been used against many of them.

Such are only a few historical facts. But can it be said that Lenin did not decide to use even the most severe means against enemies of the revolution when this was actually necessary? No, no one can say this. Vladimir Ilyich demanded uncompromising dealings with the enemies of the revolution and of the working class and when necessary resorted ruthlessly to such methods. You will recall only V. I. Lenin's fight with the Socialist Revolutionary organizers of the anti-Soviet uprising, with the counterrevolutionary kulaks in 1918 and with others, when Lenin without hesitation used the most extreme methods against the enemies. Lenin used such methods, however, only against actual class enemies and not against those who blunder, who err, and whom it was possible to lead through ideological influence and even retain in the leadership. Lenin used severe methods only in the most necessary cases, when the exploiting classes were still in existence and were vigorously opposing the revolution, when the struggle for survival was decidedly assuming the sharpest forms, even including a civil war.

Stalin, on the other hand, used extreme methods and mass repressions at a time when the revolution was already victorious, when the Soviet state was strengthened, when the exploiting classes were already liquidated, and socialist relations were rooted solidly in all phases of national economy, when our party was politically consolidated and had strengthened itself both numerically and ideologically. It is clear that here Stalin showed in a whole series of cases his intolerance, his brutality and his abuse of power. Instead of proving his political correctness and mobilizing the masses, he often chose the path of repression and physical annihilation, not only against actual enemies, but also against individuals who had not committed any crimes against the party and the Soviet Government. Here we see no wisdom but only a demonstration of the brutal force which had once so alarmed V. I. Lenin....

Considering the question of the cult of an individual, we must first of all show everyone what harm this caused to the interests of our party.

Vladimir Ilyich Lenin had always stressed the party's role and significance in the direction of the Socialist government of workers and peasants; he saw in this the chief precondition for a successful building of socialism in our country. Pointing to the great responsibility of the Bolshevik Party, as ruling party of the Soviet state, Lenin called for the most meticulous observance of all norms of party life; he called for the realization of the principles of collegiality in the direction of the party and the state.

Collegiality of leadership flows from the very nature of our party, a party built on the principles of democratic centralism. "This means," said Lenin, "that all party matters are accomplished by all party members—directly or through representatives—who without any exceptions are subject to the same rules; in addition, all administrative members, all directing collegia, all holders of party positions are elective, they must account for their activities and are recallable."

It is known that Lenin himself offered an example of the most careful observance of these principles. There was no matter so important that Lenin himself decided it without asking for advice and approval of the majority of the Central Committee members or of the members of the Central Committee's Political Bureau. In the most difficult period for our party and our country, Lenin considered it necessary regularly to convoke congresses, party conferences, and plenary sessions of the Central Committee at which all the most important questions were discussed and where resolutions, carefully worked out by the collective of leaders, were approved.

We can recall, for example, the year 1918 when the country was threatened by the attack of the imperialistic interventionists. In this situation the 7th party congress was convened in order to discuss a vitally important matter which could not be postponed—the matter of peace. In 1919, while the civil war was raging, the 8th party congress convened which adopted a new party program, decided such important matters as the relationship with the peasant masses, the organization of the Red Army, the leading role of the party in the work of the Soviets, the correction of the social composition of the party, and other matters. In 1920 the 9th party congress was convened which laid down guiding principles pertaining to the party's work in the sphere of economic construction. In 1921 the 10th party congress accepted Lenin's New Economic Policy and the historical resolution called "About Party Unity."

During Lenin's life, party congresses were convened regularly; always when a radical turn in the development of the party and the country took place, Lenin considered it absolutely necessary that the party discuss at length all the basic matters pertaining to internal and foreign policy and to questions bearing on the development of party and government.

It is very characteristic that Lenin addressed to the party congress as the highest party organ his last articles, letters and remarks. During the period between congresses, the central committee of the party, acting as the most authoritative leading collective, meticulously observed the principles of the party and carried out its policy.

So it was during Lenin's life. Were our party's holy Leninist principles observed after the death of Vladimir Ilyich?

Whereas, during the first few years after Lenin's death, party congresses and central committee plenums took place more or less regularly; later, when Stalin began increasingly to abuse his power, these principles were brutally violated. This was especially evident during the last 15 years of his life. Was it a normal situation when 13 years elapsed between the 18th and 19th party congresses, years during which our party and our country had experienced so many important events? These events demanded categorically that the party should have passed resolutions pertaining to the country's defense during the Patriotic War [World War II] and to peacetime construction after the war. Even after the end of the war a congress was not convened for over seven years. Central committee plenums were hardly ever called. It should be sufficient to mention that during all the years of the Patriotic War not a single central committee plenum took place. It is true that there was an attempt to call a central committee plenum in October 1941, when central committee members from the whole country were called to Moscow. They waited two days for the opening of the plenum, but in vain. Stalin did not even want to meet and talk to the Central Committee members. This fact shows how demoralized Stalin was in the first months of the war and how haughtily and disdainfully he treated the Central Committee members.

In practice, Stalin ignored the norms of party life and trampled on the Leninist principle of collective party leadership.

Stalin's willfulness *vis-à-vis* the party and its central committee became fully evident after the 17th party congress which took place in 1934.

Having at its disposal numerous data showing brutal willfulness toward party cadres, the central committee has created a party commission under the control of the central committee presidium; it was charged with investigating what made possible the mass repressions against the majority of the central committee members and candidates elected at the 17th Congress of the All-Union Communist Party (Bolsheviks).

The commission has become acquainted with a large quantity of materials in the NKVD archives and with other documents and has established many facts pertaining to the fabrication of cases against Communists, to false accusations, to glaring abuses of socialist legality, which resulted in the death of innocent people. It became apparent that many party, Soviet and economic activists who were branded in 1937-1938 as "enemies" were actually never enemies, spies, wreckers, etc., but were always honest Communists; they were only so stigmatized and, often, no longer able to bear barbaric tortures, they charged themselves (at the order of the investigative judges—falsifiers) with all kinds of grave and unlikely crimes. The commission has presented to the central committee presidium lengthy and documented materials pertaining to mass repressions against the delegates to the 17th party congress and against members of the central committee elected at that congress. These materials have been studied by the presidium of the central committee.

It was determined that of the 139 members and candidates of the party's Central Committee who were elected at the 17th congress, 98 persons, i.e. 70 percent, were arrested and shot (mostly in 1937-1938). [Indignation in the Hall.] What was the composition of the delegates to the 17th Congress? It is known that 80 percent of the voting participants of the 17th Congress joined the party during the years of conspiracy before the revolution and during the civil war; this means before 1921. By social origin the basic mass of the delegates to the congress were workers (60 percent of the voting members).

For this reason, it was inconceivable that a congress so composed would have elected a central committee a majority of whom would prove to be enemies of the party. The only reason why 70 percent of central committee members and candidates elected at the 17th Congress were branded as enemies of the party and of the people was because honest Communists were slandered, accusations against them were fabricated, and revolutionary legality was gravely undermined.

The same fate met not only the central committee members but also the majority of the delegates to the 17th party congress. Of 1,966 delegates with either voting or advisory rights, 1,108 persons were arrested on charges of antirevolutionary crimes, i.e., decidedly more than a majority. This very fact shows how absurd, wild and contrary to common sense were the charges of counterrevolutionary crimes made out as we now see, aqainst a majority of participants at the 17th party congress. [Indignation in the hall.]

We should recall that the 17th party congress is historically known as the Congress of Victors. Delegates to the congress were active participants in the building of our socialist state; many of them suffered and fought for party interests during the pre-Revolutionary years in the conspiracy and at the civil-war fronts; they fought their enemies valiantly and often nervelessly looked into the face of death. How then can we believe that such people could prove to be "two-faced" and had joined the camps of the enemies of socialism during the era after the political liquidation of Zinovievites, Trotskyites and rightists and after the great accomplishments of socialist construction? This was the result of the abuse of power by Stalin, who began to use mass terror against the party cadres.

What is the reason that mass repressions against activists increased more and more after the 17th party congress? It was because at that time Stalin had so elevated himself above the party and above the nation that he ceased to consider either the central committee or the party. While he still reckoned with the opinion of the collective before the 17th congress, after the complete political liquidation of the Trotskyites, Zinovievites and Bukharinites, when as a result of that fight and socialist victories the party achieved unity, Stalin ceased to an ever greater degree to consider the members of the party's central committee and even the members of the Political Bureau. Stalin thought that now he could decide all things alone and all he needed were statisticians; he treated all others in such a way that they could only listen to and praise him.

After the criminal murder of S[ergei] M. Kirov, mass repressions and brutal acts of violation of socialist legality began. On the evening of December 1, 1934, on Stalin's initiative (without the approval of the Political Bureau—which was passed two days later, casually), the Secretary of the Presidium of the Central Executive Committee, Yenukidze, signed the following directive:

"1. Investigative agencies are directed to speed up the cases of those accused of the preparation or execution of acts of terror.

"2. Judicial organs are directed not to hold up the execution of death sentences pertaining to crimes of this category in order to consider the possibility of pardon, because the Presidium of the Central Executive Committee [of the] U.S.S.R. does not consider as possible the receiving of petitions of this sort.

"3. The organs of the Commissariat of Internal Affairs are directed to execute the death sentences against criminals of the above-mentioned category immediately after the passage of sentences."

This directive became the basis for mass acts of abuse against socialist legality. During many of the fabricated court cases the accused were charged with "the preparation" of terroristic acts; this deprived them of any possibility that their cases might be re-examined, even when they stated before the court that their confessions were secured by force, and when, in a convincing manner, they disproved the accusations against them.

It must be asserted that to this day the circumstances surrounding Kirov's murder hide many things which are inexplicable and mysterious and demand a most careful examination. There are reasons for the suspicion that the killer of Kirov, Nikolayev, was assisted by someone from among the people whose duty it was to protect the person of Kirov....

Mass repressions grew tremendously from the end of 1936 after a telegram from Stalin and [Andrei] Zhdanov, dated from Sochi on September 25, 1936, was addressed to Kaganovich, Molotov and other members of the Political Bureau. The content of the telegram was as follows:

"We deem it absolutely necessary and urgent that Comrade Yezhov be nominated to the post of People's Commissar for Internal Affairs. Yagoda has definitely proved himself to be incapable of unmasking the Trotskyite-Zinovievite bloc. The OGPU is four years behind in this matter. This is noted by all party workers and by the majority of the representatives of the NKVD."

Strictly speaking we should stress that Stalin did not meet with and, therefore, could not know the opinion of party workers.

This Stalinist formulation that the "NKVD is four years behind" in applying mass repression and that there is a necessity for catching up with the neglected work directly pushed the NKVD workers on the path of mass arrests and executions.

We should state that this formulation was also forced on the February-March plenary session of the central committee of the All-Union Communist Party (Bolsheviks) in 1937. The plenary resolution approved it on the basis of Yezhov's report, "Lessons flowing from the harmful activity, diversion and espionage of the Japanese-German-Trotskyite agents," stating: "The plenum of the central committee of the All-Union Communist Party (Bolsheviks) considers that all facts revealed during the investigation into the matter of an anti-Soviet Trotskyite center and of its followers in the provinces show that the People's Commissariat of Internal Affairs has fallen behind at least four years in the attempt to unmask these most inexorable enemies of the people."

The mass repressions at this time were made under the slogan of a fight against the Trotskyites. Did the Trotskyites at this time actually constitute such a danger to our party and to the Soviet state? We should recall that in 1927, on the eve of the 15th party congress, only some 4,000 votes were cast for the Trotskyite-Zinovievite opposition while there were 724,000 for the party line. During the 10 years which passed between the 15th party congress and the February-March central committee plenum, Trotskyism was completely disarmed; many former Trotskyites had changed their former views and worked in the various sectors building socialism. It is clear that in the situation of socialist victory there was no basis for mass terror in the country.

Stalin's report at the February-March central committee plenum in 1937, "Deficiencies of party work and methods for the liquidation of the Trotskyites and of other two-facers," contained an attempt at theoretical justification of the mass terror policy under the pretext that as we march forward toward socialism class war must allegedly sharpen. Stalin asserted that both history and Lenin taught him this.

Actually Lenin taught that the application of revolutionary violence is necessitated by the resistance of the exploiting classes, and this referred to the era when the exploiting classes existed and were powerful. As soon as the nation's political situation had improved, when in January 1920 the Red Army took Rostov and thus won a most important victory over [White General Anton] Denikin, Lenin instructed [Cheka chief Felix] Dzerzhinsky to stop mass terror and to abolish the death penalty. Lenin justified this important political move of the Soviet state in the following manner in his report at the session of the All-Union Central Executive Committee on

February 2, 1920:

"We were forced to use terror because of the terror practiced by the Entente, when strong world powers threw their hordes against us, not avoiding any type of conduct. We would not have lasted two days had we not answered these attempts of officers and White Guardists in a merciless fashion; this meant the use of terror, but this was forced upon us by the terrorist methods of the Entente.

"But as soon as we attained a decisive victory, even before the end of the war, immediately after taking Rostov, we gave up the use of the death penalty and thus proved that we intend to execute our own program in the manner that we promised. We say that the application of violence flows out of the decision to smother the exploiters, the big landowners and the capitalists; as soon as this was accomplished we gave up the use of all extraordinary methods. We have proved this in practice."

Stalin deviated from these clear and plain precepts of Lenin. Stalin put the party and the NKVD up to the use of mass terror when the exploiting classes had been liquidated in our country and when there were no serious reasons for the use of extraordinary mass terror.

This terror was actually directed not at the remnants of the defeated exploiting classes but against the honest workers of the party and of the Soviet state; against them were made lying, slanderous and absurd accusations concerning "two-facedness," "espionage," "sabotage," preparation of fictitious "plots," etc....

Using Stalin's formulation, namely, that the closer we are to socialism the more enemies we will have, and using the resolution of the February-March Central Committee plenum passed on the basis of Yezhov's report—the *provocateurs* who had infiltrated the state-security organs together with conscienceless careerists began to protect with the party name the mass terror against party cadres, cadres of the Soviet state and the ordinary Soviet citizens. It should suffice to say that the number of arrests based on charges of counterrevolutionary crimes had grown ten times between 1936 and 1937.

It is known that brutal willfulness was practiced against leading party workers. The party statute, approved at the 17th party congress, was based on Leninist principles expressed at the 10th party congress. It stated that, in order to apply an extreme method such as exclusion from the party against a central committee member, against a central committee candidate and against a member of the party control commission, "it is necessary to call a Central Committee plenum and to invite to the plenum all Central Committee candidate members and all members of the Party Control Commission"; only if two-thirds of the members of such a general assembly of responsible party leaders find it necessary, only then can a central committee member or candidate be expelled.

The majority of the Central Committee members and candidates elected at the 17th congress and arrested in 1937-1938 were expelled from the party illegally through the brutal abuse of the party statute, because the question of their expulsion was never studied at the Central Committee plenum.

Now when the cases of some of these so-called "spies" and "saboteurs" were examined it was found that all their cases were fabricated. Confessions of guilt of many arrested and charged with enemy activity were gained with the help of cruel and inhuman tortures.

At the same time Stalin, as we have been informed by members of the Political Bureau of that time, did not show them the statements of many accused political activists when they retracted their confessions before the military tribunal and asked for an objective examination of their cases. There were many such declarations, and Stalin doubtless knew of them.

The central committee considers it absolutely necessary to inform the congress of many such fabricated "cases" against the members of the party's central committee elected at the 17th party congress....

Even more widely was the falsification of cases practiced in the provinces. The NKVD headquarters of the Sverdlov Oblast discovered the so-called Ural uprising staff—and organ of the bloc of rightists, Trotskyites, Socialist Revolutionaries, church leaders—whose chief supposedly was the Secretary of the Sverdlov Oblast Party Committee and a member of the Central Committee, All-Union Communist Party (Bolsheviks), Rabakov, who had been a party member since 1914. The investigative materials of that time show that in almost all *krais, oblasts* [provinces] and republics there supposedly existed rightist Trotskyite, espionage-terror and diversionary-sabotage organizations and centers and that the heads of such organizations as a rule—for no known reason—were first secretaries of *oblast* or republic Communist party committees or central committees. [Movement in the hall.]

Many thousands of honest and innocent Communists have died as a result of this monstrous falsification of such "cases," as a result of the fact that all kinds of slanderous "confessions" were accepted, and as a result of the practice of forcing accusations against oneself and others. In the same manner were fabricated the "cases" against eminent party and state workers—Kossior, Chubar, Postyshev, Rosarev and others.

In those years repressions on a mass scale were applied which were based on nothing tangible and which resulted in heavy cadre losses to the party.

The vicious practice was condoned of having the NKVD prepare lists of persons whose cases were under the jurisdiction of the Military Collegium and whose sentences were prepared in advance. Yezhov would send these lists to Stalin personally for his approval of the proposed punishment. In 1937-1938, 383 such lists containing the names of many thousands of party, Soviet, Komsomol, army and economic workers were sent to Stalin. He approved these lists.

A large part of these cases are being reviewed now and a great part of them are being voided because they were baseless and falsified. Suffice it to say that from 1954 to the present time the Military Collegium of the Supreme Court has rehabilitated 7,679 persons, many of whom were rehabilitated posthumously.

Mass arrests of party, Soviet, economic and military workers caused tremendous harm to our country and to the cause of socialist advancement.

Mass repressions had a negative influence on the moral-political condition of the party, created a situation of uncertainty, contributed to the spreading of unhealthy suspicion, and sowed distrust among Communists. All sorts of slanderers and careerists were active.

Resolutions of the January plenum of the Central Committee, All-Union Communist Party (Bolsheviks), in 1938 had brought some measure of improvement to the party organizations. However, widespread repression also existed in 1938.

Only because our party has at its disposal such great moral-political strength was it possible for it to survive the difficult events in 1937-1938 and to educate new cadres. There is, however, no doubt that our march forward toward socialism and toward the preparation of the country's defense would have been much more successful were it not for the tremendous loss in the cadres suffered as a result of the baseless and false mass repressions in 1937-1938.

We are justly accusing Yezhov for the degenerate practices of 1937. But we have to answer these questions: Could Yezhov have arrested Kossior, for instance, without the knowledge of Stalin? Was there an exchange of opinions or a Political Bureau decision concerning this? No, there was not, as there was none regarding other cases of this type. Could Yezhov have decided such important matters as the fate of such eminent party figures? No, it would be a display of naiveté to consider this the work of Yezhov alone. It is clear that these matters were decided by Stalin, and that without his orders and his sanction Yezhov could not have done this....

In such a situation, there is no need for any sanction, for what sort of a sanction could there be when Stalin decided everything? He was the chief prosecutor in these cases. Stalin not only agreed to, but on his own initiative issued, arrest orders. We must say this so that the delegates to the congress can clearly undertake and themselves assess this and draw the proper conclusions.

Facts prove that many abuses were made on Stalin's orders without reckoning with any norms of party and Soviet legality. Stalin was a very distrustful man, sickly suspicious; we knew this from our work with him. He could look at a man and say: "Why are your eyes so shifty today?" or "Why are you turning so much today and avoiding to look me directly in the eyes?" The sickly suspicion created in him a general distrust even toward eminent party workers whom he had known for years. Everywhere and in everything he saw "enemies," "two-facers" and "spies." Possessing unlimited power he indulged in great willfulness and choked a person morally and physically. A situation was created where one could not express one's own will.

When Stalin said that one or another should be arrested, it was necessary to accept on faith that he was an "enemy of the people." Meanwhile, Beria's gang, which ran the organs of state security, outdid itself in proving the guilt of the arrested and the truth of materials which it falsified. And what proofs were offered? The confessions of the arrested, and the investigative judges accepted these "confessions." And how is it possible that a person confesses to crimes which he has not committed? Only in one way—because of application of physical methods of pressuring him, tortures bringing him to a state of unconsciousness, deprivation of his judgment, taking away of his human dignity. In this manner were "confessions" acquired.

When the wave of mass arrests began to recede in 1939, and the leaders of territorial party organizations began to accuse the NKVD workers of using methods of physical pressure on the arrested, Stalin dispatched a coded telegram on January 20, 1939 to the committee secretaries of *oblasts* and *krais* to the central committees of republic Communist parties, to the People's Commissars of Internal Affairs and to the heads of NKVD organizations. This telegram stated:

> The Central Committee of the All-Union Communist Party (Bolsheviks) explains that the application of methods of physical pressure in NKVD practice is permissible from 1937 on in accordance with permission of the Central Committee of the All-Union Communist Party (Bolsheviks).... It is known that all bourgeois intelligence services use methods of physical influence against the representatives of the socialist proletariat and that they use them in their most scandalous forms. The question arises as to why the socialist intelligence service should be more humanitarian against the mad agents of the bourgeoisie, against the deadly enemies of the working class and of the *kolkhoz* workers. The Central Committee of the All Union Communist Party (Bolsheviks) considers that physical pressure should still be used obligatorily, as an exception applicable to known and obstinate enemies of the people, as a method both justifiable and appropriate.

Thus, Stalin had sanctioned in the name of the Central Committee of the All-Union Communist Party (Bolsheviks) the most brutal violation of socialist legality, torture and oppression, which led as we have seen to the slandering and self-accusation of innocent people.

Not long ago—only several days before the present Congress—we called to the Central Committee Presidium session and interrogated the investigative judge Rodos, who in his time investigated and interrogated Kossior, Chubar and Kosarev. He is a vile person, with the brain of a bird, and morally completely degenerate. And it was this man who was deciding the fate of prominent party workers; he was making judgments also concerning the politics in these matters, because having established their "crime," he provided therewith materials from which important political implications could be drawn.

The question arises whether a man with such an intellect could alone make the investigation in a manner to prove the guilt of people such as Kossior and others. No; he could not have done it without proper directives. At the Central Committee Presidium session he told us: "I was told that Kossior and Chubar were people's enemies and for this reason I, as an investigative judge, had to make them confess that they are enemies." [Indignation in the hall.]

He could do this only through long tortures, which he did, receiving detailed instructions from Beria. We must say that at the Central Committee Presidium session he cynically declared: "I thought that I was executing the orders of the party." In this manner, Stalin's orders concerning the use of methods of physical pressure against the arrested were in practice executed.

These and many other facts show that all norms of correct party solution of problems were invalidated and everything was dependent upon the willfulness of one man....

We should, in all seriousness, consider the question of the cult of the individual. We cannot let this matter get out of the party, especially not to the press. It is for this reason that we are considering it here at a closed Congress session. We should know the limits; we should not give ammunition to the enemy; we should not wash our dirty linen before their eyes. I think that the delegates to the Congress will understand and assess properly all these proposals. [Tumultuous applause.]

Comrades, we must abolish the cult of the individual decisively, once and for all; we must draw the proper conclusions concerning both ideological-theoretical and practical work. It is necessary for this purpose:

First, in a Bolshevik manner to condemn and to eradicate the cult of the individual as alien to Marxism-Leninism and not consonant with the principles of party leadership and the norms of party life, and to fight inexorably all attempts at bringing back this practice in one form or another.

To return to and actually practice in all our ideological work the most important theses of Marxist-Leninist science about the people as the creator of history and as the creator of all material and spiritual good of humanity, about the decisive role of the Marxist party in the revolutionary fight for the transformation of society, about the victory of communism.

In this connection we will be forced to do much work in order to examine critically from the Marxist-Leninist viewpoint and to correct the widely spread erroneous views connected with the cult of the individual in the sphere of history, philosophy, economy and of other sciences, as well as in literature and the fine arts. It is especially necessary that in the immediate future we compile a serious textbook of the history of our party which will be edited in accordance with scientific Marxist objectivism, a textbook of the history of Soviet society, a book pertaining to the events of the Civil War and the Great Patriotic War.

Secondly, to continue systematically and consistently the work done by the party's Central Committee during the last years, a work characterized by minute observation in all party organizations, from the bottom to the top, of the Leninist principles of party leadership, characterized, above all, by the main principle of collective leadership, characterized by the observation of the norms of party life described in the statutes of our party, and, finally, characterized by the wide practice of criticism and self-criticism.

Thirdly, to restore completely the Leninist principles of Soviet socialist democracy, expressed in the Constitution of the Soviet Union, to fight willfulness of individuals abusing their power. The evil caused by acts violating revolutionary socialist legality which have accumulated during a long time as a result of the negative influence of the cult of the individual has to be completely corrected.

Comrades, the 20th Congress of the Communist Party of the Soviet Union has manifested with a new strength the unshakable unity of our party, its cohesiveness around the Central Committee, its resolute will to accomplish the great task of building communism. [Tumultuous applause.] And the fact that we present in all their ramifications the basic problems of overcoming the cult of the individual which is alien to Marxism-Leninism, as well as the problem of liquidating its burdensome consequences, is an evidence of the great moral and political strength of our party. [Prolonged applause.]

We are absolutely certain that our party, armed with the historical resolutions of the 20th Congress, will lead the Soviet people along the Leninist path to new successes, to new victories. [Tumultuous, prolonged applause.]

Long live the victorious banner of our party—Leninism! [Tumultuous, prolonged applause ending in ovation. All rise.]

20. Tatyana Tolstoya

IN CANNIBALISTIC TIMES

Last year Robert Conquest's *The Great Terror* was translated into Russian and published in the USSR in the journal NEVA. (Unfortunately, only the first edition was published. I hope that the second, revised and enlarged edition will be published as well, if it is not suppressed by the censorship so recently revived in the Soviet Union.) The fate of this book in the USSR is truly remarkable. Many of those who opened NEVA in 1989-1990 exclaimed: "But I know all this stuff already!" How did they know it? From Conquest himself.

The first edition appeared twenty years ago in English, was translated into Russian and infiltrated what was then a closed country. It quickly became an underground bestseller, and there's not a thinking person who isn't acquainted with the book in one form or another: those who knew English read it in original, others got hold of the Russian text, made photocopies at night, and passed them on. The book gave birth to much historical (underground and émigré) research, the facts were assimilated, reanalyzed, argued, confirmed, elaborated, in short, the book almost achieved the status of folklore, and many Soviet people measure their own history "according to Conquest," sometimes without realizing that he actually exists. This is why many readers, especially the younger ones, thought of Conquest's book as a compilation of commonly known facts when they read it for the first time. The author should be both offended and flattered.

This is a book about the Stalinist terror, about the Great Terror, which began in the thirties and continued—growing and fading—until the death of the Great Tyrant in 1953.

The very expression "Great Terror" leads to the idea of the "Little Terror" which remains necessarily outside the confines of this book. Of course, no one can write a book about Russia that includes everything, explains everything, and weaves together the facts and motifs of history, revealing the root system that every so often puts out shoots and blossoms into the frightful flower of a Great Terror. I'm reminded of the protagonist of Borge's story "Aleph", who tried to create a poem that described the entire universe—but failed, of course. No one person can possible accomplish such a task.

The Little Terror in Russia has been around from time immemorial. It has lasted for centuries and continues to this very day. So many books have been written about the Little Terror! Virtually all the literature of the nineteenth century, which is so valued in the West, tells the story of the Little Terror, sometimes with indignation, sometimes as something to be taken for granted, and tries to understand its causes, explain its mechanisms, give detailed portraits of its victims: individual personalities, entire classes, and the country as a whole. What is Russian society and why is it the way it is? What can and must be done in order to free ourselves of this all-permeating terror, of total slavery, of fear of any and every one? How do we ensure that an individual's fate does not depend on others' whims? Why is it that any revolution, any attempt to rid Russian of terror, leads to an even greater terror?

Russia didn't begin yesterday and won't end tomorrow. The attempts of many writers and researchers to explain Russian horrors by the Bolshevik rise to power are naive. The sigh of relief that in recent years has been heard more and more often in the West is naive as well: the cold war is over, Gorbachev has come, everything will soon be just fine. (The events of the last few months have shown the West what has been clear to Soviet people for almost two years: nothing good can be expected from Gorbachev.)

Human life is short. For many people, delving into history's depths is boring, frightening and they have no time for it. Furthermore, in the West the sense of history has weakened or completely vanished: the West does not live in history, it lives in civilization, (by which I mean the self-awareness of transnational technological culture, as opposed to the subconscious, unquestioned stream of history.) But in Russia there is practically no civilization, and history lies in deep untouched layers over the villages, over the small towns that have reverted to near wilderness, over the large, uncivilized cities, in those places where they try not to let foreigners in, or where foreigners themselves don't go. Even in the middle of Moscow, within a ten minute walk from the Kremlin, live people with the consciousness of the fifteenth or eleventh century (the eleventh century was better, more comprehensible to us, because at that time culture and civilization were more developed in Russia than in the fifteenth century.) When you have any dealings with these people, when you start a conversation, you feel that you've landed in an episode of "The Twilight Zone". The constraints of a short article don't allow me to adequately describe this terrifying feeling, well known to Europeanized Russians, of coming into contact with what we call the absurd, a concept in which we invest far greater meaning than Western people do. Here one needs literature—Kafka, Ionesco; one needs academic scholars like Levy-Bruhl with his study of prelogical thought.

Archeological digs have been carried out in the ancient Russian city of Novgorod, once an independent republic carrying on trade with the West. The earth reveals deep layers of the city's history. In the early ones, from the eleventh or twelfth century, there are many birch-bark documents and letters written by simple people that testify to the literacy of the population. And there are also remains of good leather footwear. In the fifteenth and the sixteenth century, when Novgorod was conquered by Moscow, letters disappear, and instead of leather boots, lapti appear, a kind of shoe made from bast.

The sixteenth century, when Ivan the Terrible ruled, was also a time of Great Terror, perhaps even the first government-wide terror on the territory of what was then Russia, a terror that is horribly reminiscent of Stalinist times. It is particularly appalling in what would seem to be its inexplicableness, its lack of precedent: after all, there wasn't any Lenin, there were no Bolsheviks or revolutions preceding Ivan the Terrible. It was during his reign that someone said: "We Russians don't need to eat; we eat one another and this satisfies us."

The backward motion of history, the submersion of culture under a thick layer of gilded, decorative "Asiatic savagery", governmental piracy, guile elevated to principle, unbridled caprice, an extraordinary passivity and lack of will combined with an impulsive cruelty; incompletely suppressed paganism, undeveloped Christianity; a blind superstitious belief in the spoken, and especially in the written, word; the sense of sin as a secret and repulsive pleasure (What

Russians call Dostoevskyism). How can all this be described, how can one give a sense of the ocean from which the huge wave of a Great Terror periodically rises?

Robert Conquest investigates only the Great Terror, not touching on the Little one. He sees its roots in the Soviet regime that formed before Stalin, in the very principles and organization of the Soviet state. In his own way he is absolutely right; this is true, and every investigation must begin somewhere. I merely wish to remind the reader once again (and Robert Conquest knows this very well) that the Soviet state was not created out of thin air, that its inhabitants were the inhabitants of yesterday's Russian state who awoke one fine morning to find themselves under the so-called Soviet regime. The Revolution and the civil war that soon followed led to the exile and destruction or decivilizing of the Europeanized Russian population (by Europeanized, I mean people who were literate, educated, who possessed a work ethic, a developed religious consciousness, respect for law and reason, and who were also familiar with Europe and the achievements of world culture.) Those who survived and remained in Russia lost the right to speak their minds and were too frightened or weak to influence anything. Russian society, though it wandered in the dark for centuries, had nonetheless by 1917 given birth not only to an educated class, but to a large number of people with high moral standards and a conscience, to honest people who were not indifferent to issues of social good. This is the intelligentsia—not really a class, but a fellowship of people "with moral law in their breast," as Kant put it. Lenin hated them more than anyone else, and they were the first to be slaughtered. When Gorky wrote to Lenin in their defense, saying that "the intelligentsia is the brain of the nation," Lenin answered with the famous phrase: "It's not the brain, it's the shit."

The savage, barbaric, "Asiatic" part of the Russian empire was invited to participate in the "construction of a new world," and its members received certain privileges, some people in word alone, others in fact. What this section of the population really represented, what it was capable of and what it aspired to, no one actually knew, particularly the Soviet leaders, whose notions about the "people" derived exclusively from their own theories, while the model for the worker was taken from the German or English working class and the peasant was entirely dreamed up. Arrogant, impatient, cruel, barely literate people took advantage of the historical moment (the war dragging on, the military leadership's lack of talent, thievery in the army and the rear guard; a weak tsar; and after the February Revolution, a weak transitional government, widespread disorder, chaos, a dissatisfied people, etc.) to carry out what they called a revolution but was actually a counterrevolutionary coup.

As is well known, Lenin's initial idea was to hold onto power for no less of a period than the French Commune once did. This desire to become a chapter heading in a history textbook is quite characteristic of bookish, theoretical thinking. Then he intended to suffer a defeat, go underground, and work for a real coup. However, no one ended up taking power away from the Bolsheviks: they were better organized and much more cynical and unscrupulous than any of their opponents. Seizing power turned out not to be too difficult. But governing the Russian empire was almost impossible. (Even today no one knows how.) Terror came into use.

In one of his telegrams Lenin exclaimed indignantly: "We're not shooting enough professors." Isn't this a portent of typical Stalinist methods: destruction by category? Under Stalin arrest by category became a regular thing: today they're killing miners, tomorrow they're destroying railway engineers, then they'll get around to peasants, the historians of local customs (students of local lore, history and economy were almost completely destroyed for being "spies"). One of my grandfathers, Mikhail Lozinsky, a well-known translator of the poetry of

Shakespeare, Lope de Vega, Corneille, who spoke six languages fluently, was frequently interrogated in the early 1920's for participating in the "Poets Guild" literary group; the ignorant investigator kept trying to find out where the "Guild" kept their weapons. This was under Lenin, not Stalin. His wife (my grandmother) was jailed for several months at the same time, perhaps because so many of her friends were members of the Social Revolutionary party. She later remembered that she had never before or since had such a pleasant time with so many intelligent and educated people. In 1921 my mother's godfather, the poet Nicolai Gumilev, was shot on a false accusation of involvement in a "monarchist plot." (There were other deaths in our family, but fewer than in some. The hatred many felt toward our family because of this was typical and was expressed in the following way: "Why is it that they've lost so few family members?") Gumilev's wife, the famous poet Anna Akhmatova, referred to these relatively peaceful times as "vegetarian."

Cannibalistic times didn't emerge out of thin air. The people willing to carry out Bolshevik orders had to ripen for the task. They matured in the murk of Russian villages, in the nightmare of factory work conditions, in the deep countryside, and in the capitals, Moscow and Petersburg. They were already there, there were a lot of them, and they could be counted on. "God forbid we should ever witness a Russian revolt, senseless and merciless," our brilliant poet Pushkin remarked as early as the first quarter of the nineteenth century. He knew what he was talking about. Was Lenin counting on the senselessness and mercilessness of the Russians, or did he simply fail to take them into account? Whatever the case, by fate's inexorable law, he, too, was victimized by his own creation: his mistress, Inessa Armand, was apparently killed; power was torn from his paralyzed hands during his lifetime; it is rumored that Stalin murdered Lenin's wife, Nadezha Krupskaya, by sending her a poisoned cake. Apparently it is rumored, because no one knows precisely. (The vision of this somewhat stupid, self-assured old woman—who forbade children's stories because they were "unrealistic," but who was honest in her own way and not malicious—eating a spoonful of cake with icing and poison provokes mixed images in me. Mea culpa.)

And how could a Russian revolt be anything but senseless and merciless when the Russian government had exhibited a senseless lack of mercy toward its own people for centuries? From time immemorial the subjugated Russian classes have been required to inform their sovereign of anyone who for whatever reason seemed suspicious to them. From the mid-seventeenth century on, the law prescribed the death penalty for failure to report a crime committed or intended. Not only the criminal, but all of his relatives must be reported. Thus, for example, since unauthorized flight abroad was considered a crime, the escapee's entire family became criminals and death awaited them all, because it was supposed that they could not have been ignorant of the intended betrayal. Interrogation was carried out under torture and of course everyone "confessed."

The Stalinist regime didn't invent anything three hundred years later; it simply reproduced the political investigation techniques that were already a longstanding tradition in the Russian state. Only more of the population was included, and the pretexts for arrest became more trivial. But perhaps there was no significant difference? After all, neither the seventeenth nor the eighteenth century had their Conquest, someone to describe in scrupulous detail every aspect of what occurred.

The parallels between arrests in the eighteenth century and the twentieth are so close that it's hard to shake the feeling that time has stopped. In an article on the history of denunciation by the Soviet historian Evgeny Anisimov, I read about something that happened in 1732. A man informed on a certain merchant and called him a "traitor." The merchant was arrested (pronouncing "indecent words" was a political crime which brought suffering, torture, Siberia). With great difficulty the merchant was able to prove that the word "traitor" referred not to the other man, but to a dog sitting on the porch (the merchant was speaking out loud about the fact that the dog would betray him: it would follow whoever fed it better). A witness was found who confirmed that a dog was actually wandering around the porch during the conversation. This saved the merchant.

Two hundred years later, in the 1930s, a herdsman was arrested and sent to the Stalinist camps for referring to a cow as a "whore" because she made advances to another cow. His crime was formulated as "slandering the communal farm herd."

Of course, those who don't agree with me, who see a fundamental difference between the Russian and Soviet approaches, will say that totalitarian thinking in the Soviet period becomes all-encompassing. Previously, a dog was simply a dog, an animal; but now a cow becomes an integral part of the regime; he who affronts the cow's honor is aiming—in the final analysis—at the well-being and morals of the People. And they are also right. I only want to say that totalitarian thinking was not invented by the Soviet regime, but arose in the bleak depths of Russian history and was subsequently developed and fortified by Lenin, Stalin, and hundreds of their comrades in arms, talented students of past tyrants, sensitive sons of the people. This idea, on which I will insist, is extremely unpopular. In certain Russian circles it is considered simply obscene. Solzhenitsyn had often denounced those who think as I do; others will inevitably try to unearth my Jewish ancestors and this explanation will pacify them. I'm speaking not only of our nationalists and fascists, but about a more subtle category: about those liberal Russians who forbid one to think that Russians *forbid thinking*.

In 1953, when Stalin died, I was two years old. In one of my earliest childhood memories it is summer. There's a green lawn, bushes and trees—and suddenly from the bushes emerge two huge people, many time greater than life size; they are wearing long white overalls and pillows take the place of their heads; eyes and laughing mouths are drawn on the pillows. Instead of legs they have stilts. I remember the childlike feeling of happiness and wonder, and something similar to a promise that life would contain many more such wondrous surprises. Many years later in a chance conversation, I learned that this small group of merrymakers was imprisoned that summer for an unheard of crime: "vulgarity."

When I read *The Great Terror*, I carefully followed Conquest's detailed descriptions of the lengthy, notorious trials of the 1930s, the investigation of the police apparatus's cumbersome mechanisms, the network of destinies, biographies. This is all assembled into such a complex architectural edifice that I cannot help but admire the author who undertook an investigation so grandiose in scale. The reader comes away feeling that the author knows every event of the Soviet years, that no remotely accessible document has escaped his attention, that he hasn't neglected a single publication in the smallest provincial newspaper if it might throw light on one or another event. Ask him what happened to the wife of comrade X or the son of comrade Y—he knows. The only question he can't answer is: Why?

Conquest does ask this question in regard to Stalin and his regime; he meticulously and wittily examines the possible motives of Stalin's behavior, both rational and irrational; he shows the deleterious effect of Bolshevik ideology on the mass consciousness, how it prepared the way for the Terror. A particularly wonderful quality of this book is also that when questions, ideas or suppositions arise in you, reader, the author invariably answers those mental queries a few pages later, develops the thought you've had and figures things out along with you, bringing in more arguments on both sides than you ever thought possible. I was especially struck by this in the third chapter, "Architect of Terror," which sketches a psychological portrait of Stalin, and in the fifth chapter, "The Problem of Confession" where Conquest explores the motivations and behavior of Stalin's victims.

This book is not a storeroom of facts, but a profoundly analytical investigation. Instead of getting tangled up in the abundance of information, you untangle the knots of the Soviet nightmare under the author's patient direction. Having finished this book, no one can ever again say: "I didn't know." Now we all know.

But the question Why? remains unanswered. Perhaps the only answer is "Because." Period.

My first English teacher, the daughter of Russian-Ukrainian immigrants was once married to an American. They lived several years in America and in the mid 1930s, like many other naive Western people who believed in socialism, they came to the USSR. They were immediately arrested and sent to prison. Her husband didn't return but she survived. "But I'm not guilty of anything!" she screamed at the investigator. "No one here is guilty of anything," answered the exhausted investigator. "But why, then?" "Just because," was the answer.

What lies behind this "just because"? Why were two merrymakers arrested for "vulgarity?" After all, someone took the trouble to inform, someone else to listen and apprise the authorities, a third person took the trouble to be on guard, a fourth to think about it, a fifth to send an armed group to arrest them, a sixth... and so on. Why, in a small, sleepy provincial town in the 1930s did the head of the police, sitting on his window sill in an unbelted shirt, waving away the flies, amuse himself by beckoning passers-by and arresting those who approached (they disappeared forever)? Why, in 1918, as the writer Ivan Bunin wrote, did peasants plundering an estate pluck the feathers off the peacocks and let them die to the accompaniment of all around approving laughter? Why, in 1988, in Los Angeles (I witnessed this) did a Soviet writer, in America for the first time, take in at a glance the pink, luxurious mass of the Beverly Hills hotel, and daydream out loud: "Ah, they should drop a good-size bomb here..."? Why, in Moscow, in our time, did a woman, upon seeing a two-year old child sit down on the floor of a shop and refuse to get up, start yelling: "Those kinds of kids should be sent to jail! They're all bandits!" And why did a group of women, including the saleswomen and cashiers, gather around her and join in: "To jail, to jail!," they shouted. Why do Russians immediately start stamping their feet and waving their hands, hissing "damned beasts" if a cat or dog runs by?

This question Why? has been asked by all of Russian literature, and, of course, no historian can answer it. He almost doesn't have the right—facts are his domain. Only some sort of blind bard, a muttering poet or absurdist playwright can answer this question.

In Russia, in contrast to the West, reason has traditionally been seen as a source of destruction, emotion (the soul) as one of creation. How many scornful pages have great Russian writers dedicated to Western pragmatism, materialism, rationalism! They mocked the English with their machines, the Germans with their order and precision, the French with their logic and finally the Americans with their love of money. As a result, in Russia we have neither machines, nor order, nor logic, nor money. "We eat one another and this satisfies us...." Rejecting reason, the Russian universe turns in an emotional whirlwind and can't manage to get on even footing. Looking into the depths of Russian history, one is horrified: it's impossible to figure out when this senseless mess started. What is the source of these interminable Russian woes? The dogmatism of the Russian Orthodox Church? The Mongol invasions? The formation of the empire? Genetics? Everything together? There is no answer, or there are too many answers. You feel there's an abyss under your feet.

The enslavement of the peasants, which continued for three hundred years, provokes such a feeling of guilt in the free, educated classes of Russian society that nothing disparaging could be said about the peasants. If they have certain obvious negative characteristics, then we ourselves are to blame — that is the leitmotif of the nineteenth century. All manner of extraordinary qualities — spirituality, goodness, justice, sensitivity, and charity—are ascribed to the Russian peasant and to the simple people as a whole—everything that a person longing for a normal life among normal people might hope to find. Some voices of alarm break through Russian literature, the voices of people trying to speak about the dark side of the Russian people, but they are isolated, unpopular, misinterpreted. Everyone deceives everyone else and themselves into the bargain. The revolution comes, then another, then a third—and a wave of darkness engulfs the country. The cultured classes are destroyed, the raw elements burst forth.

Cultural taboos forbid us to judge "simple people"—and this is typical not only of Russia. This taboo demands that a guilty party be sought "high up." It's possible that such a search is partially justified, but, alas, it doesn't lead to anything. Once an enemy is found "up above," the natural movement is to destroy him, which is what happens during a revolution. So he's destroyed, but what has changed? Life is just as bad as ever. And people begin over new quests for enemies, detecting them in non-Russians, in people of a different faith, and in their neighbors. But they forget to look at themselves.

During Stalin's time, as I see it, Russian society, brutalized by centuries of violence, intoxicated by the feeling that everything was allowed, destroyed everything "alien": "the enemy," "minorities"—any and everything the least bit different from the "average." At first this was simple and exhilarating: the aristocracy, foreigners, ladies in hats, gentlemen in ties, everyone who wore eyeglasses, everyone who read books, everyone who spoke a literary language and showed some signs of education; then it became more and more difficult, the material for destruction began to run out, and society turned inward and began to destroy itself. Without popular support Stalin and his cannibals wouldn't have lasted for long. The executioner's genius expressed itself in his ability to feel and direct the evil forces slumbering in the people; he deftly manipulated the choice of courses, knew who should be the hors d'oeuvres, who the main course and who should be left for dessert; he knew what honorific toasts to pronounce and what inebriating ideological cocktails to offer (now's the time to serve subtle wines to this group, later that one will get strong liquor).

It is this hellish cuisine that Robert Conquest examines. And the leading character of this fundamental work, whether the author intends it or nor, is not just the butcher, but all the sheep that collaborated with him, slicing and seasoning their own meat for a monstrous shiskabob.

21. Yevgeny Yevtushenko

BABII YAR[1]

No monument stands over Babii Yar.[2]
A drop sheer as a crude gravestone.
I am afraid.
        Today I am as old in years
as all the Jewish People.
Now I seem to be
        a Jew.
Here I plod through ancient Egypt.
Here I perish crucified, on the cross,
and to this day I bear the scars of nails.
I seem to be
        Dreyfus.
The Philistine
        is both informer and judge.
I am behind bars.
        Beset on every side.
Hounded,
        spat on,
        slandered.
Squealing, dainty ladies in flounced Brussels lace
stick their parasols into my face.
I seem to be then
        a young boy in Byelostok.
Blood runs, spilling over the floors.
The barroom rabble-rousers
give off a stench of vodka and onion.
A boot kicks me aside, helpless.
In vain I plead with these pogrom bullies.
While they jeer and shout,
        "Beat the Yids. Save Russia!"
some grain marketeer beats up my mother.
O my Russian people!
        I know
        you

are international to the core.
But those with unclean hands
have often made a jingle of your purest name.
I know the goodness of my land.
How vile these anti-Semites—
                           without a qualm
they pompously called themselves
"The Union of the People"!
I seem to be
              Anne Frank
transparent
              as a branch in April.
And I love.
              And have no need of phrases.
My need
         is that we gaze into each other.
How little we can see
                   or smell!
We are denied the leaves,
                        we are denied the sky.
Yet we can do so much—
                     tenderly
embrace each other in a dark room.
They're coming here?
                   Be not afraid. Those are the booming
sounds of spring:
                spring is coming here.
Come then to me.
              Quick, give me your lips.
Are they smashing down the door?
                              No, it's the ice breaking…
The wild grasses rustle over Babii Yar.
The trees look ominous,
                      like judges.
Here all things scream silently,
                              and, baring my head,
slowly I feel myself
                   turning gray.
And I myself
            am one massive, soundless scream
above the thousand thousand buried here.
I am
     each old man
               here shot dead.

I am
     every child
             here shot dead.
Nothing in me
          shall ever forget!
The "Internationale," let it
              thunder
when the last anti-Semite on earth
is buried forever.
In my blood there is no Jewish blood.
In their callous rage, all anti-Semites
must hate me now as a Jew.
For that reason
          I am a true Russian!

1961
Translated by George Reavey

NOTES

1   This is one of five Yevtushenko poems on which Dmitri Shostakovich based his Thirteenth Symphony.
2   Babii Yar is a ravine in the suburbs of Kiev where Nazi forces murdered tens of thousands of Soviet Jews and others during World War II. For a long time there was no monument at the site of the atrocity.

22. Andrei D. Sakharov

THE SAKHAROV DIALOGUE

The following is the text of a dialogue between Andrei D. Sakharov, the Soviet dissident physicist and civil rights advocate, and Mikhail P. Malyarov, First Deputy Prosecutor General of the Soviet Union, whose post as the nation's second-ranking law enforcement official corresponds roughly to that of the Deputy Attorney General in the United States. The dialogue was reconstructed by Mr. Sakharov from memory and was made available to Western newsmen. The translation is by the Moscow bureau of The New York Times. Mr. Sakharov's text follows:

MOSCOW—On Aug. 15, I received a telephone call from the Deputy Prosecutor General and was asked to come to see him. He did not say what it was about, asserting simply that it would be a man-to-man talk. I arrived at the Prosecutor's office on August 16 at noon and was met at the gate by an employee who took me into the building; another then accompanied me to an office, where I was received by M.P. Malyarov, the Deputy Prosecutor General, and another man who introduced himself only as Malyarov's assistant. He took notes and participated in the conversation.

Below I have reproduced the seventy-minute conversation from memory, and the reconstruction may therefore contain some paraphrases, minor unintentional abridgments and inversions in sequence.

Malyarov— This conversation is intended to be in the nature of a warning and not all my statements will be supported by detailed proof, but you can believe me that we have such proof. Please listen to me attentively and try not to interrupt.

Sakharov— I am listening.

Malyarov— When you began a few years ago to engage in what you call public activity, we could not possibly ignore it and we paid close attention. We assumed that you would express your opinions as a Soviet citizen about certain shortcomings and errors, as you see them, without attacking the Soviet social and political system as such. To be sure, even then your statements were being published in the anti-Soviet press abroad and they

From *The New York Times*, August 29th, 1973.

caused noticeable harm to our country. Lately your activity and statements have assumed an even more harmful and openly anti-Soviet character and cannot be overlooked by the Prosecutor's office, which is charged with enforcing the law and protecting the interests of society. You are seeing foreigners and giving them material for anti-Soviet publications. That applies in particular to your interview with the Swedish Radio. In that interview you denounced the Socialist system in our country, calling it a system of maximum nonfreedom, a system that is undemocratic, closed, deprived of economic initiative, and falling to pieces.

Sakharov— I did not say "falling to pieces."

Malyarov— You keep meeting with reactionary newsmen, like the Swedish Radio correspondent Stenholm, and give them interviews that are then used for subversive propaganda and are printed by Possev, the publication of the N.T.S. [A Russian émigré organization with headquarters in Frankfurt, West Germany.] You must be aware that the N.T.S. program calls for overthrow of the Soviet regime. Possev publishes more of your writings than anyone else, and in your interview you adopted in effect the same anti-Soviet subversive position.

Sakharov— I am not familiar with the N.T.S. program. If it does indeed include such a plank, it would be fundamentally opposed in my views, as stated, for example, in the interview with the Swedish Radio. There I spoke about the desirability of gradual change, about democratization within the framework of the present system. Of course, I am also referring to what I consider serious faults in the system and do not conceal my pessimism (with regard to possible changes in the near future). As for those publications, I never handed over any material for the N.T.S. or for Possev, and my writings have appeared in many foreign mass media besides Possev. For example, in Der Spiegel [West Germany newsmagazine], which the Soviet press has regarded as rather progressive so far.

Malyarov's assistant— But you never protested publication in Possev. We found that most of your writings appeared in Possev, Grani [another publication of the Possev publisher] and in the White Guards newspaper Russkaya Mysl [of Paris].

Sakharov— I would be very glad to have my writings published in the Soviet press. For example, if, in addition to [Yuri] Kornilov's critical article, Literaturnaya Gazeta [Soviet weekly] had also published my interview [with the Swedish Radio]. In that case, Kornilov would not have been able to distort the interview. But that is obviously out of the question. I consider openness of publications far more important than the place of publication.

Malyarov's assistant— Even if they appear in anti-Soviet publications for anti-Soviet purposes, as in Possev?

Sakharov— I consider Possev's publishing activities highly useful. I am grateful to that publisher. I reserve the right not to identify Possev with the N.T.S. and not to approve of the N.T.S. program, with which I am not even familiar, or to condemn those aspects of N.T.S. activities that may be viewed as provocative (like sending Sokolov as a witness to the Galanskov-Ginsburg trial, which did have such consequences).[The reference is to Nicholas Brocks-Sokolov, an N.T.S. courier, who was arrested on arriving in the Soviet Union and testified for the prosecution in the 1968 trial of two dissidents.

Malyarov's assistant— We are not talking about that now, that was a long time ago.

Sakharov— To go back, you called Stenholm [of the Swedish Radio] a reactionary journalist. That is unfair. He is a Social Democrat, he is far more of a Socialist or Communist than I am, for example.

Malyarov's assistant— The Social Democrats were the ones who murdered Rosa Luxemburg [German Communist, in 1919]. As for that "Communist" of yours, he evidently inserted into your interview that our system was "falling to pieces," if indeed you did not say it.

Sakharov— I am convinced that Stenholm quoted me correctly.

Malyarov— Let me go on. Please listen closely. By nature of your previous work, you had access to state secreets of particular importance. You signed a commitment not to divulge state secrets and not to meet with foreigners. But you do meet with foreigners and you are giving them information that may be of interest to foreign intelligence agencies. I am asking you to consider this a serious warning and to draw your conclusions.

Sakharov— What sort of information are you talking about? What do you have in mind, specifically?

Malyarov— I told you that our meeting was meant to be a warning. We have the information, but we will not go into details now.

Sakharov— I insist that I have never divulged any military or military-technical secrets that I may have known by nature of my work from 1948 to 1968. And I never intend to do so. I also want to call your attention to the fact that I have been out of secret work for the last five years.

Malyarov— But you still have your head on your shoulders, and your pledge not to meet with foreigners is still in effect. You are beginning to be used not only by anti-Soviet forces hostile to our country, but also by foreign intelligence.

Sakharov— As for meetings with foreigners, I know many people who used to be in my position and who now meet freely with foreign scholars and ordinary citizens. I do meet with some foreign journalists, but those meetings have no bearing whatever on any state, military, or military-technical secrets.

Malyarov's assistant— Those meetings are of benefit to our enemies.

Malyarov— We have now warned you. It is up to you to draw your conclusions.

Sakharov— I repeat. I would prefer to be published in the Soviet press and to deal with Soviet institutions. But I see nothing illegal in meeting with foreign journalists.

Malyarov's assistant— But you are still a Soviet citizen. Your qualification shows your real attitude toward our system.

Sakharov— Soviet institutions ignore my letters and other forms of communcation. If we just take the Prosecutor's office, I remember that in May, 1970 (I think it was May 17), several persons, including myself, addressed a complaint to comrade [Roman A.] Rudenko, the Prosecutor General, in the case of [Maj.Gen. Pyotr G.] Grigorenko [a dissident committed to a psychiatric hospital in 1969]. There were many gross violations of the law in that case. There has been no reply to that complaint to this day. Many times I did not even receive confirmation of the delivery of my letters. The late Academician Petrovsky, who was a member of the Presidium of the Supreme Soviet of the U.S.S.R. [Ivan G. Petrovsky, rector of Moscow University, died this year] promised to look into the case of the psychiatrist Semyon Gluzman, sentenced in Kiev in 1972 in a trial fraught with violations of the law. That was the only time anyone promised to look into a case for me. But Petrovsky is now dead. And how about the Amalrik case? [Andrei A. Amalrik, dissident author]. He was unjustly sentenced to three years, he lost his health, suffered from meningitis, and now he has been sentenced in a labor-camp court to another three years. It is an absolute disgrace. He was in fact sentenced once again for his convictions, which he has refused to recant and does not force on anyone. And a labor-camp court! What kind of public proceeding, what kind of justice is that?

Malyarov— That Amalrik is a half-educated student. He contributed nothing to the state. He was a parasite. And Böll [Heinrich Böll,West German author] writes about him as if he were an outstanding historian. Is that the kind of information Böll has?

Sakharov— Böll and many others demonstrate a great deal of interest in Amalrik's fate. A labor-camp court is in fact a closed court.

Malyarov— I suppose you would have brought him to Moscow for trial?

Sakharov— In view of the wide public interest, that would have made sense. If I had known that I could attend Amalrik's trial, I would have done so.

Malyarov— Amalrik caused a great deal of harm to our society. In one of his books he tried to show that Soviet society would not survive until 1984, and in so doing he called for violent action. Any society has the right to defend itself. Amalrik violated the law, and he must take the punishment. In camp he again violated the law. You know the law, I don't have to tell you what it is. Abroad they wrote that Amalrik was deprived of a lawyer. That is a lie. Shveisky [Vladimir Shveisky, Amalrik's lawyer] attended the trial, and you know that.

Malyarov's assistant— In contrast to that dropout, you did make contributions to society.

Malyarov— Who gave you the right to doubt our system of justice? You did not attend the trial. You base yourself on rumors, and they are often wrong.

Sakharov— When proceedings are not public, when political trials are consistently held under conditions allowing for violations, there are grounds for doubting the fairness of the court. I consider it undemocratic to prosecute under Articles 190-1 [On circulating false information defaming the Soviet State] and 70 [On anti-Soviet agitation and propaganda]. All the cases with which I am familiar confirm this. Take the recent case of Leonid Plyushch [a Kiev mathematician]. In that case, the court accepted the most grievous of three contradictory psychiatric findings without checking any of them. Although the court reduced the sentence, it was restored upon protest by the prosecution. Plyushch is being kept in a special [psychiatric] hospital, and his wife has not seen him for more than a year and a half.

Malyarov— You keep dealing in legal questions, but you don't seem to know them very well. The court has the power to determine the form of compulsory treatment regardless of the findings of an expert commission.

Sakharov— I am unfortunately all too familiar with that. And therefore, even when the expert commission recommends an ordinary hospital, there are grounds for fearing the worst. You say that I always rely on rumor. That is not so. I try to get reliable information. But it is becoming increasingly difficult in this country to know what is going on. There is no publication with complete and precise information about violations [of due process].

Malyarov's assistant— You mean the Chronicle [The Chronicle of Current Events, an underground publication that has not appeared since October, 1972]?

Sakharov — Of course.

Malyarov's assistant— You will soon be hearing about the Chronicle. You know what I mean. But now we are talking about more important matters.

Malyarov— You don't seem to like the fact that our [Criminal] Code contains Article 190-1 and 70. But there they are. The state has the right to defend itself. You must know what you are doing. I am not going to try to convince you. I know that would be useless. But you must understand what is involved here. And who is supporting you, anyway, who needs you? Yakir, whom you know well, was written about constantly in the antii-Soviet press abroad as long as he provided it with propaganda. As soon as he changed his views, he was forgotten. [Pyotr Yakir was arrested in

June, 1972, and is now being tried.]

Sakharov— To say that I know him well is not correct. I hardly know him. But I do know that there is great interest in his case. Everyone is wondering when the trial will begin. Do you know?

Malyarov's assistant— No. When the trial starts, you will probably know about it yourself.

Malyarov— Your friend Chalidze [Valery Chalidze, now living in the United States] was quite famous in the West as long as he came out with anti-Soviet statements, and when he stopped, he was also soon forgotten. Anti-Soviet circles need people like [Julius] Telesin, [Vladimir] Telnikov [dissidents living in Great Britain] and Volpin [Alexander Yesenin-Volpin], who keep slandering their former homeland.

Sakharov— I don't think that Chalidze ever engaged in anti-Soviet activity. The same goes for the others. You mentioned Volpin. As far as I know he is busy with mathematics in Boston.

Malyarov— That may be, but we also have reliable information about his anti-Soviet activity.

Sakharov— You say that no one is supporting me. Last year I took part in two collective appeals, for amnesty and for abolition of the death penalty. Each of these appeals was signed by more than fifty persons.

Malyarov— Only asking that the matter be considered?

Sakharov— Yes. And we are quite distressed when the law on amnesty turned out to be a very limited one, and the death penalty was not abolished.

Malyarov— You did not seriously expect a change in the l;aw just because you wanted it. This is not the time to abolish the death penalty. Murderers and rapists who commit serious crimes cannot go unpunished. [The death penalty also applies to serious crimes against the state, such as treason and espionage.]

Sakharov— I am talking about abolishing the very institution of the death penalty. Many thoughtful people are of the view that this institution has no place in a humane society and that it is amoral. We have serious crime despite the existence of the death penalty. The death penalty does not help make society more humane. I heard that abolition of the death penalty has been under discussion in Soviet legal circles.

Malyarov— No. One jurist raised the question, but he found no support. The time is not ripe.

Sakharov— The issue is now being debated throughout the world. Many countries have abolished the death penalty. Why should we be different?

Malyarov— They abolished it in the United States, but now they are forced to restore it. You've been reading about the crimes that have occurred there. Nothing like that happens here. You seem to like the American way of life, even though they permit the unrestricted sale of guns, they murder their Presidents, and now they've got this demagogic fraud of the Watergate case. Sweden, too, is proud of her freedom, and there they have pornographic pictures on every street. I saw them myself. Don't tell me you are for pornography, for that kind of freedom?

Sakharov— I am not familiar with either the American or the Swedish way of life. They probably have their own problems and I would not idealize them. But you mentioned the Watergate case. To me, it is a good illustration of American democracy.

Malyarov— It is calculated to be just a show. All Nixon has to do is show a little firmness, and the whole thing will come to nothing. That's their democracy for you, nothing but fraud. I think we better end this conversation. There was one more thing. You seem to have a high opinion of Belinkov [Arkady V. Belinkov, a Soviet writer, who defected to the West in 1968 and died two years later]. You know that name, don't you?

Sakharov— I consider Belinkov an outstanding writer on public affairs. I particularly appreciated his letter to the Pen Club in 1968 [protesting curbs on intellectual freedom in the Soviet Union].

Malyarov— Are you aware that Belinkov was once arrested and imprisoned for having distributed leaflets calling for the killing of Communists?

Sakharov— I don't know anything about that. That probably happened a long time ago under Stalin. How can you take that seriously? At that time anyone could be arrested as a terrorist.

Malyarov— No, Belinkov was imprisoned twice, the second time not so long ago. And how about your Daniel [Yuli M. Daniel, dissident writer, who served five years at hard labor, 1966-1970]? Didn't he call openly for the murder of leaders of the party and Government in his story "Day of Open Murders"? And Amalrik, is he any better? You better think about it.

Sakharov— "Day of Open Murders" is a work of fiction, an allegory, directed in spirit against the terror of the Stalin years which was still very fresh at that time, in 1956. Daniel made that quite clear in his trial. As for [Amalrik's] "Will the U.S.S.R. Survive until 1984" that, too, is an allegory. You know that the date stems from Orwell's story.

Malyarov— We better stop. I just want you to give serious thought to my warnings. Any state has the right to defend itself. There are appropriate articles in the Criminal Code, and no one will be permitted to violate them.

Sakharov— I have been listening closely and I will certainly bear in mind every word you said. But I cannot agree that I have been violating the law. In particular, I cannot agree with your statement that my meetings with foreign correspondents are illegal or that they endanger state secrets. Good-by.

Malyarov— Good-by.

23. Mikhail S. Gorbachev

EXCERPTS FROM REMARKS BEFORE THE PARTY CENTRAL COMMITTEE

February 6, 1990

A Pivotal Gathering

Comrades, I think you will agree that we have gathered for a very important plenary meeting, a meeting which Communists and all society have been waiting for with immense interest and impatience.

The Central Committee has received thousands of letters with suggestions and wishes from party members and nonparty people, from party organizations and committees, from work collectives, factory workers and farmers, intellectuals, scientists, veterans and youth.

Telegrams continue to pour in. You too have seen rallies and meetings at which the most vital problems were discussed from various positions, in an acute and interested way. Their participants also wanted to make their viewpoint known to the party Central Committee.

All this combined is a phenomenon that reflects profound changes that have already occurred and are occurring in our society along the tracks of perestroika and in conditions of democratization and glasnost.

The main thing that now worries Communists and all citizens of the country is the fate of perestroika, the fate of the country and the role of the Soviet Communist Party at the current, probably most crucial, stage of revolutionary transformation.

Society wants to know the party's position, and this determines the significance of our plenum. During preparations for the meeting we were faced with the question of when to hold the 28th Party Congress.

Last December the Central Committee considered it necessary to bring forward the convocation of the congress by six months. But the course of developments is so fast that it is necessary to review this issue.

Having assessed the entire situation and examined petitions from Communists and party organizations, the Politburo submits the following proposal for your consideration: to hold the 28th Communist Party Congress late in June, early in July this year. We are convinced that the proposal will be approved at this plenum.

The congress should be preceded, in our view, with a full report-and election campaign in all links of the party with a broad debate on the platform and the draft new rules of the Soviet Communist Party. Overdue personnel issues will be resolved and new elected party bodies will be formed during the reports and elections. This will create a totally different situation for holding the congress.

At this plenum we are to adopt the Central Committee's draft platform for the congress. In a month or, better, three weeks from now, not later, we will probably have to gather again for a plenary meeting to consider the draft new rules and have them published for public discussion...

The Party's Renewal

Of no less importance is the understanding of the fact, which is the other aspect of the problem that also demands the bringing forward of the congress, is that the party will only be able to fulfill the mission of political vanguard if it drastically restructures itself, masters the art of political work in the present conditions and succeeds in cooperating with forces committed to perestroika.

The crux of the party's renewal is the need to get rid of everything that tied it into the authoritarian-bureaucratic system, a system that left its mark not only on methods of work and inter-relationships within the party, but also on ideology, ways of thinking and notions of socialism.

The platform says: our ideal is a humane, democratic socialism, expressing the interests of the working class and all working people and relying on the legacy of Marx, Engels and Lenin, the Soviet Communist Party is creatively developing socialist ideals to match present day realities and with due account for the entire experience of the 20th century.

The platform states clearly what we should abandon. We should abandon the ideological dogmatism that became ingrained during past decades, outdated stereotypes in domestic policy and outmoded views on the world revolutionary process and world development as a whole.

We should abandon everything that led to the isolation of socialist countries from the mainstream of world civilization. We should abandon the understanding of progress as a permanent confrontation with a socially different world...

At the Vanguard, Legally

The Party's renewal presupposes a fundamental change in its relations with state and economic bodies and the abandonment of the practice of commanding them and substituting for their functions.

The party in a renewing society can exist and play its role as vanguard only as a democratically recognized force. This means that its status should not be imposed through constitutional endorsement.

The Soviet Communist Party, it goes without saying, intends to struggle for the status of the ruling party.

But it will do so strictly within the framework of the democratic process by giving up any legal and political advantages, offering its program and defending it in discussions, cooperating with other social and political forces, always working amidst the masses, living by their interests and their needs.

The extensive democratization currently under way in our society is being accompanied by mounting political pluralism. Various social and political organizations and movements emerge. This process may lead at a certain stage to the establishment of parties.

The Soviet Communist Party is prepared to act with due account for these new circumstances, cooperate and conduct a dialogue with all organizations committed to the Soviet Constitution and social system endorsed in this Constitution...

Enriching the People

I think that comrades have also noticed that after human rights in the draft, the need is stressed to adopt a range of measures to enrich the spiritual world of the people, to raise society's education and cultural level. Unfortunately, this factor has been in the background for some time now and has been regarded as almost a balance for industrial growth figures.

We had to pay for this by seriously lagging behind and we will be paying for it for a long time. We were nearly one of the last to realize that in the age of information science the most expensive asset is knowledge, the breadth of mental outlook and creative imagination...

People are especially dissatisfied with the food situation. The question should be posed squarely. We worked out an innovative agrarian policy and voted for it at the March plenary. We see it as progressive and pointing to real ways out of food crisis.

The main outcome of the plenum was that it lifted all restrictions on the use of diverse forms of land tenure. This conclusion was drawn on the basis of experience of many collectives. Several regions managed to blunt the acuteness of the situation at the food market. Nevertheless on the scale of the country, no fundamental improvement has taken place. The reason is that many people in localities are in the sway of old attitudes and methods of management.

Yes, There Are Shortages

Yes, there are shortages of resources and technology. Yes, social transformations must be conducted on a different scale and at different rates. All this is true. But primary importance should be assigned to restructuring relations of production in the village. And the crux of the matter now is the position of our cadre at the center and localities.

This is a political rather than an economic question. All obstacles should be removed in the way of the farmer; he should be given a free hand. This is how the draft platform poses the problem.

Food is the only part of the problem normalizing the consumer market. The draft stresses the importance of a range of measures to improve finances and monetary circulation, and to strengthen the purchasing power of the ruble as an urgent task for the next two years...

Comrades, our society is concerned no less with the situation in the economy than with a number of complex problems that arose in the inter-ethnic field, which affect the future of the Soviet federation. In working on the draft of the document that we are now discussing, we drew on the platform on inter-ethnic issues adopted at the September 1989 plenum.

We think that the platform on inter-ethnic issues can serve as a departure for transforming our federation.

At the same time, we tried to take into account several developments. The pre-congress platform points to the possibility of and the need for the further development of the treaty principle of the Soviet federation.

This would involve the creation of legal conditions that would open the possibility for the existence of diverse forms of federative ties. We stand for the diversity of modes of ethnic life in an integral and united state.

We have all lately had the possibility to think seriously of the state of affairs and developments in the sphere of ethnic relations...

To a Stronger Future

The sooner decisions are taken to delimit the competence of the union and that of republics, to actually strengthen their political and economic independence, to broaden the rights of ethnic autonomies and to achieve the harmonious development of all languages and cultures, the sooner the people will see the enormous advantages of the new federation.

Separatists, chauvinists and nationalists of all kinds understand this well and are trying to use the growth of peoples' national self-consciousness for their selfish aims. They evidently want to deliver a preventative strike at perestroika, which threatens to thwart their far-reaching plans.

This has been patently manifest in the recent development in Azerbaijan and Armenia. I don't think I should describe in detail the history of conflict which is rooted in the distant past. I would like to draw your attention to the principled aspect of the problem. The conflict is centered around Nagorno-Karabakh...

Unfortunately, many representatives of the intelligentsia in Azerbaijan and Armenia failed to correctly assess the situation, to find the real causes of the conflict and exert a positive influence on developments.

Meanwhile, corrupted anti-perestroika forces managed to take the lead and direct misled people's actions into the destructive channel.

I should say that there has been, perhaps, no other issue in the past two years that has been given so much attention in Moscow.

Cooling Ethnic Tensions

The initial position of the center was that the Nagorno-Karabakh conflict should be settled in such a way that would leave no winners and no losers. Otherwise, new flare-ups of hostility and violence, new victims and losses would be inevitable.

We continued to adhere to this position also at the height of the conflict. And still, we failed to check the aggravation of the situation.

Late last year, in a difficult situation, the supreme bodies of power in both republics took decisions that aggravated the situation still more. The republics found themselves on the brink of all-out war. Armed groups from both sides began clashing, they began to seize weapons and attack troops and law enforcement bodies and tightened the blockade of railways and roads.

Baku became the scene of brutal pogroms. If the state of emergency had not been introduced in Nagorno-Karabakh, in same border areas and then in Baku, the blood of not dozens, but thousands upon thousands of people would have been shed...

The great and responsible role played by the party, local government and state bodies, our cadres and the intelligentsia, has became more obvious now. It must be clear that those who depart from principled positions, follow in the wake of obsolete sentiments or fall under the influence of nationalist passions will find themselves outside political life.

It is not only the principled stance of our cadres that matters. Of no less importance is the ability to resolve practical problems that worry people. We know how hard and painful perestroika processes are proceeding in these two republics. This is one of the reasons why nationalist forces have succeeded in winning over the people...

I have already said that a greater tragedy was prevented thanks to resolute actions. The safety of several thousand people was jeopardized. This was the main motive of the decision taken. The key fact is that nationalist, anti-Soviet groups openly encroached on the constitutional system, strove for power and sought to establish a dictatorship, not a democracy, by naked force and through militant nationalism.

This was in fact a coup attempt, nothing more, nothing less...

Grief for the Dead

We express condolences to all Armenians, Azerbaijanis, Russians, and people of other nationalities, who lost dear ones or themselves suffered during those tragic days. The party and the Soviet Government will do everything possible to alleviate the plight of the refugees and help them return to normal life.

Soldiers and officers of the Soviet Army and Interior Ministry troops displayed a lofty sense of responsibility before the people, courage and restraint, and thus averted the escalation of bloodshed, saved thousands of lives and created conditions for defusing the situation...

Comrades, the logic of the struggle for perestroika has looked to new major decisions. The Supreme Soviet will soon adopt laws on ownership, on land, on local self-government and local economy, on the tax system, on the delineation of the competence of the union as a whole and of the constituent republics, and other fundamental legislative acts.

The second stage of political reform has been launched, encompassing the formation of governing bodies at republican and local levels.

Outlines of Federation

Real outlines of a new Soviet federation begin to emerge. As a matter of fact, new forms of our entire political, economic and public life are taking shape together with a new system of bodies of power, which are characterized by profound democratization and self-governing principles.

Indeed society is acquiring a new quality. But the processes that the party consciously activated, which will undoubtedly bring forth positive results, have not been insured, as we already see, against manifestations of instability, weakened management and centrifugal tendencies...

I will not dwell now on other issues of the political and legal reform, which are laid down, although in a concentrated but rather full way, in the draft platform. They were formulated in line with the decisions of the 19th party conference and, certainly, with account of the experience gained by our society over the time that has passed since then.

Democratization and creating a law-based state and a self-governing socialist society remain the principle direction of our development.

Comrades, naturally, the draft platform speaks about the international aspect of perestroika, about the modern world outlook which defines our foreign policy strategy...

Dangers Do Remain

The all-important thing for us now is to push forward the disarmament negotiating process, deepen dialogue and mutual understanding on crucial sections of international development, and facilitate in every way efforts to expand and strengthen the ground which was covered in building a common European home.

It is important to upgrade within its framework allied relations with East European countries, which really need this. This approach meets with understanding and reply moves on the part of their new leaders...

The situation in the world did improve in recent years, but the danger of war is still preserved.

The doctrines and concepts of the United States and NATO, which are far from being defensive, remain in force. Their armies and military budgets also exist.

This is why we need well-trained and well-equipped armed forces. Certainly, they need improvement and restructuring. But there should be a more responsible approach to changing the principle of their staffing and their construction as a whole in the context of changes in the world.

Some questions have arisen in view of the ongoing and possible reductions in troops and armaments. Specifically, apprehensions are expressed if this does not weaken the country's defense capability. Evidently, additional explanations are necessary here to show that the reduction and reorganization of the armed forces are being carried out strictly in conformity with the principle of reasonable sufficiency for defense, reliable defense...

Some social problems have arisen, especially those of housing provisions to servicemen and persons who retired or were transferred to reserve, and their employment. The Defense Ministry cannot cope with them. The government passed decisions that took the heat out of that issue, but evidently much still has to be done to rid officers and their families of the feeling that they lack social protection, which has emerged lately.

These decisions should be implemented. It also is deemed necessary to draft and endorse a special program of the social security of servicemen and members of their families and also of officers and warrant officers in reserve service...

Freedom at All Levels

Comrades, I want to say for one more time that the pivotal idea of restructuring the party itself is in asserting the power of party masses. In this connection, we are to recomprehend, among others, the role of primary organizations in what concerns admission to the party and quitting it, using membership dues, and implementing the tasks related to the new role of the party as the vanguard.

The role of district and city organizations should be revised and their rights should be considerably broadened. We should change the system of forming party bodies at all levels...

The rules should definitely say that elective bodies, from top to bottom, must be under control of and accountable to Communists and that the apparatus must be under control of and accountable to elective bodies...

One may ask, Why reduce the Central Committee? Let us discuss it. We proceeded from the need to turn the Central Committee into a body working on a permanent basis.

We should also depart from the principle of electing to the Central Committee many people holding state posts. This principle was actually an expression of the party-and-state system of power in the country.

We think these changes will help strengthen the Central Committee's ties with party organizations, because these ties will be maintained not through the apparatus but mainly through elected members of the Central Committee commission, actually becoming politicians of the party-wide rank.

It would be appropriate to speak here also about the central party apparatus. It is clear that the change of the party's role should entail changes in the qualitative composition of the apparatus. It should become an assistant of the Central Committee and work strictly under its control...

I will not speak about other issues raised in the draft platform. The Politburo hopes that by joint efforts we will work out a document that will give answers to all questions vital to Communists and all Soviet people and that perestroika in the country will thus receive a new powerful, positive impetus.

24. Yevgeny Yevtushenko

HALF-MEASURES

Half-measures
        can kill,
when,
     chafing at the bit in terror,
we twitch our ears,
        all lathered in foam,
on the brink of precipices,
because we can't jump halfway across.
Blind is the one
        who only half-sees
            the chasm.
Don't half-recoil,
        lost in broad daylight,
half-rebel,
     half-suppressor
of the half-insurrection
        you gave birth to!
With every half-effective
        half-measure
half the people
      remain half-pleased.
The half-sated
      are half-hungry.
The half-free
      are half-enslaved.
We are half-afraid,
        halfway on a rampage…
A bit of this,
     yet also half of that
party-line
     weak-willed "Robin Hood" [1]
who half-goes
     to a half-execution.

"Half-Measures" by Yevgency Yevtushenko, from *20th Century Russian Poetry*, ed. A. C. Todd & M. Hayward, pp. 818-819. Copyirhgt ©1993 by Doubleday. Used by permission of Doubleday, a division of Bantam Doubleday Dell Publishing Group, Inc.

Opposition has lost
           its resolution.
By swashbuckling jabs
             with a flimsy sword
you cannot be half
           a guard for the Cardinal
and half
     a King's Musketeer.
Can there be
     with honor
a half-motherland
         and a half-conscience?
Half-freedom
     is perilous,
and saving the Motherland halfway
              will fail.

1989
Translated by Albert C. Todd

1. The Russian character is Stenka Razin, a Don Cossack who led a mixed Russian and non-Russian peasant rebellion (1670-1671) that engulfed the southeastern steppe region. Celebrated in folk songs and tales, he was finally captured and taken to Moscow where he was publicly quartered alive.

TRADITIONAL CHINA,
NATIONALIST CHINA
AND THE
PEOPLE'S REPUBLIC OF CHINA

OLD AND NEW SPELLINGS OF CHINESE NAMES

Wade Giles	*Pin-Yin*
Ching Dynasty	Qing Dynasty
Lin Tse-hsü	Lin Zexiu
Hong Hsiu-chian	Hong Xiuguan
Tseng Kuo-fan	Zeng Guofan
Li Hung-chang	Li Hongshang
Tz'u-hsi	Cixi
T'ung-chih Restoration	Tongzhi Restoration
Tsungli Yamen	Zonghi Yamen
K'ang Yu-wei	Kang Youwei
Liang Chi-chao	Liang Qichao
Yuan Shih-Kai	Yuan Shikai
Kuomintang (KMT)	Guomindang (GMD)
Ch'en Tu-hsiu	Chen Duxiu
Yu Hsun	Lu Xun
Hu Shih	Hu Shi
Pai-hua	Bai Hua
Li Ta-chao	Li Dazhao
Tuan Ch'i-jui	Duan Jirui
Chou En-lai	Zhou Enlai
Yin Pao	Lin Bao
Chu Teh	Zhu De
Chang Hsueh-liang	Zhang Zueliang
Chungking*	Chongqing*
Canton*	Guanzhou*
Peking*	Beijing*
hsia-feng	xiafeng
Yiu Shao-chi	Liu Shaoqi
R'eng Teh-hui	Peng Dehuai
Deng Hsiao-p'ing	Deng Xiaoping
Chiang Ch'ing	Jiang Qing
Hua Kuo-feng	Hua Guofang
Mao Tse-t'ung	Mao Zedong

*These are cities.

25. Lin Zexiu

LETTER TO QUEEN VICTORIA

1839

The Way of Heaven is fairness to all; it does not suffer us to harm others in order to benefit ourselves. Men are alike in this all the world over; that they cherish life and hate what endangers life. Your country lies twenty thousand leagues away; but for all the Way of Heaven holds good for you as for us, and your instincts are too different from ours; for nowhere are there men so blind as not to distinguish between what brings life and what brings death, between what brings profit and what does harm. Our Heavenly Court treats all within the Four Seas as one great family; the goodness of our great Emperor is like Heaven, that covers all things. There is no region so wild or so remote that he does not cherish and tend it. Ever since the port of Canton was first opened, trade has flourished.[1] For some hundred and twenty or thirty years the natives of the place have enjoyed peaceful and profitable relations with the ships that come from abroad. Rhubarb,[2] tea, silk are all valuable products of ours, without which foreigners could not live. The Heavenly Court, extending its benevolence to all alike, allows these things to be sold and carried away across the sea, not grudging them even to remote domains, its bounty matching the bounty of Heaven and Earth.

But there is a class of evil foreigner that makes opium and brings it for sale, tempting fools to destroy themselves, merely in order to reap a profit. Formerly the number of opium smokers was small; but now the vice has spread far and wide and the poison penetrated deeper and deeper. If there are some foolish people who yield to this craving to their own detriment, it is they who have brought upon themselves their own ruin, and in a country so populous and flourishing, we can well do without them. But the great, unified Manchu Empire regards itself as responsible for the habits and morals of its subjects and cannot rest content to see any of them become victims to a deadly poison. For this reason we have decided to inflict very severe penalties on opium dealers and opium smokers, in order to put a stop forever to the propagation of this vice. It appears that this poisonous article is manufactured by certain devilish persons in places subject to your rule. It is not, of course, either made or sold at your bidding, nor do all the countries you rule produce it, but only certain of them. I am told that in your own country opium smoking is forbidden under severe penalties. This means that you are aware of how harmful it is. But better than to forbid the smoking of it would be to forbid the sale of it and, better still, to forbid the production of it, which is the only way of cleansing the contamination at its source. So long as you do not take it yourselves, but continue to make it and tempt people of China to buy it, you will be showing yourselves careful of your own lives, but careless of the lives of other people, indifferent in your greed to human feeling and at variance with the Way of Heaven.

From *Sources of Chinese Tradition* by William T. de Bary (ed.), 1989, © Columbia University Press, New York. Reprinted with the permission of the publisher.

The laws against the consumption of opium are now so strict in China that if you continue to make it, you will find that no-one buys it and no more fortunes will be made. Rather than waste your efforts on a hopeless endeavour, would it not be better to devise some other form of trade? All opium discovered in China is being cast into burning oil and destroyed. Any foreign ships that in the future arrive with opium on board, will be set fire to, and any other goods they are carrying will inevitably be burned along with the opium. You will then not only fail to make any profit out of us, but ruin yourselves into the bargain. Intending to harm others, you will be the first to be harmed. Our Heavenly Court would not have won the allegiance of innumerable lands did it not wield superhuman power. Do not say you have not been warned in time. On receiving this, Your Majesty will be so good as to report to me immediately on the steps that have been taken at each of your ports.

NOTES

1 That is, since the port was opened in the middle of the eighteenth century to British trade under the [Guangzhou] system of the Cohong.
2 At that time the Chinese were convinced that "red-haired barbarians" could not do without Chinese rhubarb, for use as a laxative.

26. THE TAIPING ECONOMIC PROGRAM

The following selection is taken from The Land System of the Heavenly Kingdom, *which was included in the list of official Taiping publications promulgated in 1853. Its precise authorship is uncertain, and there is no evidence of a serious attempt having been made to put this system into effect in Taiping-controlled areas. Nevertheless, as a statement of Taiping aims the document carried with it all the weight of Hung Hsiu-ch'uan's authority and that of the Eastern King, Yang Hsiu-ch'ing, then at the height of his power. It reflects one of the chief appeals which the movement made to the Chinese peasantry.*

The plan set forth here amounts to a blueprint for the total organization of society, and especially of its human resources. If its initial concern is with the land problem, as the title indicates, it quickly moves on to other spheres of human activity and brings them under a single pattern of control. The basic organization is military in nature, reminiscent of the farmer-soldier militia of earlier dynasties. In its economic egalitarianism, totalitarian communism, authoritarian hierarchy and messianic zeal, this Taiping manifesto seems to foreshadow the Chinese Communist movement of the twentieth century, while at the same time it echoes reformers and rebels in the past. Most typically it recalls the fondness of earlier Chinese thinkers for what might be described as the "completely-designed" society—their vision of a neat symmetrical system embodying the supreme values of Chinese thought: order, balance, and harmony.

Nevertheless, we can appreciate how conservative Confucianists would have recoiled at the thought of so much economic regimentation. Tseng Kuo-fan, their great leader in the struggle against the Taipings, commented: "The farmer cannot till his own land and [simply] pay taxes on it; the land is all considered to be the land of the Heavenly King [and all produce goes directly to the communal treasury]. The merchant cannot engage in trade for himself and profit thereby; all goods are considered to be the goods of the Heavenly King."

The organizational note is struck at the outset with an explanation of the system of army districts and military administration (omitted here). We reproduce below only the basic economic program.

[From Hsiao I-shan, *T'ai-p'ing t'ien-kuo-shu*, Series I, t'se 4, pp. 1a-3a]

All officials who have rendered meritorious service are to receive hereditary stipends from the court. For the later adherents to the Taiping cause, every family in each military district (chun) is to provide one man to serve as a militia man. During an emergency they are to fight under the command of their officers to destroy the enemy and to suppress bandits. In peacetime they are to engage in agriculture under the direction of their officers, tilling the land and providing support for their superiors...

The distribution of all land is to be based on the number of persons in each family, regardless of sex. A large family is entitled to more land, a small one to less. The land distributed should not be all of one grade, but mixed. Thus for a family of six, for instance, three are to have fertile land and three barren land—half and half of each.

All the land in the country is to be cultivated by the whole population together. If there is an insufficiency [of land] in this place, move some of the people to another place. If there is an insufficiency in another place, move them to this one. All lands in the country are also to be mutually supporting with respect to abundance and scarcity. If this place has a drought, then draw upon the abundant harvest elsewhere in order to relieve the distress here. If there is drought there, draw upon the abundant harvest here in order to relieve distress distress there. Thus all the people of the country may enjoy the great blessings of the Heavenly Father, Supreme Ruler, and Lord God-on-High. The land is for all to till, the food for all to eat, the clothes for all to wear, and money for all to spend. Inequality shall exist nowhere; none shall suffer from hunger or cold.

Every person sixteen or over, whether male or female, is entitled to a share of land; those fifteen or under should receive half the share of an adult...

THE PRINCIPLES OF THE HEAVENLY NATURE

> This official work, dated 1854, was written after the Taipings had established their capital at Nanking and the first flush of victory gave way to a seeming let-down in morale, discipline, and zeal for the cause. It served to restate the religious creed of the Taipings and emphasize those qualities—self-sacrifice, loyalty, and solidarity—which had contributed to their amazing successes. The appeal throughout is to a dedicated and crusading military elite.
>
> Another important purpose of the book was to enhance and consolidate the position of the Taiping leadership, especially that of the Eastern King, Yang Hsiu-ch'ing, who was virtual prime minister of the regime and the one who inspired the writing of this document. We see here in a strange new garb the old conception of the ruler as commissioned with the divine powers to unite the world and establish peace. Both Hung and Yang are thus represented as in some degree sharing the rule of Jesus Christ as saviors of the world. Since it would not have done for any of the "kings" to engage openly in such self-glorification, nominal authorship is attributed to the "marquises" who constituted the next highest ranks in the Taiping hierarchy.
>
> Extant editions of the text appear to date from about 1858, by which time rivalries and mistrust had split the leadership, Yang had been assassinated, and his assassin, the Northern King, murdered by Hung. Though there are many direct and indirect evidences of dissension, the text has not been amended or adjusted to these later developments except to strip the Northern King of his rank.
>
> The translation here has been adapted from that of C.T. Hu for the documentary history of the Taiping Rebellion being prepared by the Modern Chinese History Project of the Far Eastern and Russian Institute, University of Washington.

[From Hsiao, *T'ai-p'ing t'ien-kuo ts'ung-shu*, ts'e 5, pp. 1-37]

With regard to human life, reverence for Heaven and support of the Sovereign begin with loyalty and uprightness; to cast off the devil's garb and become true men —— this must come about through awakening. Now, the Heavenly Father and the Heavenly Elder Brother have displayed the heavenly favor and specially commended our Heavenly King to descend into the world and be the true Taiping sovereign of the ten thousand states of the world; they have also sent the Eastern King to assist in court policy, to save the starving, to redeem the sick and, together with the Western and Northern Kings, [Wei] Ch'ang-hui, and the Assistant King, to take part in the prosperous rule and assist in the grand design. As a result, the mortal world witnesses the blessing of resurrection, and our bright future is the symbol of renewal.

We marquises and chancellors hold that our brothers and sisters have been blessed by the Heavenly Father and Heavenly Elder Brother, who saved the ensnared and drowning and awakened the deluded; they have cast off the worldly sentiments and now follow the true Way. They cross mountains and wade rivers, not even ten thousand *li* being too far for them to come, to uphold together the true Sovereign. Armed and bearing shield and spear, they carry righteous banners that rise colorfully. Husband and wife, men and women, express common indignation and lead the advance. It can be said that they are determined to uphold Heaven and to requite the nation with loyalty.

You younger brothers and sisters have now experienced the heavenly days of Great Peace (Taiping), and have basked in the glory of the Heavenly Father, the Supreme Ruler and Lord God-on High. You must be aware of the grace and virtue of the Heavenly Father, the Supreme ruler and Lord God-on-High, and fully recognize that the Heavenly Father, the Supreme Ruler and Lord God-on-High, is alone the one true God. Aside from the Heavenly Father, the Supreme Ruler and Lord God-on-High, there is no other god. Moreover, there is nothing which can usurp the merits of the Heavenly Father, the Supreme Ruler and Lord God-on-High. In the ten thousand nations of the world everyone is given life, nourished, protected, and blessed by the Heavenly Father, the Supreme Ruler and Lord God-on-High, is the universal father of man in all the ten thousand nations of the world. There is no man who should not be grateful, there is no man who should not reverently worship Him. Have you not seen the Heavenly King's "ode on the Origin of Virtue and the Saving of the World," which reads: "The true God who created Heaven and earth is none but God; all, whether noble or mean, must worship Him piously"? This is precisely our meaning!...

27. Zeng GuoFan and Li Hongzhang

ON SENDING YOUNG MEN ABROAD TO STUDY

Last autumn when I [Tseng] was at Tientsin, Governor Ting Jihch'ang frequently came to discuss with me proposals for the selection of intelligent youths to be sent to the schools of various Western countries to study military administration, shipping administration, infantry tactics, mathematics, manufacturing, and other subjects. We estimated that after more than ten years their training would have been completed, and they could return to China so that other Chinese might learn thoroughly the superior techniques of the Westerners. Thus we could gradually plan for self-strengthening...After Mr. Pin Chu'un and two other gentlemen, Chih-kang and Sun Chia-ku had traveled in various countries at imperial command, they saw the essential aspects of conditions overseas, and they found that cartography, mathematics, astronomy, navigation, ship-building, and manufacturing are all closely related to military defense. It is the practice of foreign nations that those who have studied abroad and have learned some superior techniques are immediately invited upon their return by academic institutions to teach the various subjects and to develop their fields. Military administration and shipping are considered as important as the learning that deals with the mind and body, and nature and destiny of man. Now that the eyes of the people have been opened, if China wished to adopt Western ideas and excel in Western methods, we should immediately select intelligent boys and send them to study in foreign countries...

Some may say: "Arsenals have been established in Tientsin, Shanghai and Foochow for shipbuilding and the manufacturing of guns and ammunition. The T'ung-wen College [for foreign languages] has been established in Peking for Manchu and Chinese youths to study under Western instructors. A language school has also been opened in Shanghai for the training of young students. It seems, therefore, that a beginning has been made in China and that there is no need for studying overseas." These critics, however, do not know that to establish arsenals for manufacturing and to open schools for instruction is just the beginning of our effort to rise again. To go to distant lands for study, to gather ideas for more advantageous use, can produce far-reaching and great results. Westerners seek knowledge for practical use. Whether they be scholars, artisans, or soldiers, they all go to school to study and understand the principles, to practice on the machines, and to participate personally in the work. They all exert themselves to the utmost of their ingenuity, and learn from one another, in the hope that there will be monthly progress and yearly improvement. If we Chinese wish to adopt their superior techniques and suddenly try to buy all their machines, not only will our resources be insufficient to do so, but we will be unable to master the fundamental principles or to understand the complicated details of the techniques, unless we have actually seen and practiced with them for a long time...

We have heard that youths of Fukien, Kwangtung, and Ningpo also occasionally have gone abroad to study, but they merely attempted to gain a superficial knowledge of foreign written and

From *Sources of Chinese Tradition* by William T. de Bary (ed.), Vol. II, pp. 49-51. Copyright ©1960 Columbia University Press, New York. Reprinted with the permission of the publisher.

spoken languages in order to do business with the foreigners for the purpose of making a living. In our plan, we must be doubly careful at the beginning of selection. The students who are to be taken to foreign countries will all be under the control of the commissioners. Specializing in different fields, they will earnestly seek for mastery of their subjects. There will be interpreters, and instructors to teach them Chinese literature from time to time, so that they will learn the great principles for the establishment of character, in the hope of becoming men with abilities of use to us.

28. Chen Duxiu

THE WAY OF CONFUCIUS AND MODERN LIFE

The pulse of modern life is economic and the fundamental principle of economic production is individual independence. Its effect has penetrated ethics. Consequently the independence of the individual in the ethical field and the independence of property in the economic field bear witness to each other, thus reaffirming the theory [of such interaction]. Because of this [interaction], social mores and material culture have taken a great step forward.

In China, the Confucianists have based their teachings on their ethical norms. Sons and wives possess neither personal individuality nor personal property. Fathers and elder brothers bring up their sons and younger brothers and are in turn supported by them. It is said in chapter thirty of *The Book of Rites* that "While parents are living, the son dares not regard his person or property as his own." This is absolutely not the way to personal independence...

In all modern constitutional states, whether monarchies or republics, there are political parties. Those who engage in party activities all express their spirit of independent conviction. They go their own way and need not agree with their fathers or husbands. When people are bound by the Confucian teachings of filial piety and obedience to the point of the son not deviating from the father's way even three years after his death and the woman obeying not only her father and husband but also her son, how can they form their own political party and make their own choice? The movement of women's participation in politics is also an aspect of women's life in modern civilization. When they are bound by the Confucian teaching that "To be a woman means to submit," that "The wife's words should not travel beyond her own apartment," and that "A woman does not travel beyond her own apartment," and that "A woman does not discuss affairs outside the home," would it not be unusual if she participated in politics?

In the West some widows choose to remain single because they are strongly attached to their late husbands and sometimes because they prefer a single life: they have nothing to do with what is called the chastity of widowhood. Widows who remarry are not despised by society at all. On the other hand, in the Chinese teaching of decorum, there is the doctrine of "no remarriage after the husband's death." It is considered to be extremely shameful and unchaste for a woman to serve two husbands or a man to serve two rulers. *The Book of Rites* also prohibits widows from wailing at night and people from being friends with sons of widows. For the sake of their family reputation, people have forced their daughters-in-law to remain widows. These women have had no freedom and have lived a physically and spiritually abnormal life. All this is a result of Confucian teachings of decorum [or rites].

In today's civilized society, social intercourse between men and women is a common practice. Some even say that because women have a tender nature and can temper the crudeness of man, they are necessary in public or private gatherings. It is not considered improper even for strangers to sit or dance together once they have been introduced by the host. In the way of

Confucian teaching, however, "Men and women do not sit on the same mat," "Brothers- and sisters-in-law do not exchange inquiries about each other," "Married sisters do not sit on the same mat with brothers or eat from the same dish," "Men and women do not know each other's name except through a matchmaker and should have no social relations or show affection until after marriage presents have been exchanged," "Women must cover their faces when they go out," "Boys and girls seven years or older do not sit or eat together," "Men and women have no social relations except through a matchmaker and do not meet until after marriage presents have been exchanged," and "Except in religious sacrifices, men and women do not exchange wine cups." Such rules of decorum are not only inconsistent with the mode of life in Western society: they cannot even be observed in today's China.

Western women make their own living in various professions such as that of a lawyer, physician, and store employee. But in the Confucian way, "In giving or receiving anything, a man or woman should not touch the other's hand," "A man does not talk about affairs inside [the household] and a woman does not talk about affairs outside [the household]," and "They do not exchange cups except in sacrificial rites and funerals." "A married woman is to obey" and the husband is the standard of the wife. Thus the wife is naturally supported by the husband and needs no independent livelihood.

A married woman is at first a stranger to her parents-in-law. She has only affection but no obligation toward them. In the West parents and children usually do not live together, and daughters-in-law, particularly, have no obligation to serve parents-in-law. But in the way of Confucius, a woman is to "revere and respect them and never to disobey day or night," "A woman obeys, that is, obeys her parents-in-law," "A woman serves her parents-in-law as she serves her own parents," she "never should disobey or be lazy in carrying out the orders of parents and parents-in-law." "If a man is very fond of his wife, but his parents do not like her, she should be divorced." (In ancient times there were many such cases, like that of Lu Yu [1125-1210].) "Unless told to retire to her own apartment, a woman does not do so, and if she has an errand to do, she must get permission from her parents-in-law." This is the reason why the tragedy of cruelty to daughters-in-law has never ceased in China.

According to Western customs, fathers do not discipline grown-up sons but leave them to the law of the country and the control of society. But in the way of Confucius, 'when one's parents are angry and not pleased and beat him until he bleeds, he does not complain but instead arouses in himself the feelings of reverence and filial piety." This is the reason why in China there is the saying, "One has to die if his father wants him to, and the minister has to perish if his ruler wants him to"...

Confucius lived in a feudal age. The ethics he promoted were the ethics of the feudal age. The social mores he taught and even his own mode of living were teachings and modes of a feudal age. The political institutions he advocated were those of a feudal age. The objectives, ethics, social norms, mode of living, and political institutions did not go beyond the privilege and prestige of a few rulers and aristocrats and had nothing to do with the happiness of the great masses. How can this be shown? In the teachings of Confucius, the most important element in social ethics and social life is the rules of decorum and the most serious thing in government is punishment. In chapter one of *The Book of Rites*, it is said that "The rules of decorum do not go down to the common people and the penal statutes do not go up to great officers." Is this not solid proof of the [true] spirit of the way of Confucius and the spirit of the feudal age?

29. Sun Yatsen

THE THREE PEOPLE'S PRINCIPLES

China as a Heap of Loose Sand

For the most part the four hundred million people of China can be spoken of as completely Han Chinese. With common customs and habits, we are completely of one race. But in the world today what position do we occupy? Compared to the other peoples of the world we have the greatest population and our civilization is four thousand years old; we should therefore be advancing in the front rank with the nations of Europe and America. But the Chinese people have only family and clan solidarity; they do not have national spirit. Therefore even though we have four hundred million people gathered together in one China, in reality they are just a heap of loose sand. Today we are the poorest and weakest nation in the world, and occupy the lowest position in international affairs. Other men are the carving knife and serving dish; we are the fish and the meat. Our position at this time is most perilous. If we do not earnestly espouse nationalism and weld together our four million people into a strong nation, there is danger of China's being lost and our people being destroyed. If we wish to avert this catastrophe, we must espouse nationalism and bring this national spirit to the salvation of the country.

China as a "hypo-colony"

Since the Chinese Revolution, the foreign powers have found that it was much less easy to use political force in carving up China. A people who had experienced Manchu oppression and learned to overthrow it, would now, if the powers used political force to oppress it, be certain to resist, and thus make things difficult for them. For this reason they are letting up in their efforts to control China by political force and instead are using economic pressure to keep us down .... As regards political oppression people are readily aware of their suffering, but when it comes to economic oppression most often they are hardly conscious of it. China has already experienced several decades of economic oppression by the foreign powers, and so far the nation has for the most part shown no sense of irritation. As a consequence China is being transformed everywhere into a colony of the foreign powers.

Our people keep thinking that China is only a "semi-colony"—a term by which they seek to comfort themselves. Yet in reality the economic oppression we have endured is not just as the colony of every nation with which it had concluded treaties; each of them is China's master. Therefore China is not just the colony of one country; it is the colony of many countries. We are not just the slaves of one country, but the slaves of many countries. In the event of natural disasters like flood and drought, a nation which is sole master appropriates funds for relief and distrib-

From *Sources of Chinese Tradition* by William T. de Bary (ed.), Vol. II, pp. 105-120. Copyright ©1960 Columbia University Press, New York. Reprinted with the permission of the publisher.

utes them, thinking this its own duty; and the people who are its slaves regard this relief work as something to which their masters are obligated. But when North China suffered drought several years ago, the foreign powers did not regard it as their responsibility to appropriate funds and distribute relief; only those foreigners resident in China raised funds for the drought victims, whereupon Chinese observers remarked on the great generosity of the foreigners who bore no responsibility to help....

From this we can see that China is not so well off as Annam [under the French] and Korea [under the Japanese]. Being the slaves of one country represents a far higher status than being the slaves of many, and is far more advantageous. Therefore, to call China a "semi-colony" is quite incorrect. If I may coin a phrase, we should be called a "hypo-colony." This is a term that comes from chemistry, as in "hypo-phosphite." Among chemicals there are some belonging to the class of phosphorous compounds but of lower grade, which are called phosphites. Still another grade lower, and they are called hypophosphites....The Chinese people, believing they were a semi-colony, thought it shame enough; they did not realize that they were lower even than Annam or Korea. Therefore we cannot call ourselves a "semi-colony" but only a "hypo-colony."

Nationalism and Cosmopolitanism

A new idea is emerging in England and Russia, proposed by the intellectuals, which opposes nationalism on the ground that it is narrow and illiberal. This is simply a doctrine of cosmopolitanism. England now and formerly Germany and Russia, together with the Chinese youth of today who preach the new civilization, support this doctrine and oppose nationalism. Often I hear young people say: "The Three Principles of the People do not fit in with the present world's new tendencies; the latest and best doctrine in the world is cosmopolitanism." But is cosmopolitanism really good or not? If that doctrine is good, why is it that as soon as China was conquered, her nationalism was destroyed? Cosmopolitanism is the same thing as China's theory of world empire two thousand years ago. Let us now examine that doctrine and see whether in fact it is good or not. Theoretically, we cannot say it is no good. Yet it is because formerly the Chinese intellectual class had cosmopolitan ideas that, when the Manchus crossed China's frontier, the whole country was lost to them ....

We cannot decide whether an idea is good or not without seeing it in practice. It the idea is of practical value to us, it is good; if it is impractical, it is bad. It if is useful to the world, it is good; if it is not, it is no good. The nations which are employing imperialism to conquer others and which are trying to retain their privileged positions as sovereign lords are advocating cosmopolitanism and want the whole world to follow them.

Nationalism and Traditional Morality

If today we want to restore the standing of our people, we must first restore our national spirit.... If in the past our people have survived despite the fall of the state [to foreign conquerors], and not only survived themselves but been able to assimilate these foreign conquerors, it is because of the high level of our traditional morality. Therefore, if we go to the root of the matter, besides arousing a sense of national solidarity uniting all our people, we must recover and restore our characteristic, traditional morality. Only thus can we hope to attain again the distinctive position of our people.

This characteristic morality the Chinese people today have still not forgotten. First comes loyalty and filial piety, then humanity and love, faithfulness and duty, harmony and peace. Of these traditional virtues, the Chinese people still speak, but now, under foreign oppression, we have been invaded by a new culture, the force of which is felt all across the nation. Men wholly intoxicated by this new culture have thus begun to attack the traditional morality, saying that with the adoption of the new culture, we no longer have need of the old morality....They say that when we formerly spoke of loyalty, it was loyalty to princes, but now in our democracy there are no princes, so loyalty is unnecessary and can be dispensed with. This kind of reasoning is certainly mistaken. In our country princes can be dispensed with, but not loyalty. If they say loyalty can be dispensed with, then I ask: "Do we, or do we not, have a nation? Can we, or can we not, make loyalty serve the nation? If indeed we can no longer speak of loyalty to princes, can we not, however, speak of loyalty to our people?"

The Principle of Democracy
Separation of Sovereignty and Ability

How can a government be made all-powerful? Once the government is all-powerful, how can it be made responsive to the will of the people?... I have found a method to solve the problem. The method which I have thought of is a new discovery in political theory and is a fundamental solution of the whole problem.... It is the theory of the distinction between sovereignty and ability.

After China has established a powerful government, we must not be afraid, as Western people are, that the government will become too strange and that we will be unable to control it. For it is our plan that the political power of the reconstructed state will be divided into two parts. One is the power over the government: that great power will be placed entirely in the hands of the people, who will have a full degree of sovereignty and will be able to control directly the affairs of state—this political power is popular sovereignty. The other power is the governing power; that great power will be placed in the hands of the government organs, which will be powerful and will manage all the nation's business—this governing power is the power of the government. If the people have a full measure of political sovereignty and the methods for exercising popular control over the government are well worked out, we need not fear that the government will become too strong and uncontrollable....

It is because Europe and America lacked compact and effective methods to control their government that their governmental machines have not, until the present day, been well-developed. Let us not follow in their tracks. Let the people in thinking about government distinguish between sovereignty and ability. Let the great political force of the state be divided into two; the power of the government and the power of the people. Such a division will make the government the machinery and the people the engineer. The attitude of the people toward the government will then resemble the attitude of the engineer toward this machine. The construction of machinery has made such advances nowadays that not only men with mechanical knowledge, but even children without any knowledge of machinery are able to control it.

The Four Powers of the People

What are the newest discoveries in the way of exercising popular sovereignty? First, there is suffrage, and it is the only method practiced throughout the so-called advanced democracies. Is this one form of popular sovereignty enough in government? This one power by itself may be compared to the earlier machines which could move forward only but not back.

The second of the newly discovered methods is the right of recall. When the people have this right, they possess the power of pulling the machine back.

These two rights give the people control over officials and enable them to put all government officials in their positions or to remove them from their positions. The coming and going of officials follow the free will of the people, just as the modern machines move to and fro by the free action of the engine. Besides officials, another important thing in a state is law; "with men to govern there must also be laws for governing." What powers must the people possess in order to control the laws? If the people think that a certain law would be of great advantage to them, they should have the power to decide upon this law and turn it over to the government for execution. This third kind of popular power is called the initiative.

If the people think that an old law is not beneficial to them, they should have the power to amend it and to ask the government to enforce the amended law and do away with the old law. This is called the referendum and is a fourth form of popular sovereignty.

Only when the people have these four rights can we say that democracy is complete, and only when these four powers are effectively applied can we say that there is a thorough-going, direct, and popular sovereignty.

The Five-Power Constitution

With the people exercising the four great powers to control the government, what methods will the government use in performing its work? In order that the government may have a complete organ through which to do its best work, there must be a five-power constitution. A government is not complete and cannot do its best work for the people unless it is based on the five-power constitution [i.e., a government composed of five branches: executive, legislative, judicial, civil service examination, and censorate]....

All governmental powers were formerly monopolized by kings and emperors, but after the revolutions they were divided into three groups. Thus the United States, after securing its independence, established a government with three coordinate departments. The American system achieved such good results, that it was adopted by other nations. But foreign governments have merely a triple-power separation. Why do we now want a separation of five powers? What is the source of the two new features in our five-power constitution?

The two new features come from old China. China long ago had the independent systems of civil service examination and censorate, and they were very effective. The imperial censors of the Manchu dynasty and the official advisers of the T'ang dynasty made a fine censoring system. The power of censorship includes the power to impeach. Foreign countries also have this power, only it is placed in the legislative body and is not a separate governmental power.

The selection of real talent and ability through examinations has been characteristic of China for thousands of years. Foreign scholars who have recently studied Chinese institutions highly praise China's old independent examination system. There have been imitations of the system for the selection of able men in the West. Great Britain's civil service examinations are modeled after the old Chinese system, but they are limited to ordinary officials. The British system does not yet possess the spirit of the independent examination of China.

In old China, only three governmental powers—judicial, legislative, and executive—were vested in the emperor. The other powers of civil service examination and the censorate were independent of the Three. The old autocratic government of China can also be said to have had three separate departments and so it was very different from the autocratic governments of the West in which all power was monopolized by the king or emperor himself. During the period of autocratic government in China, the emperor did not monopolize the power of examination and the censorate.

Hence, as for the separation of governmental powers, we can say that China had three coordinate departments of government just as the modern democracies. China practiced the separation of autocratic examination and censorate powers for thousands of years. Western countries have practiced the separation of legislative, judicial, and executive powers for only a little over a century. However, the three governmental powers in the West have been imperfectly applied and the three coordinate powers of old China led to many abuses. If we now want to combine the best from China and the best from other countries and guard against all kinds of abuse, we must take the three Western governmental powers—the executive, legislative and judicial—add to them the Chinese powers of examination and censorate and make a perfect government of five powers. Such a government will be the most complete and the finest in the world, and a state with such a government will indeed be of the people, by the people and for the people.

The People's Livelihood
The Principle of Livelihood

The Kuomintang some time ago in its party platform adopted two methods by which the principle of livelihood is to be carried out. The first method is equalization of landownership: the second is regulation of capital.

Our first method consists in solving the land question. The methods for solution of the land problem are different in various countries, and each country has its own peculiar difficulties. The plan which we are following is simple and easy—equalization of landownership.

After land values have been fixed we should have a regulation by law that from that year on, all increase in land value, which in other countries means heavier taxation, shall revert to the community. This is because the increase in land value is due to improvement made by society and to the progress of industry and commerce. China's industry and commerce have made little progress for thousands of years, so land values have scarcely changed throughout these generations. But as soon as progress and improvement set in, as in the modern cities of China, land prices change every day, sometimes increasing a thousandfold and even ten thousandfold. The credit for the progress and improvement belongs to the energy and enterprise of all the people. Land increment resulting from that progress and improvement should therefore revert to the community rather than to private individuals.

Capital and the State

If we want to solve the livelihood problem in China and to "win eternal ease by one supreme effort," it will not be sufficient to depend only on the restriction of capital. The income tax levied in foreign countries is one method of regulating capital. But have these countries solved the problem of the people's livelihood?

China cannot be compared to foreign countries. It is not sufficient for us to regulate capital. Other countries are rich while China is poor; other countries have a surplus of production while China is not producing enough. So China must not only regulate private capital, but she must also develop state capital.

At present our state is split into pieces. How can we develop our state capital? It seems as if we could not find or anticipate a way. But our present disunion is only a temporary state of affairs; in the future we shall certainly achieve unity, and then to solve the livelihood problem we shall need to develop capital and promote industry.

As soon as the landowners hear us talking about the land question and equalization of landownership, they are naturally alarmed as capitalists are alarmed when they hear people talking about socialism, and they want to rise up and fight it. If our landowners were like the great landowners of Europe and had developed tremendous power, it would be very difficult for us to solve the land problem. But China does not have such big landowners, and the power of the small landowners is still rather weak. If we attack the problem now, we can solve it: but if we lose the present opportunity, we will have much more difficulty in the future. The discussion of the land problem naturally causes a feeling of fear among the landowners, but if the Kuomintang policy is followed, present landowners can set their hearts at rest.

What is our policy? We propose that the government shall levy a tax proportionate to the price of the land and, if necessary, buy back the land according to its price.

But how will the price of the land be determined? I would let the landowner himself fix the price.... Many people think that if the landowners made their own assessment, they would undervalue the land and the government would lose out.... But suppose the government makes two regulations; first, that it will collect taxes according to the declared value of the land; second, that it can also buy back the land at the value declared.... According to this plan, if the landowner makes a low assessment, he will be afraid lest the government buy the land at the declared value and make him lose his property; if he makes too high an assessment, he will be afraid of the government taxes according to the value and his loss through heavy taxes. Comparing these two serious possibilities, he will certainly not want to report the value of his land too high or too low; he will strike the mean and report the true market price to the government. In this way neither the landowner nor the government will lose.

First, we must build means of communication, railroads and waterways, on a large scale. Second, we must open up mines. China is rich in minerals, but alas, they are buried in the earth! Third, we must hasten to develop manufacturing. Although China has a multitude of workers, she has no machinery and so cannot compete with other countries. Goods used throughout China have to be manufactured and imported from other countries, with the result that our rights and interests are simply leaking away. If we want to recover these rights and interests, we must quickly employ state power to promote industry, use machinery in production, and see that all workers of the country are employed. When all the workers have employment and use machinery in production, we will have a great, new source of wealth. If we do not use state power to build up these enterprises but leave them in the hands of private Chinese or of foreign businessmen, the result will be the expansion of private capital and the emergence of a great wealth class with the consequent inequalities in society....

China is now suffering from poverty, not from unequal distribution of wealth. Where there are inequalities of wealth, the methods of Marx can, of course, be used; a class war can be advocated to destroy the inequalities. But in China, where industry is not yet developed, Marx's class war and dictatorship of the proletariat are impracticable.

30. James E. Sheridan

EMERGENCE OF THE WARLORDS

In Chinese history, the term warlord ordinarily designates a man who was lord of a particular area by virtue of his capacity to wage war. A warlord exercised effective governmental control over a fairly well-defined region by means of a military organization that obeyed no higher authority than himself. From 1916 to 1928, virtually all of China was divided among many such regional militarists, big and small: those years are therefore commonly termed the "warlord period," although warlords and warlordism remained important in Chinese politics long after 1928.

Regionalism and Militarism in the Late Ch'ing

Military regionalism did not, of course, come suddenly into being in 1916; rather, it was the culmination of a process that had begun about a century earlier. Indeed, regionalism always was latent in China, even when the central government operated at maximum effectiveness. Communication and transportation facilities never were adequate to the task of binding all parts of the vast country to its political center. There were strong local and regional variations in language, habits, and traditions. Although the Chinese traditionally took great pride in Chinese culture, incentives to national patriotism were few and weak, whereas provincial and local loyalties were powerful. As long as the central government was vigorous and reasonably efficient, there was little to arouse this latent regionalism; in any event, the central authority could check such tendencies whenever they appeared. Conversely, a decline in central power both stimulated the growth of regionalism (as an alternative to anarchy) and lessened the government's ability to restrain that growth. During the nineteenth and early twentieth centuries, the Manchu Court suffered just such a decline.

During that period, Western commercial and industrial powers used force or the threat of force to wrest economic and territorial concessions from the Manchus. Manchu prestige declined under these military and diplomatic defeats, the treasury was drained and the very premises of Chinese society were undermined by new institutions and ideas introduced by the Westerners. At the same time, the state was also beset by domestic revolt. By the early nineteenth century, agrarian distress was widespread, and in the time of the Tao Kuang emperor (1821-1850) revolts began to erupt all over the empire.

The Ch'ing military organization—enfeebled by inactivity, extreme decentralization, and especially corruption—could do little to meet these crises. Consequently, local armed forces sprang up to defend local interests. The central government, unable to prevent the formation of such forces, could only try to control those elements of local power in enlisting the support of some local forces, mostly led by gentry, in quelling local uprisings. But when the discontent in the countryside was mobilized by the Taipings into a great wave of revolution, local forces were no longer effective. A new type of armed power was necessary.

Under this stimulus, some of the local forces were brought together into larger, regional armies. The first army of this type, which set the pattern for later ones, was the Hunan army (Hsiang-chun), organized by Tseng Kuo-fan in 1853. In obedience to an imperial order to recruit and train the Hunan militia to fight the Taipings, Tseng organized an army based on existing local forces. He expanded his army by local recruiting and by incorporating new local forces, always indoctrinating the latter to ensure that they became an integral part of the larger organization. By 1856, the Hunan Army numbered about 60,000 men, and after this date it evidently grew even larger. For a number of years, Tseng's forces operated successfully against the Taiping rebels as the central government's only effective military support.

At the beginning of the 1860's, Tseng assigned a subordinate, Li Hung-chang, the task of organizing a new regional army to supplement the Hunan Army. It was called the Anhwei Army (Huai-chün), and its nucleus was formed by the spring of 1862.   By 1864, it numbered 70,000 troops. It eventually superseded the Hunan Army as the most powerful regional force, and in fact remained the largest and strongest army in China until almost the end of the century. Although the Anhwei and Hunan armies were not the only regional forces, they were the most important, both as military organizations and as manifestations of the growth of regional power.

The regional nature of the armies was implicit in their recruitment. Tseng's army was composed almost entirely of Hunanese until 1856, and Hunanese remained predominant after that date. Li's army at the outset was recruited largely from Anhwei. The leaders also sought authority over the sources of revenue in their regions, and the central government increasingly conceded financial control as it came to recognize the Court's dependence on the regional armies. Li and Tseng also acquired regional administrative authority, which facilitated the creation of personal political machines.

The Hunan and Anhwei armies were personal as well as regional, for they were virtually the private instruments of their personal loyalty to the commander-in-chief. These officers in turn selected subordinates loyal to them, and so on through the ranks. The troops' ultimate focus of loyalty was thus not the central government, but the army's commander-in-chief. At the same time, the commander's authority was qualified by the fact that the soldiers owed their most direct and strongest allegiance to their immediate superiors. For example, men of the local forces that were incorporated into the regional armies were primarily loyal to their own leaders, and only through them to the regional army leader, thus creating a hierarchy of loyalties. In sum, the Hunan and Anhwei armies were recruited and maintained regionally, and were bonded together by a complex of interrelated ties of regional feeling and personal loyalties.

When the Taiping Rebellion was finally stamped out, regional leaders controlled the only effective armies in the country. From then on, the Ch'ing government was without direct control over the major military activities of China. Regional leaders not only had political authority in their own domains, but were leading figures in the councils of the nation, the most conspicuous being the head of the Anhwei Army, Li Hung-chang, who represented China before the world for three decades. Economically, the provincial leaders had a stranglehold on regional finances. The balance between central and regional power was unequivocally and permanently altered.

It is true that this regional power was used to support the central government. Regional leaders, though they sought and acquired the substance of regional power, did not aspire to formal independence or seek the overthrow of the dynasty. Financial and other limitations combined with rivalry among the various leaders to inhibit any such aspirations. Moreover, the Ch'ing dynasty, though racially alien, defended a Confucian social order against the challenge of anti-Confucian rebels and Western barbarians, and regional leaders saw this cause as their own. But it was their power, limited not so much by the central government as by their own commitment to the social order identified with that government.

In the decades following the Taiping Rebellion, the Manchu government tried one expedient after another to regain effective control of the nation's military, but to no avail. Indeed, regionalism was an important factor in the Chinese defeat in the Sino-Japanese War of 1894-1895. Provincial autonomy had reached the point where it was difficult to obtain troops, funds, or supplies from provinces not directly involved in the fighting. As Li Hung-chang put it at one time, "One province, Chihli, is dealing with the whole nation of Japan." Five years later, during the Boxer Rebellion, there was another startling example of this provincial independence. While imperial troops fought Allied armies in Chihli, the provincial officials Liu K'un-i, Chang Chih-tung, and Yüan Shih-k'ai, together with other officials in the south, remained aloof from the struggle and observed an agreement with the foreign powers. The Manchus were unable to reduce this remarkable regionalism before the dynasty fell in 1912.

The fiasco of China's war with Japan in 1894-1895 produced one important change in the Chinese military modernization that resulted in the famous Peiyang Army[1]. After China's defeat, the court recognized the need to modernize China's military arm, and asked Yüan Shih-k'ai to draw up a program for training a new and modern army. Yüan was a protégé of Li Hung-chang; between 1885 and 1894, he had made a good reputation serving as China's commissioner in Korea, and after the war he had shown interest in military reform. Yüan submitted detailed plans for an army organized and trained on the German pattern. The court approved, and about 5,000 troops were turned over to him for training. In December 1895, Yüan, then 36, began training these troops at Hsiaochan, a small market town between Tientsin and Taku that had formerly been a station of the Anhwei Army.

Within a decade, he had created the most formidable army in China. During that period, in 1901, he succeeded Li Hung-chang as Commissioner of Trade for the Northern Ports, and his troops then became the Peiyang Army. By 1906, this army was variously estimated at 50,000 to 80,000 men, well-equipped and with Western-style training. However, Yüan's success made him enemies in some court circles, and he was eased out from direct command of his troops in 1906-1907. Two years later, after the death of the Empress Dowager had removed his most powerful friend, Yüan was dismissed from office and retired to his home in Honan, where he lived quietly until the outbreak of revolution in 1911.

Despite these setbacks, Yüan lost little effective control aver the Peiyang Army. The reason was that the Peiyang Army was a personal army, just as the earlier regional armies had been. The critical element in Yüan's control was the very same one that had allowed the earlier army leaders to control their forces— the loyalty of the officers. Yüan evidently tried also, with some success, to inculcate direct loyalty to himself in the ranks, but he gave far greater attention to the more important task of keeping the loyalty of his commanders. He was extremely careful in the selection of his officers; for example, he seldom used returned students, whose heterogeneous training and background might make it difficult to bind them to him. He cultivated a teacher-student relationship between himself and his chief subordinates, a type of connection that today is still strong in East Asia, and was much more so at the beginning of the century. Yüan made the relationship meaningful by seeing to it that both his military and civilian subordinates received rapid promotion. In this fashion, he rewarded past loyalty and hinted at what future loyalty might bring. He was also careful to protect his lieutenants. For example, when a furor erupted because a soldier struck a foreigner, it was necessary to transfer the division commander; but Yüan reinstated him in his command as soon as the affair quieted dawn. In such ways, Yüan successfully cultivated the loyalty that bound his officers to him during his absence, a loyalty that permitted him to resume command without difficulty when the revolution came.

In 1912, Yüan's Peiyang Army was the most powerful military organization in China, but it was certainly not the only one. Attempts at military modernization had added to, not replaced, the complex, antiquated, and decentralized Ch'ing military structure. The weakness of the court vis-a-vis the provinces had prevented the abolition of the old forces. Consequently, a great mishmash of military units were scattered over the country. Some were fairly new, with touches of modernity, and others were quite old-fashioned; but virtually all were under provincial authorities, and had more or less that character of personal armies.

There was a natural line of development from the personal armies of the mid-nineteenth century to the Peiyang Army. However, in the course of the development, the character of the armies changed in important ways. The first regional armies were created by civil officials who had risen in the Ch'ing bureaucracy in the traditional fashion through the examination system. Although they understood well the uses of the military power they had created, they were not fundamentally military men. They were active and successful in many fields besides the army. Their values, like their offices, were primarily civilian, and accorded little dignity to military activity. The regional leaders were willing to adopt certain Western techniques and devices, but only on a limited scale. Some Western concepts were used in training, and some Western equipment was employed; that was all. A good indication of the limits imposed by their traditional, anti-Western orientation was their refusal to grant command positions to graduates of newly established Western-style military academies. Because of this discrimination, which continued as late as the 1880's, the new learning of these graduates was largely unused. In short, the early regional forces were fundamentally traditional armies led by civilians with a profound commitment to the preservation of Confucian society.

Although the creators of the first regional armies were civil officials who had risen in the traditional fashion, their military successes opened up a new road to power for men who had neither their academic background nor their extensive civilian experience. It became possible to rise to high position through service in the regional armies. Twenty of the forty-four governors-general appointed between 1861 and 1890 rose to prominence as regional army commanders. During the same period, over half the 117 governors appointed had served as officers in the regional forces. About one fourth of the governors held neither of the two highest civil service degrees; most of this group rose to power through military service. For a time, men of this sort were still eager to don the robes of civil officials, for the prestige of officialdom was not dead. However, as the old century yielded to the new, military success gradually came to be considered sufficient in itself.

A number of circumstances conspired to that end. In the first place, the pressing need for modernization finally forced the abolition of civil service examinations in 1905. This confirmed that the old road to power was a dead end. At the same time, the long-standing contempt felt by educated Chinese toward a military career was fading. As part of its military modernization program, the Ch'ing government purposefully tried to raise the prestige of military service. The disciplined behavior of the best of the new forces contrasted well with the actions traditionally expected of soldiers, and helped the reputation of the military. The school system that emerged as part of the Manchu reform program after the Boxer catastrophe stipulated that pupils wear uniforms and that military drill be taught in all schools, including missionary institutions. In a country where the military had so long been viewed with disdain, this was a remarkable innovation.

At the same time, the continued pressure of foreign imperialism kindled the beginnings of patriotism and a martial spirit. Foreign observers noted the growth of these feelings particularly during and after the Russo-Japanese War, when the Chinese vicariously relished the victory of fellow Asians over a European power. A large proportion of the Chinese students in Japan after 1905 chose to study the art of modern war. Finally, a military career was respected in the West, and as willingness to imitate the West grew, that Western attitude also acted to alter Chinese conceptions. A military career was perhaps not yet completely respectable, but it was becoming so.

Around the turn of the century, as a result of the army's increasing power and prestige, and the simultaneous diminution of the central government's authority, army leaders no longer used their military eminence to gain civilian posts; instead they devoted themselves exclusively to the military. Many of the army leaders of the time had been trained for a military career, as distinguished from the commanders of the first regional armies, for whom military activity had been an adjunct of a civilian occupation.

Although Yüan Shih-k'ai held civilian posts, he and a number of his senior officers exemplified this trend toward professionalism. Moreover, they did not share the profound commitment of the early regional leaders to the preservation of traditional civilization, and thus to the perpetuation of Manchu rule as the bulwark of Confucian society. This was partly due to the fact that they were soldiers rather than Confucian scholar-officials. In any event, Confucian society was changing so rapidly under the impact of foreign and other pressures that its preservation was clearly an unrealistic goal. In addition, and more immediately important, Yüan's personal prospects were bleak. The ruling circles at court after 1908 disliked and feared him, and though he was at the peak of his powers, he could see little likelihood of regaining his former authority under normal circumstances. No earlier regional leader had ever suffered such a blow to his personal ambition, and thus none had ever experienced the same temptation to use his military power for personal ends.

The upshot of these social and personal factors was that Yüan and his officers were not restricted by the values and loyalties that had prevented the earlier regional leaders from asserting their independence. The early regional armies were personal armies, but the Peiyang Army was the first to became a personal army only, in the sense that it had no commitment to suprapersonal principles and goals. To that extent, it represented the beginnings of warlordism.

In sum, the last century of the Ch'ing dynasty witnessed two related developments. On the one hand, the central government steadily weakened under the blows of domestic rebellion and foreign wars; as the central power declined, regional economic and political autonomy increased. On the other hand, the influence of military men steadily grew, not only because armed force was needed to deal with internal revolt and foreign threats, but also because of the increasing respect accorded the military by proponents of nationalism and Westernization. These were two aspects of a single phenomenon. That is, as regional power increased, it tended to flow into the hands of military men. By 1911, these men had little commitment to the Confucian order: their major commitment was to personal advancement by military means.

THE WARLORD PERIOD

The most powerful man to emerge from the Revolution of 1911 was Yüan Shih-k'ai. He was legally head of state, and he personally controlled, in the Peiyang Army, the most formidable military organization in China. With these two supports, Yüan was able to maintain effective rule over most of a fairly unified country until a few months before his death in 1916. But ominous signs appeared during those years. The number of men under arms climbed as provincial leaders, and Yüan himself, steadily recruited soldiers. More important, Yüan repeatedly used his armies for domestic political purposes. To the extent that he used military force to gain his ends, he undermined the office of the presidency, and intensified the weaknesses of the political parties and republican civil authority in general. This reliance on force or the threat of force had the effect of rendering the already puny Republic virtually impotent, and of strengthening the arm that he flexed, the military. Since the republicans could not restrain Yüan by political means, they also turned to armed force. A republic of militarists came into being. The preponderant military strength of the Peiyang Army allowed it to dominate the other militarists, and thus China was assured of a kind of unity as long as the Peiyang Army remained unified. But Peiyang cohesion depended on the personal loyalty of the army's chief officers to Yüan Shih-k'ai. When Yüan died in June 1916, the keystone of the army's unity disappeared, and army authority reverted to the top commanders. The Peiyang hierarchy began to break down into its constituent hierarchies, still on the basis of personal loyalties. Non-Peiyang military units had also been organized on this basis. Now, freed from the domination of unified Peiyang power, they rose to challenge one another as well as Peiyang units. Thus began a period in which the political life of the country was dominated by incessant struggles among military men for regional or national dominance. This was the warlord period of modern Chinese history.

The constant strife, the ceaseless shifts and changes, that characterized this period make the political-military history of Chinese warlordism extraordinarily complicated and confusing. Nevertheless, it is possible to outline the main events, which fall into three phases.

Early Warlordism

The early phase of warlordism began with the death of Yüan Shih-k'ai in 1916 and lasted until the first great military expression of the Chinese nationalist movement, the Northern Expedition, which started in 1926. This was the period of "pure" warlordism, when wars and political maneuvers were solely the work of military men in quest of power and wealth. Although they rationalized their wars and policies with patriotic and altruistic slogans—many of which may even have been sincere—none of them represented any important segment of the population, nor were their struggles the expression of genuine national or social movements.

The political and military events of this phase were extremely complex. Confusing military and political maneuvering occurred on various overlapping levels. On the one hand, there was a series of contests between major warlord groupings for control of Peking and the machinery of the national government. On the other hand, within each of these groupings there were ambivalent tendencies. These was competition for control of the group, and those who hoped to profit from such control sought to strengthen and perpetuate the group as a group, irrespective of other considerations. But there was also a strong desire to maintain provincial or regional autonomy, particularly among those who were not closely connected with leading warlords. Thus there were forces working for the maintenance of warlord groups and other forces working for their disintegration. At the same time, there was rivalry between the North, where the Peiyang clique was strongest, and the South, where non-Peiyang militarists predominated.

Owing to these various conflicts, the situation was very unstable and in constant flux. From the death of Yüan Shih-k'ai in June 1916 until the spring of 1926 there were six different heads of state.[2] This includes neither the brief imperial restoration in 1917 nor the three periods of several months each when a caretaker, or regency, government existed while decisions were being made regarding a new head of state. In the same period, over twenty-five successive cabinets were formed. These rapid political changes to some extent reflected the shifting balance of power among the leading military cliques…

While the warlords were preoccupied with the struggle for power and position, the context in which their struggles took place was changing. Chinese nationalism was burgeoning, and for the first time became linked with a revolutionary social movement. The nationalism movement began among students, but spread quickly to a wider public. It was nourished not only by indignation over the political and economic concessions that foreign powers had wrung from China, but by currents from abroad, especially the fact and theory of the Russian Revolution. In 1919, when the Versailles peacemakers ignored Chinese demands and turned German concessions in Shantung over to Japan, Chinese anti-imperialist indignation found expression in the great May Fourth Movement. Two years later the Chinese Communist Party was formed, and in 1924 the Kuomintang was reorganized along Bolshevik lines with Russian assistance; both parties preached Chinese nationalism, and they soon allied to seek their common goals.

Both parties were strongly anti-imperialist, and both received ardent support from students and intellectuals. By the early 1920's, however, Chinese nationalism was fed by stronger currents than the agitation intellectuals. Among these currents was the growth of industry in China. During World War I, the industrial output of Western nations was devoted to their war effort. Chinese producers suddenly found themselves free from the crushing pressure of foreign competition, and native industry expanded rapidly. Growth was especially fast for producers of cotton textiles, flour, matches, cigarettes, cement, canned food, bean oil, and even coal and iron. As a result of this expansion, Chinese commercial and industrial leaders gained strength and confidence; in particular, they saw a great future if only national unity and independence could be achieved under a government that would protect their interests. At the same time, a small urban working class grew up, and a militant labor movement came into being with surprising speed. Peasant unions were also organized, and joined with the labor movement to seek new status and rewards.

The Communist-Kuomintang alliance channeled these new economic forces into the nationalist movement, thus fusing anti-imperialism with social revolution. For the first time in the history of China, political parties had mass support and represented national aspirations. The first step toward the realization of those aspirations was a military expedition to eliminate the warlords and unify the country under a revolutionary government. When this was attempted, warlordism moved into its second phase.

Residual Warlordism

It has often been asserted that the success of the Northern Expedition in 1928 marked the end of the warlord period, which is commonly described as lasting from 1916 to 1928. This is misleading. Many warlords continued to command personal armies, control territory, and retain tax revenues after 1928; and in general warlordism remained a conspicuous feature of political life under the Nationalist government.

Such residual warlordism was at least partly the product of the National Revolutionary Army's policies during the Northern Expedition. Many warlords chose not to fight the advancing army as it marched north, but to join it with their forces intact. The Kuomintang leadership "reorganized" such units, not by changing their structure or shifting key personnel, but by giving them numbers to identify them as units of the National Revolutionary Army; that was all. Units that joined in this fashion—with no genuine commitment to Kuomintang principles or the goals of the revolution, or anything but their own self-preservation—ultimately far outnumbered the original National Revolutionary Army. By the time the army reached the Yangtze, thirty-four warlords and their troops had joined it. Within six months after the beginning of the Northern Expedition, the army was nearly three times its original size, primarily as a result of the adherence of warlord units. By April 1928, on the eve of the expedition's last stage, the National Revolutionary Army consisted of fifty separate armies. Well over half of them had originally been warlord armies: and in a very real sense they continued to be, despite their changed status.

Top officials of the Nationalist government certainly had few illusions that the end of the Northern Expedition meant the elimination of the warlords. For example, the Minister of Finance, reporting on the state of the country's financial unification in early 1929, said:

> There is today little if any improvement from conditions existing during the period of warfare. Thus the national revenues from such provinces as Hunan, Hupeh, Kwangtung, Kwangsi, Shensi, Kansu, Honan, Shansi, and Suiyuan, not to mention those from the Three Eastern Provinces [Manchuria], Szechwan, Yunnan, and Kweichow, are entirely appropriated by the localities mentioned. In the provinces of Hapei (Chihli), Shantung, and Fukien, the revenue officials are at least commissioned by the Central Government, but in other provinces they are appointed by local and military authorities and most of them fail even to render accounts.

When the government attempted to transform its nominal authority into genuine control, the result was war. In the spring of 1929, government forces engaged a group of warlords called the Kwangsi clique. Shortly thereafter, a pair of warlords—Feng Yuhsiang and Yen Hsi-shan—challenged the government and here began a sporadic but bloody war that lasted until the fall of 1930. In subsequent years, there were not warlord wars on this scale (the war with the Communists cannot be considered in this category), but there were smaller outbreaks. There was also continuing political competition between the Nanking government and regional militarists as the former sought to make its authority genuinely national.

The extent and nature of residual warlordism after 1928 is a subject that merits serious investigation. To what degree did it render the government less able to counter the Communist challenge and the Japanese invasion? Or was it perhaps a symptom, rather than a cause, of weakness? Was its existence a measure of the extent to which Kuomintang nationalism under Chiang

Kai-shek had become attenuated and adulterated? Many such questions might be asked, and hopefully will one day be answered. Here it is enough to note that the government's control after 1928 was sufficiently loose and qualified to allow residual warlordism to exist, and thus to offer defeated warlords—such as Feng Yü-hsiang—the hope that they might someday rise again.

WARLORDS AND WARLORDISM

Although the warlord period lasted for years, and warlordism came to dominate the entire country of China, there are very few monographs relating to individual warlords or to events in specific geographic regions during the warlord period. General statements on these subjects are therefore more hazardous than most, particularly since there is enough information already available to indicate that there was probably greater diversity in warlordism than has usually been assumed. Nevertheless, some tentative generalizations must be attempted.

The Warlord

As mentioned at the beginning of this chapter, a warlord was one who established and maintained control over territory by the use of his personal army. All warlord armies, of course, were personal. Indeed, they were often referred to in terms of the commander's name rather than whatever formal designation they might have had; the troops of Feng Yü-hsiang, for example, were often called the Feng-chun, or army of Feng. Identification sometimes extended to unit commanders, a reflection of the hierarchy of loyalties mentioned earlier. Thus, a soldier might say that he was from the Li division or the Wang brigade of the army of such-and-such a general...

Territorial jurisdiction was the second essential characteristic of a warlord. The extent of the territory could vary tremendously. Major warlords sometimes controlled areas as large as or larger than chief states of Western Europe, with many millions of inhabitants. Petty warlords might control two or three districts, or perhaps only a very few villages. Historically, the petty warlords were very important, and though specific allusions to them are few, it should be remembered that there were sometimes many pockets actually ruled by minor warlords within the area ostensibly controlled by a major warlord. The customary terminology of warlordism ignores this phenomenon and is consequently misleading. When a warlord occupied the capital of a province, especially if he did so with the approval of the government in Peking, it was customary to consider him in control of that province. Journalists and historians have continued to err in this fashion, and maps of warlord-controlled areas—including maps in this book—follow the same practice, largely because so little is yet known about the configuration of control outside the capital area.

Control of territory was important for obvious reasons. It provided a warlord with a military base for defensive and offensive purposes, a source of foodstuffs and other supplies, and a source of revenue. A warlord needed funds for arms, ammunition, and other military supplies, and for personal enrichment. Most important, he needed money to pay his troops, without whom he could not control his territory. Unless he had funds to pay his soldiers—or an area that the soldiers could exploit in some fashion in lieu of pay—he could not control his army. His position thus rested on these two interrelated supports—army and territory. Or, to phrase it differently, a warlord needed an army to gain control of territory so that be could pay his army.

Because of the rapacity displayed by some warlords in the administration of their territories, the question arises whether "warlord" was simply a euphemism for "bandit." The chaos of the warlord period brought many bandit gangs into existence. Some were very large, equivalent to warlord armies. But bandits ordinarily did not control territory, and this was the essential difference. Bandits had to loot and run in order to survive as bandits; they had no semblance of legality and recognized no obligation to their victims. Warlords, on the contrary, could levy taxes; they were not forced to loot to maintain themselves, and many did not.

Moreover, warlords assumed the burdens of government for the areas they controlled. The governments they established were not always praiseworthy, but they were governments and usually maintained some degree of order. It has been asserted that many warlords were simply bandit chieftains who amassed great power. To the extent this was true, it can be said that a bandit became a warlord at the point where he acquired acknowledged control over a specific area and assumed the tasks of governing it. Actually, however, none of the most important warlords became warlords in this fashion. Virtually all the major ones came out of the regular army, though some had been bandits before their army service.

The origins of the outstanding warlords were diverse. Many rose from very low estate; others had the advantages of wealth and education. Chang Tso-lin was a brigand in the pay of the Japanese during the Russo-Japanese War. He then became an officer in the regular Chinese army, went to Manchuria in 1911, and rose to be military governor of Fengtien. Yen Hsi-shan, a battalion commander in the Manchu army, was head of a revolutionary faction in an army garrison in Shansi when the Revolution of 1911 broke out. He ousted the Manchu authorities and became military governor of the province, a position he held against all comers for two decades. Wu P'ei-fu was an officer in the Peiyang Army, and became a protégé of his division commander. As the commander rose, so did Wu. He ultimately became effective head of the Chihli clique, although his patron was still nominally his superior. Some men, like Feng Yü-hsiang and Ts'ao K'un, rose from the ranks. Others, such as Tuan Ch'i-jui and Feng Kuo-chang, were early leaders in the army modernization program directed by Yüan Shih-k'ai. But regardless of their diverse origins, most of them began their careers in the regular army.

Notwithstanding the military reforms of the late Ch'ing period, very few Chinese officers had the experience and training of the ordinary military leader in the West. In lieu of extensive training, the Chinese warlord depended on boldness, shrewdness, a certain resourcefulness, and a talent for personal leadership. An English diplomat with some forty years' experience in China asserted that under other conditions "China could have easily produced some very great military leaders from among the War Lords."

Perhaps the cliché most persistently applied to the warlords is that they "sought power." This phrase suggests that they sought power for exclusively selfish ends, such as the accumulation of wealth. Certainly this was often true, but there were many exceptions—warlords who combined personal ambition with social and national concerns. Indeed, into this category fall most of the best known warlords, notably Feng Yü-hsiang, Yen His-shan, Ch'en Chiungming, Chang Tso-lin, and Wu P'ei-fu.

Some warlords were illiterate, their schooling limited to the story-teller's booth or theatrical performances. But they had great self-confidence and native intelligence. There were few mediocrities among them. On the basis of an intimate knowledge of the Chinese scene, Pearl Buck has written:

Without exception, the war lords I have known have been men of unusual native ability, gifted with peculiar personal charm, with imagination and strength, and often with a rude poetic quality. Above all, they carry about with them, in them, a sense of high drama. The war lord sees himself great—and great in the traditional manner of heroes of ancient fiction and history who are so inextricably mingled in the old Chinese novels. He is, in effect, an actor by nature, as Napoleon was. The war lord is a creature of emotion; cruel or merciful, as the whim is; dangerous and unstable as friend or enemy; licentious and usually fond of luxury.

The warlord personality, with its flair for the theatrical, made the period colorful even while it was tragic. The common people, who suffered most from the warlords' acts, where nevertheless fascinated by them. They could tell innumerable stories abut a warlord's temper tantrums, his extravagances, his reckless courage, his bold idiosyncrasies. There were tales explaining his origin: he was the personification of some god, some star, some magic creature. Warlords assumed something of the stature of folk heroes.

Warlordism

The term warlordism refers to the aspects and conditions of warlord rule. One such aspect has already been mentioned: the growth of an essentially mercenary spirit as the loyalty of a warlord's subordinates come increasingly to be conditioned on his prospects of success. In earlier years, the relationship between a military or civil official and his subordinates had been more or less analogous to that between a teacher and his students. A talented subordinate advanced thanks to his superior, not by usurping his superior's position or by finding a more powerful patron. Indeed, the warlords tried to cultivate this type of relationship with their subordinates, and with some success.

As a result, the offer of money and position to entice officers to switch sides (a tactic known as using "silver bullets") became an important weapon in the warlord wars. It was essential, of course, that the defecting officer bring his troops with him, thus weakening his former leader while strengthening his new one. When the stakes of war were high, the bribes offered to officers were proportionately huge. Less mercenary methods were also employed. As a result of the constant shuffling of military units, friends and relatives sometimes found themselves in opposing armies. In such cases, a commander might send men to lure their kinsmen or comrades away from an enemy force. "Conditions in our army are much better," they might argue. Or, "Come to our side, and we can all be together." These tactics—particularly the use of "silver bullets"—brought about many defections, some of great significance. The defection of key subordinates was a factor in limiting the size of the territory a warlord could successfully control. Wartime commanders had to keep in mind the possibility of treachery which could turn apparent victory into sudden defeat. In 1924, on the eve of the Second Chih-Feng War, an official of the Chihli clique epitomized the situation nicely. "We shall undoubtedly win," he said. "It is simply a matter of waiting for treason."

The importance of defections illustrates once again the individualistic character of warlordism: personal preferences, aspirations, policies, and whims were little hampered by ideological or social restraints. Consequently the elimination of a single key person could drastically alter the total power situation, and murder was therefore a common warlord tactic. A favorite method was to invite an intended victim to a banquet, where he was seized and shot.

Two or more warlords frequently found it expedient or necessary to combine in an alliance or confederation. For example, warlords of roughly equal strength might unite to resist the threat of a more powerful nearby warlord, or a number of small warlords might came into the orbit of an important militarist in hopes that the alliance would achieve gains in which all would share. It was also possible for a single warlord organization to expand to the point where the leaders of its constituent elements were for all practical purposes independent, thus transforming a relationship of subordination into one of alliance. Indeed, this was essentially what took place in the two wings of the Peiyang Army after the death of Yüan Shih-k'ai. Generally, a warlord alliance could realistically plan only short-term cooperation, for the warlord system was subject to so many and such sudden changes that the long-range future was always uncertain.

Perhaps the most obvious characteristic of warlordism was war. Not all warlords were ambitious to expand their holding, but all were interested in maintaining what they had against those who sought more. And since there were always those who sought more, local and regional wars were frequent.

The control of Peking was a prize sought by the most powerful northern warlords. There were several reasons for this. First, those who controlled the capital controlled such national administrative machinery as continued to function, and this had a basis for claiming the allegiance of the country. Secondly, until 1928, foreign nations dealt with the Peking government as the government of China. Therefore, the warlord of Peking could assert a claim to any surplus from the customs collections and the salt gabelle after loan and indemnity charges defrayed from these sources had been met. Finally, there was always the hope that one might contract foreign loans in the name of the nation. These attractions were responsible for some of the major warlord conflicts in northern China. At the outset of the warlord period, the chief militarists themselves assumed high office in the Peking government, but this was seldom done after the early 1920s. Warlords, however, wanted the stamp of legitimacy, and the Peking government was invariably called upon to formalize changes wrought by warfare. This meant, of course, that whenever the distribution of armed and territorial power altered, there soon followed corresponding changes in the composition of the Peking government.

There exists a widespread impression that wars between Chinese warlords were something like televised wrestling matches in the United States: a good deal of grunting and groaning, of posturing and grimacing, but little serious attempt to hurt each other. Many writers—especially "old China hands" but also scholars and Chinese authors—have written of the "comic-opera Chinese wars." The essence of such opinions was expressed in an after-dinner statement attributed to a Chinese admiral. "China's wars," he said, "are always civil"...

The warlords tapped almost every conceivable source of revenue, and in the process worked tremendous hardships on the people. The land tax, which was completely in the hands of provincial military leaders after 1919, became an instrument of terrible exploitation. The tax was increased in many areas. For example, after Chang Tsung-ch'ang became the warlord of Shantung, land taxes rose to five or six times their former amount. In some areas, there was a proliferation of supplementary taxes, which after a few years became the normal taxes to which further supplements might be added. Large taxes were sometimes collected far in advance. Pearl Buck writes of one region where the warlord collected the land tax for ten years in advance, even though the area was swept by famine.

When such a rapacious warlord was ousted from control of a region, his successor had the choice of collecting the taxes dating from the year reached by his predecessor, or declaring that the latter's exactions were illegal and starting collections from the current year. From the peasant's point of view, of course, the difference was academic; it all added up to his paying the taxes several times over. In Kwangtung there even instances of people taxed for land held by their ancestors that was no longer in their hands.

Many additional taxes were also created. After the terms of a foreign loan in 1913 had placed control of the salt gabelle in the hands of foreigners, regional authorities countered by adding other taxes to salt: a salt transportation tax, a price tax, and so on. In Szechwan there were twenty-six types of taxes added to the basic salt tax by 1924. In Kwangtung there were areas where one was taxed for owning a pig, taxed if one's daughter married, taxed for owning geese, and taxed for many other reasons. The government at Changhsa imposed a tax on postal parcels coming from outside the province. In Fukien, where tax collectors were particularly imaginative, door plates were among the many items taxed.

Many special taxes were levied at irregular intervals for particular purposes, or ostensibly particular purposes. There were taxes for "university expenses," "military expenses," "self-government expenses," and so forth. In 1927, Sun Ch'uan-fang, a warlord opposing the northern advance of the National Revolutionary Army ordered all districts in the area under his control to pay a special land tax to finance a last desperate stand. In Shantung there were a number of special taxes, including, when the harvest was particularly good, a "rich harvest tax." The following list, which illustrates the extraordinary tax burdens of the time, shows the taxes levied in Amoy as of January 1924:

pork tax
pig tax
pig slaughter tax
pig-rearing tax
pig-inspecting tax
surtax on pork for educational expenses
fish tax
tax on fish hongs
tax on fish shops
cockle, crab, and prawn tax
sea product tax
night soil tax
fruit tax
bamboo shoot tax
fuel and rice tax
wine tax (local wine)
onion and garlic tax
oyster shell tax
lime tax
narcissus bulb tax
chicken and duck tax
paper tax
transportation, or sea protection tax on employees of fishing boats

superstition tax (on candles, paper money for funerals,etc.)
trade tax
householders' protection tax
opium-smoking lamp tax
license fee on opium smoking
license fee on milk
passenger tax for water police
pig seller' s tax
shoe tax
tax on opium cultivation
gambling tax (on gambling houses)
water boat tax
cow and horse sanitation tax
vegetable tax
shop tax
theater tax
tea tax
tinfoil tax
brothel tax
brothel license fee
sanitation tax (for cleaning streets)
sugar malt tax

brick and tile tax
lumber tax
land tax
deed stamping fee
street lamp tax
surtax for electric lamps
police tax
cotton tax
hawker's tax
flour tax
license fee for prostitute on call
firecracker tax
deed inspecting fee
lower-class prostitute singing tax
field tax
likin
beancake tax
examination fee for prepared medicine
license fee for discharging goods from steamer
piece goods tax
rice and wheat
venmicelli tax
cotton yarn and cotton thread tax
bean, sugar, and oil tax

The warlords exploited many other sources of revenue in ways that directly or indirectly imposed hardships on all classes of the Chinese population. Railroads were a major source of revenue, and were taxed for all they were worth.[3] Heavy freight charges plus special taxes and surtaxes were even wrung from exasperated foreigners, contrary to treaty arrangements, by the simple expedient of not having freight cars available for those who did not pay. Transit taxes for likin, were exacted time after time on a single shipment of goods. For example, a shipment of paper worth $1,350 when landed at Shanghai was shipped up the Yangtze to Chengtu. It passed through eleven tax stations, the last being at the very gates of Chengtu, and the illegal taxation collected on it by regional authorities totaled $2,150. In some cases, warlords acquired revenue by establishing state monopolies over the manufacture of certain goods. Forced loans, for which bonds were issued that were presumably redeemable over a period of years, were sometimes exacted from certain sections of the populace. Contributions were forced from chambers of commerce by threatening to loot their cities. Opium monopolies were auctioned off. Many of the so-called Opium Suppression Bureaus were actually warlord agencies for taxing opium in the guise of fines. Warlords sometimes issued their own currency; in at least one province, these provincial notes were stamped to the effect that they would be redeemed for silver "after the war." Finally, there were foreign loans. Tuan Ch'i-jui, for example, received large sums from the Japanese—the so-called Nishihara loans....

Although some warlords had nationalistic ideas and aspirations, warlordism as a social phenomenon was the essence of anti-nationalism. Nationalism aspired to a unified nation; warlordism thrived on division. It inhibited the growth of new intellectual and economic forces that could develop the productive capacities of the nation's physical and human resources. Nationalism demanded the elimination of foreign controls and privileges; warlordism facilitated foreign military invasion, political intervention, and economic exploitation. Nationalism called for pride in the nation's past and present, and hope in its future; warlordism fostered demoralization and hopelessness at home, and destroyed the prestige of the nation abroad. Nationalism meant patriotism; warlordism meant self-seeking. Warlordism, indeed, could exist only at nationalism's expense.

However, warlordism was the context from which the most important Chinese nationalist movements arose. The Kuomintang was reorganized and expanded at the height of the warlord period. At almost the same time, Chinese communism was born and began its early development. A whole generation of Chinese intellectuals came of age under warlord governments. The cumulative influence of warlordism on millions of Chinese children and adults is incalculable, but clearly enormous. The precise nature of the influence is obscure, and must remain obscure until we know more about the major warlords themselves.

NOTES

1   The name "Peiyang" comes from Pei-yang ta-chen, the Commissioner of Trade for the Northern Ports. This position, which was held by Li Hung-chang from 1870 to 1901 and thereafter by Yüan Shih-k'ai, entailed various military responsibilities: the forces involved came to be known as the Peiyang Army. Although thus name was current under Li as well as Yüan, in current usage it refers nearly always to Yüan's army.

2   Li Yüan-hung served twice as President, both times being counted to make six terms.

3   Not infrequently, two or more warlords would control sections of a railroad. This could lead to a
    virtual standstill of traffic, for each warlord was unwilling to permit rolling stock to enter an area
    controlled by a rival or a potential rival. Therefore, nothing moved; at least nothing moved very
    far. This occasionally created serious situations. For example, in January, 1925, when Peking
    badly needed fuel and food, which were ordinarily shipped to the city in large quantities over the
    Peking-Hankow Railroad, the warlord of Honan refused to permit railroad cars on this line to
    leave his own domain. Incidentally, the warlord of Hunan at that time was supposed to be a close
    ally and subordinate of the warlord of Peking.

31. Mao Zedong

REPORT ON AN INVESTIGATION OF THE HUNAN PEASANT MOVEMENT

THE IMPORTANCE OF THE PEASANT PROBLEM

During my recent visit to Hunan I conducted an investigation on the spot into the conditions in the five counties of Siangtan, Siangsiang, Henghsan, Liling, and Changsha. In the thirty-two days from January 4 to February 5, [1925] in villages and in country towns, I called together for fact-finding conferences experienced peasants and comrades working for the peasant movement, listened to their reports, and collected a lot of material. Many of the hows and whys of the peasant movement were quite the reverse of what I had heard from the gentry in Hankow and Changsha. And many strange things there were that I had never seen or heard before. I think these conditions exist in many other places.

All kinds of arguments against the peasant movement must be speedily set right. The erroneous measures taken by the revolutionary authorities concerning the peasant movement must be speedily changed. Only thus can any good be done for the future of the revolution. For the rise of the present peasant movement is a colossal event. In a very short time, in China's central, southern, and northern provinces, several hundred million peasants will rise like a tornado or tempest, a force so extraordinarily swift and violent that no power, however great, will be able to suppress it. They will break all trammels that now bind them and rush forward along the road to liberation. They will send all imperialists, warlords, corrupt officials, local bullies, and bad gentry to their graves. All revolutionary parties and all revolutionary comrades will stand before them to be tested, and to be accepted or rejected as they decide.

To march at their head and lead them? Or to follow at their rear, gesticulating at them and criticizing them? Or to face them as opponents?

Every Chinese is free to choose among the three alternatives, but circumstances demand that a quick choice be made.

DOWN WITH THE LOCAL BULLIES AND BAD GENTRY!

All Power to the Peasant Association!

The peasants attack as their main targets the local bullies and bad gentry and the lawless landlords, hitting in passing against patriarchal ideologies and institutions, corrupt officials in the cities, and evil customs in the rural areas. In force and momentum, the attack is like a tempest or hurricane; those who submit to it survive and those who resist it perish. As a result, the privileges which the feudal landlords have enjoyed for thousands of years are being shattered to pieces. The dignity and prestige of the landlords are dashed to the ground. With the fall of the sole organ of authority, and what people call "All power to the peasant association" has come to pass. Even such a trifle as a quarrel between man and wife has to be settled at the peasant association. Nothing can be settled in the absence of people from the association. The association is actually dictating in all matters in the countryside, and it is literally true that "whatever it says, goes." The public can only praise the association and must not condemn it. The local bullies and bad gentry and the lawless landlords have been totally deprived of the right to have their say, and no one dared mutter the word "No." To be safe from the power and pressure of the peasant associations, the top local tyrants and evil gentry have fled to Shanghai, those of second rank to Hankow, . . . and the still lesser fry surrender to the peasant associations in the villages.

"I'll donate ten dollars, please admit me to the peasant association," one of the smaller gentry would say.

"Pshaw! Who wants your filthy money!" the peasants would reply.

Many middle and small landlords, rich peasants and middle peasants, formerly opposed to the peasant association, now seek admission in vain. Visiting various places, I often came across such people, who solicited my help. "I beg," they would say, "the committeeman from the provincial capital to be my guarantor."

The census book compiled by the local authorities under the Manchu regime consisted of a regular register and a special register; in the former honest people were entered, and in the latter burglars, bandits, and other undesirables. The peasants in some places now use the same method to threaten people formerly opposed to the association: "Enter them in the special register!"

Such people, afraid of being entered in the special register, try various means to seek admission to the association and do not feel at ease until, as they eagerly desire, their names are entered in its register. But they are as a rule sternly turned down, and so spend their days in a constant state of suspense; barred from the doors of the association, they are like homeless people. In short, what was generally sneered at four months ago as the "peasants' gang" has now become something most honorable. Those who prostrated themselves before the power of the gentry now prostrate themselves before the power of the peasants. Everyone admits that the world has changed since last October.

"AN AWFUL MESS!" AND "VERY GOOD INDEED!"

The revolt of the peasants in the countryside disturbed the sweet dreams of the gentry. When news about the countryside reached the cities, the gentry there immediately burst into an uproar. When I first arrived in Changsha, I met people from various circles and picked up a good deal of street gossip. From the middle strata upwards to the right-wingers of the Kuomintang, there was not a single person who did not summarize the whole thing in one phrase: "An awful mess!" Even quiet revolutionary people, carried away by the opinion of the "awful mess" school which prevailed like a storm over the whole city, become downhearted at the very thought of the conditions in the countryside, and could not deny the word "mess." Even very progressive people could only remark: "Indeed a mess, but inevitable in the course of the revolution." In a word, nobody could categorically deny the word "mess."

But the fact is, as stated above, that the broad peasant masses have risen to fulfill their historic mission, that the democratic forces in the rural areas have risen to overthrown the rural feudal power. The patriarchal-feudal class of local bullies, bad gentry, and lawless landlords has formed the basis of autocratic government for thousands of years, the cornerstone of imperialism, warlordism and corrupt officialdom. To overthrow this feudal power is the real objective of the national revolution. What Dr. Sun Yat-sen wanted to do in the forty years he devoted to the national revolution but failed to accomplish, the peasants have accomplished in a few months. This is a marvelous feat which has never been achieved in the last forty or even thousands of years. It is very good indeed. It is not "a mess" at all. It is anything but "an awful mess."

THE QUESTION OF "GOING TOO FAR"

There is another section of people who say: "Although the peasant association ought to be formed, it has gone rather too far." This is the opinion of the middle-of-the-roaders. But how do matters stand in reality? True, the peasants do in some ways "act unreasonably" in the countryside. The peasant association, supreme in authority, does not allow the landlords to have their say and makes a clean sweep of all their prestige. This is tantamount to trampling the landlords underfoot after knocking them down. The peasants threaten: "Put you in the special register"; they impose fines on the local bullies and bad gentry and demand contributions; they smash their sedan-chairs. Crowds of people swarm into the homes of the local bullies and bad gentry who oppose the peasant association, slaughtering their pigs and consuming their grain. They may even for a minute or two loll on the ivory beds of the young mesdames and mademoiselles in the families of the bullies and gentry. At the slightest provocation they make arrests, crown the arrested with tall paper-hats, and parade them through the villages: "You bad gentry, now you know who we are!" Doing whatever they like and turning everything upside down, they have even created a kind of terror in the countryside. This is what some people call "going too far," or "going beyond the proper limit to right a wrong," or "really too outrageous."

The opinion of this group, reasonable on the surface, is erroneous at bottom.

First, the things described above have all been the inevitable results of the doings of the local bullies and bad gentry and lawless landlords themselves. For ages these people, with power in their hands, tyrannized over the peasants and trampled them underfoot; that is why the peasants have now risen in such a great revolt. The most formidable revolts and the most serious troubles invariably occur at places where the local bullies and bad gentry were the most ruthless in their evil deeds. The peasants' eyes are perfectly discerning. As to who is bad and who is not, who is the most ruthless and who is less so, and who is to be severely punished and who is to be dealt with lightly, the peasants keep perfectly clear accounts and very seldom has there been any discrepancy between the punishment and the crime.

Secondly, a revolution is not the same as inviting people to dinner, or writing an essay, or painting a picture, or doing fancy needlework; it cannot be anything so refined, so calm and gentle, or so mild, kind, courteous, restrained, and magnanimous. A revolution is an uprising, an act of violence whereby one class overthrows another. A rural revolution is a revolution by which the peasantry overthrows the authority of the feudal landlord class. If the peasants do not use the maximum of their strength, they can never overthrow the authority of the landlord which has been deeply rooted for thousands of years. In the rural areas, there must be a great fervent revolutionary upsurge, which alone can arouse hundreds and thousands of the people to form a great force. All the actions mentioned above, labeled as "going too far," are caused by the power of the peasants, generated by a great, fervent, revolutionary upsurge in the countryside. Such actions were quite necessary in the second period of the peasant movement (the period of revolutionary action). In this period, it was necessary to establish the absolute authority of the peasants. It was necessary to stop malicious criticisms against the peasant association. It was necessary to overthrow all the authority of the gentry, to knock them down and even trample them underfoot. All actions labeled as "going too far" had a revolutionary significance in the second period. To put it bluntly, it was necessary to bring about a brief reign of terror in every rural area; otherwise one could never suppress the activities of the counter-revolutionaries in the countryside or overthrow the authority of the gentry. To right a wrong it is necessary to exceed the proper limits, and the wrong cannot be righted without the proper limits being exceeded.

VANGUARD OF THE REVOLUTION

The main force in the countryside which has always put up the bitterest fight is the poor peasants. Throughout both the period of underground organization and that of open organization, the poor peasants have fought militantly all along. They accept most willingly the leadership of the Communist Party. They are the deadliest enemies of the local bullies and bad gentry and attack their strongholds without the slightest hesitation.

Without the poor peasants (the "riffraff" as the gentry call them) it would never have been possible to bring about in the countryside the present state of revolution, to overthrow the local bullies and bad gentry, or to complete the democratic revolution. Being the most revolutionary, the poor peasants have won the leadership in the peasant association. . .This leadership of the poor peasants is absolutely necessary. Without the poor peasants there can be no revolution. To reject them is to reject the revolution. To attack them is to attack the revolution. Their general direction of the revolution has never been wrong.

OVERTHROWING THE CLAN AUTHORITY OF THE ELDERS AND ANCESTRAL TEMPLES, THE THEOCRATIC AUTHORITY OF THE CITY GODS AND LOCAL DEITIES, AND THE MASCULINE AUTHORITY OF THE HUSBANDS.

A man in China is usually subjected to the domination of three systems of authority:
1) the system of the state (political authority), ranging from the national, provincial, and county government to the township government;
2) the system of the clan (clan authority), ranging from the central and branch ancestral temples to the head of the household; and
3) the system of gods and spirits (theocratic authority), including the system of the nether world ranging from the King of Hell to the city gods and local deities, and that of supernatural beings ranging from the Emperor of Heaven to all kinds of gods and spirits.

As to women, apart from being dominated by the three systems mentioned above, they are further dominated by men (the authority of the husband). These four kinds of authority—political authority, clan authority, theocratic authority, and the authority of the husband—represent the whole ideology and institution of feudalism and patriarchy, and are the four great cords that have bound the Chinese people and particularly the peasants. We have already seen how the peasants are overthrowing the political authority of the landlords in the countryside. The political authority of the landlords is the backbone of all other systems of authority. Where it has already been overthrown, clan authority, theocratic authority, and the authority of the husband are all beginning to totter. Where the peasant association is powerful, the clan elders and administrators of temple funds no longer dare oppress members of the clan or embezzle the funds. The bad clan elders and administrators have been overthrown as local bullies and bad gentry. No ancestral temple dare any longer, as it used to do, inflict cruel corporal and capital punishments like "beating," "drowning," and "burying alive." The old rule that forbids women and poor people to attend banquets in the ancestral temple has also been broken. On one occasion the women of Paikwo, Henghsan, marched into their ancestral temple, sat down on the seats and ate and drank, while the grand patriarchs could only look on. At another place the poor peasants, not admitted to the banquets in the temples, swarmed in and ate and drank their fill, while the frightened local bullies, bad gentry, and gentlemen in long gowns all took to their heels.

Theocratic authority begins to totter everywhere as the peasant movement develops. In many places the peasant associations have taken over the temples of the gods as their offices. Everywhere they advocate the appropriation of temple properties to maintain peasant schools and to defray association expenses, calling this, "public revenue from superstition." Forbidding superstition and smashing idols has become quite the vogue in Liling. In its northern districts the peasants forbade the festival processions in honor of the god of pestilence. There were many idols in the Taoist temple on Fupo hill, Lukow, but they were all piled up in a corner to make room for the district headquarters of the Kuomintang, and no peasant raised any objection. When a death occurs in a family, such practices as sacrifice to the gods, performance of Taoist or Buddhist rites, and offering of sacred lamps are becoming rare. It was Sun Hsiao-shan, the chairman of the peasant association, who proposed all this, so the local Taoist priests bear him a grudge. In the Lungfeng Nunnery in the North Third district, the peasants and school teachers chopped up the wooden idols to cook meat. More than thirty idols in the Tungfu Temple in the South district were burnt by the students together with the peasants; only two small idols, generally known as "His excellency Pao," were rescued by an old peasant who said, "Don't commit a sin!" In places where the power of the peasants is predominant, only the older peasants and the women still believe in gods while among the young and middle-aged peasants who are in control of the peasant association, the movement to overthrow theocratic authority and eradicate superstition is going on everywhere.

As to the authority of the husband, it has always been comparatively weak among the poor peasants, because the poor peasant women, compelled for financial reasons to take more part in manual work than women of wealthier classes, have obtained more right to speak and more power to make decisions in family affairs. In recent years rural economy has become even more bankrupt and the basic condition for men's domination over women has already been undermined. And now, with the rise of the peasant movement, women in many places have set out immediately to organize the rural women's association; the opportunity has come for them to lift up their heads, and the authority of the husband is tottering more and more every day. In a word, all feudal and patriarchal ideologies and institutions are tottering as the power of the peasant rises. In the present period, however, the peasants' efforts are concentrated on the destruction of the landlords' political authority. Where the political authority of the landlords is already completely destroyed, the peasants are beginning their attacks in the other three spheres, namely, the clan, the gods, and the relationship between men and women. At present, however, such attacks have only just "begun" and there can be no complete overthrow of the three until after the complete victory of the peasants' economic struggle. Hence at present our task is to guide the peasants to wage political struggles with their utmost strength so that the authority of the landlords may be thoroughly uprooted. An economic struggle should also be started immediately in order that the land problem and other economic problems of the poor peasants can be completely solved.

The abolition of the clan system, of superstitions, and of inequality between men and women will follow as a natural consequence of victory in political and economic struggles. If we crudely and arbitrarily devote excessive efforts to the abolition of such things, we shall give the local bullies and bad gentry a pretext for undermining the peasant movement by raising such slogans of counter-revolutionary propaganda as "The peasant association does not show piety towards ancestors," "The peasant association abuses the gods and destroys religion," and "The peasant association advocates the community of women." Clear proof has been forthcoming recently at both Siangsiang in Hunan and Yangsin in Hupeh, where the landlords were able to take advantage of peasant opposition to the smashing of idols. The idols were set up by the peasants, and in time they will pull them down with their own hands; there is no need for anybody else prematurely to pull down the idols for them. The agitational line of the Communist Party in such matters should be: "Draw the bow to the full without letting go the arrow, and be on the alert." The idols should be removed by the peasants themselves, and the temples of martyred virgins and the arches for chaste and filial widowed daughters-in-law should likewise be demolished by the peasants themselves: it is wrong for anyone else to do these things for them.

In the countryside I, too, agitated among the peasants for abolishing superstitions. What I said was:

> One who believes in the Eight Characters hopes for good luck; one who believes in geomancy hopes for the beneficial influence of the burial ground. This year the local bullies, bad gentry, and corrupt officials all collapsed within a few months. It is possible that till a few months ago they were all in the good luck and all under the beneficial influence of their burial grounds, while in the last few months they have all of a sudden been in bad luck and their burial grounds all ceased to exert any beneficial influence of them?

> The local bullies and bad gentry jeer at your peasant association, and say: "How strange! It has become a world of committeemen; look, you can't even go the latrines without meeting one of them!" Quite true, in the towns and in the villages, the trade unions, the peasant association, the Kuomintang, and the Communist Party all have their committee members—it is indeed world of committeemen. But is this due to the Eight Characters and the burial grounds? What a strange thing! The Eight Characters of all the poor wretches in the countryside have suddenly changed for the better! And their burial grounds have suddenly started to exert a beneficial influence!

The gods? They may quite deserve our worship. But if we had no peasant association but only the Emperor Kuan and the Goddess of Mercy, could we have knocked down the local bullies and bad gentry? The gods and goddesses are indeed pitiful; worshipped for hundreds of years, they have not knocked down for you a single bully or a single one of the bad gentry!

Now you want to have your rent reduced. I would like to ask: How will you go about it? Believe in the gods, or believe in the peasant association?

These words of mine made the peasants roar with laughter.

CULTURAL MOVEMENT

With the downfall of the power of the landlords in the rural areas, the peasants' cultural movement has begun. And so the peasants, who hitherto bitterly hated the schools, are now zealously organizing evening classes. The "foreign-style schools" were always unpopular with the peasants. In my student days I used to stand up for the "foreign-style schools" when, upon returning to my native place, I found the peasants objecting to them. I was myself identified with the "foreign-style students" and "foreign-style teachers," and always felt that the peasants were somehow wrong. It was during my six months in the countryside in 1925, when I was already a Communist and had adopted the Marxist viewpoint, that I realized I was mistaken and that the peasants' views were right. The teaching materials used in the rural primary schools all dealt with city matters and were in no way adapted to the needs of the rural areas. Besides, the primary school teachers behaved badly towards the peasants, who, far from finding them helpful, grew to dislike them. As a result, the peasants wanted old-style rather than modern schools—"Chinese classes," as they call them, rather than "foreign classes"—and they preferred the masters of the old-style school to the teachers in the primary schools.

Now the peasants are energetically organizing evening classes, which they call peasant school. Many such schools have been opened and others are being established; on the average there is one school to every township. The peasants are very enthusiastic about establishing such schools, and regard only such schools as their own. The funds for evening classes come from the "public revenue from superstitious practices," the funds of ancestral temples and other kinds of public funds or public property that have been lying idle. The country education boards wanted to use these public funds for establishing primary schools, that is, "foreign-style schools" not adapted to the needs of the peasants, while the peasants wanted to use them for peasant schools; as a result of the dispute, both sides got part of the funds, thought in certain places the peasants got the whole. As a result of the growth of the peasant movement, the cultural level of the peasants has risen rapidly. Before long there will be tens of thousands of schools sprouting up in the rural areas throughout the whole province, and that will be something quite different from the futile clamor of the intelligentsia and so-called "educators" for "popular education," which for all their hullabaloo has remained an idle phrase.

32. John S. Service

THE SITUATION IN CHINA AND SUGGESTIONS REGARDING AMERICAN POLICY

June 20, 1944

I. THE SITUATION IN CHINA IS RAPIDLY BECOMING CRITICAL

A. The Japanese strategy in China, which has been as much political as military, has so far been eminently successful.

Japan has had the choice of two alternatives:
1) It could beat China to its knees. But this would have required large military operations and a large and continuing army of occupation. And there was the danger that it might have driven the Kuomintang to carry out a real mobilization of the people, thus making possible effective resistance and perhaps rendering the Japanese task as long and costly as it has been in North China.
2) Or Japan could maintain just enough pressure on China to cause slow strangulation. Based on the astute use of puppets, the understanding of the continuing struggle for power within China (including the Kuomintang-Communist conflict), and the knowledge that Chiang expects to have the war won for him outside of China by his allies, this policy had the advantage that as long as the Kuomintang leaders saw a chance for survival they would not take the steps necessary to energize an effective war. It would thus remove any active or immediate threat to Japan's flank, and permit the accomplishment of these aims at a relatively small cost.

Japan chose the second alternative, accepting the gamble that the Kuomintang would behave exactly as it has. Like many other Japanese gambles, it has so far proved to have been nicely calculated. China *is* dying a lingering death by slow strangulation. China *does not* now constitute any threat to Japan. And China *cannot*, if the present situation continues, successfully resist a determined Japanese drive to seize our offensive bases in East China.

B. The position of the Kuomintang and the Generalissimo is weaker than it has been for the past ten years.

China faces economic collapse. This is causing disintegration of the army and the government's administrative apparatus. It is one of the chief causes of growing political unrest. The Generalissimo is losing the support of a China which, by unity in the face of violent aggression, found a new and unexpected strength during the first two years of the war with Japan. Internal weaknesses are become accentuated and there is taking place a reversal of the process of unification.

1) Morale is low and discouragement widespread. There is a general feeling of hopelessness.

2) The authority of the Central Government is weakening in the areas away from the larger cities. Government mandates and measures of control cannot be enforced and remain ineffective. It is becoming difficult for the Government to collect enough food for its huge army and bureaucracy.

3) The governmental and military structure is being permeated and demoralized from top to bottom by corruption, unprecedented in scale and openness.

4) The intellectual and salaried classes, who have suffered the most heavily from inflation, are in danger of liquidation. The academic groups suffer not only the attrition and demoralization of economic stress; the weight of years of political control and repression is robbing them of the intellectual vigor and leadership they once had.

5) Peasant resentment of the abuses of conscription, tax collection and other arbitrary impositions has been widespread and is growing. The danger is ever-increasing that past sporadic outbreaks of banditry and agrarian unrest may increase in scale and find political motivation.

6) The provincial groups are making common cause with one another and with other dissident groups, and are actively consolidating their positions. Their continuing strength in the face of the growing weakness of the Central Government is forcing new measures of political appeasement in their favor.

7) Unrest within the Kuomintang armies is increasing, as shown in one important instance by the "Young Generals Conspiracy" late in 1943. On a higher plane, the war-zone commanders are building up their own spheres of influence and are thus creating a "new warlordism."

8) The break between the Kuomintang and the Communists not only shows no signs of being closed, but has grown more critical with the passage of time; the inevitability of civil war is now generally accepted.

9) The Kuomintang is losing the respect and support of the people by its selfish policies and its refusal to heed progressive criticism. It seems unable to revivify itself with fresh blood, and its unchanging leadership shows a growing ossification and loss of a sense of reality. To combat the dissensions and cliquism within the Party, which grow more rather than less acute, the leadership is turning toward the reactionary and unpopular Ch'en brothers clique.

10) The Generalissimo shows a similar loss of realistic flexibility and a hardening of narrowly conservative views. His growing megalomania and his unfortunate attempts to be "sage" as well as leader—shown, for instance, by *China's Destiny* and his book on eco-

nomics—have forfeited the respect of many intellectuals, who enjoy in China a position of unique influence. Criticism of his dictatorship is becoming more outspoken.

These symptoms of deterioration and internal stress have been increased by the defeat in Honan and will be further accelerated if, as seems likely, the Japanese succeed in partially or wholly depriving the Central Government of East China south of the Yangtze.

In the face of the grave crisis with which it is confronted, the Kuomintang is ceasing to be the unifying and progressive force in Chinese society, the role in which it made its greatest contribution to modern China.

C. The Kuomintang is not only proving itself incapable of averting a debacle by its own initiative: on the contrary, its policies are precipitating the crisis.

Some war-weariness in China must be expected. But the policies of the Kuomintang under the impact of hyper-inflation and in the presence of obvious signs of internal and external weakness must be described as bankrupt…

1. *On the internal political front the desire of the Kuomintang leaders to perpetuate their own power overrides all other considerations: the result is the enthronement of reaction.*

The Kuomintang continues to ignore the great political drive within the country for democratic reform. The writings of the Generalissimo and the Party press show that they have no real understanding of that term…

On the contrary, the trend is still in the other direction. Through such means as compulsory political training for government posts, emphasis on the political nature of the Army, thought control and increasing identification of the Party and Government, the Kuomintang intensifies its drive for "*Ein Volk, Ein Reich, Ein Fuhrer*"—even though such a policy in China is inevitably doomed to failure.

The Kuomintang shows no intention of relaxing the authoritarian controls on which its present power depends. Far from discarding or reducing the paraphernalia of a police state—the multiple and omnipresent secret-police organizations, the gendarmerie, and so forth—it continues to strengthen them as its last resort for internal security. (For the reinforcement of the most important of these German-inspired and Gestapo-like organizations we must, unfortunately, bear some responsibility.)

Obsessed by the growing and potential threat of the Communists, who it fears may attract the popular support its own nature makes impossible, the Kuomintang, despite the pretext—to meet foreign and Chinese criticism—of conducting negotiations with the Communists, continues to adhere to policies and plans which can only result in civil war. In so doing it shows itself blind to the facts: that its internal political and military situation is so weak that success without outside assistance is most problematic; that such a civil war would hasten the process of disintegration and the spread of chaos: that it would prevent the prosecution of any effective war against Japan; and that the only parties to benefit would be Japan immediately and Russia eventually. Preparations for this civil war include an alliance with the present Chinese puppets which augurs ill for future unity and democracy in China.

2. *On the economic front the Kuomintang is unwilling to take any effective steps to check inflation which would injure the landlord-capitalist class.*

It is directly responsible for the increase of official corruption, which is one of the main obstacles to any rational attempt to ameliorate the financial situation. It does nothing to stop large-scale profiteering, hoarding and speculation—all of which are carried on by people either powerful in the Party or with intimate political connection...

It refuses to attack the fundamental economic problems of China such as the growing concentration of land holdings, extortionate rents and ruinous interest rates, and the impact of inflation.

3. *On the external front the Kuomintang is showing itself inept and selfishly short-sighted by progressive estrangement of its allies.*

By persistence in tactics of bargaining, bluff and blackmail—most appropriate to its circumstances—and its continuing failure to deal openly and frankly and to extend wholehearted cooperation—which its own interests demand— the Kuomintang is alienating China's most important ally, the United States. It has already alienated its other major potential ally, Soviet Russia, toward which its attitude is as irrational and short-sighted as it is toward the Communists. The latest example of this is the irresponsible circulation of the report that Soviet Russia and Japan have signed a secret military agreement permitting Japanese troop withdrawal from Manchuria.

It is allowing this situation to develop at a time when its survival is dependent as never before upon foreign support. But the Kuomintang is endangering not only itself by its rash foreign policy: there are indications that it is anxious to create friction between the United States and Great Britain and Russia. When speedy victory—and any victory at all—demands maximizing of agreements and the minimizing of frictions, such maneuvers amount to sabotage of the war effort of the United Nations.

4. *On the military front the Kuomintang appears to have decided to let America win the war and to have withdrawn for all practical purposes from active participation.*

Its most important present contribution is to allow us—at our own and fantastic cost—to build and use air bases in China...

It fails to make effective use of American equipment given to it as it also failed with earlier Russian supplies. Equipment brought into China has often not been transported to the fighting fronts. In other cases it has been known to have been hoarded or diverted to nonmilitary purposes...

It has allowed military cooperation to be tied up with irrelevant financial demands which can only be described as a form of blackmail...

It remains uncooperative and at times obstructive in American efforts to collect vital intelligence regarding the enemy in China. This attitude is exemplified by the disappointing fruits of promised cooperation by Chinese espionage organizations (toward which we have expended great effort and large sums); by the continued obstruction, in the face of agreement, to visits by American observers to the actual fighting fronts; and by the steadfast refusal to permit any contact with the Communist areas...

In its own war effort a pernicious and corrupt conscription system works to ensure the selection and retention of the unfit—since the ablest and strongest can either evade conscription, buy their way out or desert. It starves and maltreats most of its troops to the degree that their military effectiveness is greatly impaired and military service is regarded in the minds of the people as a sentence of death. At the same time it refuses to follow the suggestion that the army should be reduced to the size that could be adequately fed, medically cared for, trained and armed. It bases this refusal on mercenary political considerations—the concentration on the continuing struggle for power in China, and the ultimate measurement of power in terms of armies.

For the same reason it refuses to mobilize its soldiers and people for the only kind of war which China is in a position to wage effectively—a people's guerrilla war. Perhaps our entry into the war has simplified the problems of the Kuomintang. As afraid of the forces within the country—its own people—as it is of the Japanese, it now seeks to avoid conflict with the Japanese in order to concentrate on the perpetuation of its own power.

The condition to which it has permitted its armies to deteriorate is shown most recently by the defeat in Honan, which is due not only to lack of heavy armament but also to the poor morale and miserable condition of the soldiers, absence of support by the people—who have been consistently mistreated—lack of leadership, and prevalent corruption among the officers through such practices as trade with the occupied areas.

If we accept the obvious indications that the present Kuomintang leadership does not want to fight the Japanese any more that it can help, we must go further and recognize that it may even seek to prevent China from becoming the battleground for large-scale campaigns against the Japanese land forces. This helps to explain the Kuomintang's continued dealings with the Japanese and puppets. Thus the Kuomintang may hope to avert determined Japanese attack, maintain its own position and power, save the East China homes of practically all of its officials, and preserve its old economic-industrial base in the coastal cities.

If this analysis is valid, it reveals on the part of the Kuomintang leadership—which means the Generalissimo—a cynical disregard of the added cost of the inevitable prolongation of the war in American lives and resources.

D. These apparently suicidal policies of the Kuomintang have their roots in the composition and nature of the Party.

In the view of the above it becomes pertinent to ask *why* the Kuomintang has lost its power of leadership; *why* it neither wishes actively to wage war against Japan itself nor to cooperate wholeheartedly with the American Army in China: and *why* it has ceased to be capable of unifying the country.

The answer to all these questions is to be found in the present composition and nature of the Party. Politically, a classical and definitive American description becomes ever more true: the Kuomintang is a congerie of conservative political cliques interested primarily in the preservation of their own power against all outsiders and in jockeying for position among themselves. Economically, the Kuomintang rests on the narrow base of the rural gentry landlords, the militarists, the higher ranks of the government bureaucracy, and merchant-bankers having intimate connections with the government bureaucrats. This base has actually contracted during the war. The Kuomintang no longer commands, as it once did, the unequivocal support of China's industrialists, who as a group have been much weakened economically, and hence politically, by the Japanese seizure of the coastal cities.

The relation of this description of the Kuomintang to the questions propounded above is clear.

The Kuomintang has lost its leadership because it has lost touch with and is no longer representative of a nation which, through the practical experience of the war, is becoming both more politically conscious and more aware of the Party's selfish shortcomings.

It cannot fight an effective war because this is impossible without greater reliance upon and support by the people. There must be a release of national energy such as occurred during the early period of the war. Under present conditions, this can be brought about only by reform of the Party and greater political democracy. What form this democracy takes is not as important as the genuine adoption of a democratic philosophy and attitude; the threat of foreign invasion is no longer enough to stimulate the Chinese people and only real reform can now regain their enthusiasm. But the growth of democracy, though basic to China's continuing war effort, would, to the mind of the Kuomintang's present leaders, imperil the foundations of the Party's power because it would mean that the conservative cliques would have to give up their closely guarded monopoly. Rather than do this, they prefer to see the war remain in its present state of passive inertia. They are thus sacrificing China's national interests to their own selfish ends...

The Kuomintang cannot unify the country because it derives its support from the economically most conservative groups, who wish the retention of China's economically and socially backward agrarian society. These groups are incapable of bringing about China's industrialization, although they pay this objective elaborate lip service. They are also committed to the maintenance of an order which by its very nature fosters particularism and resists modern centralization . . . .

E. The present policies of the Kuomintang seem certain of failure: if that failure results in a collapse of China it will have consequences disastrous both to our immediate military plans and our long-term interests in the Far East.

The present policies of the Kuomintang seem certain to fail because they run counter to strong forces within the country and are forcing China into ruin. Since these policies are not favorable to us, nor of assistance in the prosecution of an effective war by China, their failure would not of itself be disastrous to American interests. For many reasons mentioned above we might welcome the fall of the Kuomintang if it could immediately be followed by a progressive government able to unify the country and help us fight Japan.

But the danger is that the present drifting and deterioration under the Kuomintang may end in a collapse. The result would be the creation in China of a vacuum. This would eliminate any possibility in the near future of utilizing China's potential military strength. Because the Japanese and their puppets might be able to occupy this vacuum—at much less cost than by a major military campaign—it might also became impossible for us to exploit China's flank position and to continue operating from Chinese bases. The war would thus be prolonged and made more difficult.

Such a collapse would also initiate a period of internal chaos in China which would defer the emergence of a strong and stable government—an indispensable pre-condition for stability and order in the Far East.

China, which might be a minor asset to us now, would became a major liability.

F. There are, however, active and constructive forces in China opposed to the present trends of the Kuomintang leadership which, if given a chance, might avert the threatened collapse.

These groups, all increasingly dissatisfied with the government and the Party responsible for it, include:

the patriotic younger army officers

the small merchants

large sections of the lower ranks of the Government bureaucracy

most of the foreign-returned students

the intelligentsia, including professors, students and the professional classes

the liberal elements of the Kuomintang, who make up a sizable minority under the leadership of such men as Sun Fo,

the minor parties and groups, some of which, like the National Salvationists, enjoy great prestige

the Chinese Communist Party,

and the inarticulate but increasingly restless rural population.

The collective numbers and influence of these groups could be tremendous. A Kuomintang official recently admitted that resentment against the present Kuomintang Government is so widespread that if there were free, universal elections, 80 percent of the votes might be cast against it. But most of these groups are nebulous and unorganized, feeling—like the farmers—perhaps only a blind dislike of conditions as they are. They represent different classes and varying political beliefs—where they have any at all. They are tending, however, to draw together in the consciousness of their common interest in the change of the *status quo*. This awakening and fusion is, of course, opposed by the Kuomintang with every means at is disposal.

The danger, as conditions grow worse, is that some of these groups may act independently and blindly. The effect may be to make confusion worse. Such might be the case in a military putsch—a possibility that cannot be disregarded. The result might be something analogous to the Sian incident of 1936. But the greater delicacy and precariousness of the present situation would lend itself more easily to exploitation by the most reactionary elements of the Kuomintang, the Japanese or the puppets. Another possibility is the outbreak, on a much larger scale than heretofore, of unorganized and disruptive farmers' revolts. A disturbing phenomenon is the apparent attempt now being made by some of the minority parties to effect a marriage of convenience with the provincial warlords, among the most reactionary and unscrupulous figures in Chinese politics and hardly crusaders for a new democracy.

The hopeful sign is that all these groups are agreed that the basic problem in China today is political reform toward democracy. This point requires emphasis. It is only through political reform that the restoration of the will to fight, the unification of the country, the elimination of provincial warlordism, the solution of the Communist problem, the institution of economic policies which can avoid collapse, and the emergence of a government actually supported by the people can be achieved. *Democratic reform is the crux of all important Chinese problems, military, economic and political.*

It is clear beyond doubt that China's hope for internal peace and effective unity—certainly in the immediate future (which for the sake of the war must be our prior consideration) and probably in the long-term as well—lies neither with the present Kuomintang nor with the

Communists, but in a democratic combination of the liberal elements within the country, including those within the Kuomintang, and the probably large section of the Communists who would be willing, by their own statements and past actions, to collaborate in the resurrection of a united front...

II. IN THE LIGHT OF THIS DEVELOPING CRISIS, WHAT SHOULD BE THE AMERICAN ATTITUDE TOWARD CHINA?

It is impossible to predict exactly how far the present disintegration in China can continue without spectacular change in the internal situation and drastic effect on the war against Japan. But we must face the question whether we can afford passively to stand by and allow the process to continue to an almost certainly disastrous collapse, or whether we wish to do what we legitimately and practically can to arrest it. We need to formulate a realistic policy toward China.

A. The Kuomintang and Chiang are acutely conscious of their dependence on us and will be forced to appeal for our support.

We must realize that when the process of disintegration gets out of hand it will be to us that the Kuomintang will turn for financial, political and military salvation. The awareness of this dependence is the obvious and correct explanation of the Kuomintang's hypersensitivity to American opinion and criticism. The Kuomintang—and particularly the Generalissimo—know that we are the only disinterested, yet powerful ally to whom China can turn.

The appeal will be made to us on many grounds besides the obvious, well-worn, but still effective one of pure sentiment. They have said in the past and will say in the future that they could long ago have made peace with Japan—on what are falsely stated would have been favorable terms. They have claimed and will claim again that their resistance and refusal to compromise with Japan saved Russia, Great Britain and ourselves—ignoring the truth that our own refusal to compromise with Japan to China's disadvantage brought on Pearl Harbor and our involvement before we were ready. They have complained that they have received less support in the form of materials that any other major ally—forgetting that they have done less fighting, have not used the materials given, and would not have had the ability to use what they asked for. Finally, they have tried and will continue to try to lay the blame on us for their difficulties—distorting the effect of American Army expenditures in China and ignoring the fact that these expenditures are only a minor factor in the whole sorry picture of the mismanagement of the Chinese economy.

But however far-fetched these appeals, our flat refusal of them might have several embarrassing effects:
1) We would probably see China enter a period of internal chaos. Our war effort in this theater would be disrupted, instability in the Far East prolonged, and possible Russian intervention attracted.
2) We would be blamed by large sections of both Chinese and American public opinion for "abandoning" China after having been at least partly responsible for its collapse. (In such a measure we would have brought such blame upon ourselves because we have tended to allow ourselves to became identified not merely with China but also with the

Kuomintang and its policies. Henceforth it may be the better part of valor to avoid too close identification with the Kuomintang.)

3) By an apparent abandonment of China in its hour of need, we would lose international prestige, especially in the Far East.

On the other hand, if we came to the rescue of the Kuomintang on its own terms, we would be buttressing—but only temporarily—a decadent regime which by its existing composition and program is incapable of solving China's problems. Both China and we ourselves would be gaining only a brief respite from the ultimate day of reckoning.

It is clear, therefore, that it is to our advantage to avoid a situation arising in which we would be presented with a Hobson's choice between two such unpalatable alternatives.

B. The Kuomintang's dependence can give us great influence.

Circumstances are rapidly developing so that the Generalissimo will have to ask for the continuance and increase of our support. Weak as he is, he is in no position—and the weaker he becomes, the less he will be able—to turn down or render nugatory any coordinated and positive policy we may adopt toward China. The cards are all in our favor. Our influence, intelligently used, can be tremendous.

C. There are three general alternatives open to us:

1) We may give up China as hopeless and wash our hands of it altogether.
2) We may continue to give support the Generalissimo, when and as he asks for it.
3) We may formulate a coordinated and positive policy toward China and take the necessary steps for its implementation.

D. Our choice between these alternatives must be determined by our objective in China.

The United States, if it so desired and if it had a coherent policy, could play an important and perhaps decisive role in:

1) Stimulating China to an active part in the war in the Far East, thus hastening the defeat of Japan.
2) Staving off economic collapse in China and bringing about basic political and economic reforms, thus enabling China to carry on the war and enhancing the chances of its orderly postwar recovery.
3) Enabling China to emerge from the war as a major and stabilizing factor in postwar East Asia.
4) Winning a permanent and valuable ally in a progressive, independent and democratic China.

E. We should adopt the third alternative—a coordinated and positive policy.

This is clear from an examination of the background of the present situation in China and the proper objectives of our policy there.

The first alternative must be rejected on immediate military grounds—but also for obvious long-range considerations. It would deprive us of valuable air bases and a position on Japan's flank. Its adoption would prolong the war. We cannot afford to wash our hands of China.

The results of the second alternative—which, insofar as we have a China policy, has been the one we have been and are pursuing—speak for themselves. The substantial financial assistance we have given China has been frittered away with negligible if any effect in slowing inflation and retarding economic collapse. The military help we have given has certainly not been used to increase China's war effort against Japan. Our political support has been used for the Kuomintang's own selfish purposes and to bolster its shortsighted and ruinous policies.

The third, therefore, is the only real alternative left to us. Granted the rejection of the first alternative, there is no longer a question of helping and advising China. China itself must request this help and advice. The only question is whether we give this help within a framework which makes sense, or whether we continue to give it in our present disjointed and absent-minded manner. In the past it has sometimes seemed that our right hand did not know what the left was doing. To continue without a coherent and coordinated policy will be dissipating our effort without either China or ourselves deriving any appreciable benefit. It can only continue to create new problems, in addition to those already troubling us, without any compensating advantages beyond those of indolent short-term expediency. But most important is the possibility that this haphazard giving, this serving of short-term expediency, may not be enough to save the situation; even with it, China may continue toward collapse.

F. This positive policy should be political.

The problem confronting us is whether we are to continue as in the past to ignore political considerations of direct military significance, or whether we are to take a leaf out of the Japanese book and invoke even stronger existing political forces in China to achieve our military and long-term political objectives.

We must seek to contribute toward the reversal of the present movement toward collapse and to the rousing of China from its military inactivity. This can be brought about only by an accelerated movement toward democratic political reform within China. Our part must be that of a catalytic agent in this process of China's democratization. It can be carried out by the careful exertion of our influence, which has so far not been consciously and systematically used.

This democratic reform does not necessarily mean the overthrow of the Generalissimo or the Kuomintang. On the contrary—if they have the vision to see it—their position will be improved and the stability of the Central Government increased. The democratic forces already existing in China will be strengthened, the reactionary authoritarian trends in the Kuomintang will be modified, and a multiparty United Front government will probably emerge. It is almost certain that the Generalissimo and the Kuomintang would continue to play a dominant part in such a government.

It goes without saying that this democratization of China must be brought about by, and depend on, forces within the country. It cannot be enforced by us—or by any foreign nation. For us to dictate "democracy" would not only be paradoxical, it would also open us to the charge, which the Japanese and reactionary elements would exploit, of being "imperialistic." Our task therefore is to find means of exerting our political influence in indirect and sometimes unassuming ways and of showing to the Kuomintang and the people of China our benevolent and serious interest in democracy.

The popular desire for democracy in China is already strong. We can be sure that as our attitude becomes clear, and as our desire that China itself should be the prime mover in bringing about reform becomes apparent, steady progress will be made....

33. Mao Zedong

EXCERPTS FROM CONFIDENTIAL SPEECHES, DIRECTIVES AND LETTERS

The New York Times, March 1, 1970

Chinese-Soviet Dispute

The roots for [the conflict] were laid earlier. The episode occurred a long time ago. They did not allow China to make a revolution. This was in 1945, when Stalin tried to prevent the Chinese revolution by saying that there should not be any civil war and that we must collaborate with Chiang Kai-shek. At that time we did not carry this into effect, and the revolution was victorious. After the victory, they again suspected that China would be like Yugoslavia and I would become a Tito.

Later on, I went to Moscow to conclude the Chinese-Soviet Treaty of alliance and Mutual Assistance (Feb. 14, 1950), which also involved a struggle. He [Stalin] did not want to sign it, but finally agreed after two months of negotiations. When did Stalin begin to have confidence in us? It began in the winter of 1950, during the Resist-America Aid-Korea campaign [the Korean War]. Stalin then believed that we were not Yugoslavia and not Titoist.

—Speech to the 10th Plenary Session of the Eighth Central Committee, Sept. 24, 1962.

Great Leap Forward

Talking about it now, our country is so populous; it has such vast territory and abundant resources, a history of more than 4,000 years, and culture. What a boast, tough, it is not even as good as Belgium. Our steel production is so low, so few people are literate. We are inferior when these things are compared; but we have zeal and must catch up with Britain within 15 years.

There are two methods of leadership, one is little better than the other. For instance, on the question of cooperativization, some advocated quick action, others slower action. I consider that former better. Strike the iron when it is hot. Better to get it done in one stroke than drag on.

—Speech at Supreme State Conference, Jan. 28, 1958, just before that Great Leap Forward.

I was not in a hurry to speak, and have endured it by stiffening my scalp. For 20 days I have sown my forbearance, and now the conference will soon be adjourned.

Being an unpolished man, I am not too cultured.

Nobody can be without shortcomings; even Confucius had his mistakes. I have seen Lenin's own drafts that had been corrected pellmell. If there were no errors, why should he correct them?

It is basically impossible to anticipate some things.

Coal and iron could not walk by themselves, and had to be transported by rolling stock. I did not anticipate this point.

It was possible that I did not know about it. This is because I was not the director of the Planning Commission. Before August of last year, I devoted my main energy to revolution. Being basically not versed in construction, I knew noting about industrial planning.

However, comrades, in 1958 and 1959 the main responsibility has fallen on me and you should take me to task. Was it Ko Chingsi [head of the party's Shanghai bureau] or I who invented the massive smelting of iron and steel? I say it was I. This created a great disaster when 90 million people went ahead to smelt steel.

You have said what you wanted to say, and the minutes attest to that. If you have caught me in the wrong, you can punish me.

Next was the people's commune. I did not claim the right of inventing people's communes, but I had the right to suggest. In Shantung a reporter asked me: "Is the commune good?" I said, "Good," and he immediately published it in the newspaper. Hereafter, newspaper reporters should leave me alone.

Have we failed now? All comrades who have come to this conference have gained something. We have not failed completely. We have paid a price, blown some Communist wind, and enabled the entire nation to learn a lesson.

Comrades, you should analyze your responsibility and your stomachs will feel much more comfortable if you move your bowels and break wind.
—*Speech an the failure of the Great Leap Forward, July 23, 1959.*

Mao at Work

During the last decade there was not a single comrade who suggested and dared to expose analytically and systematically to the Central Committee the defects in our plans. I have never known such a man. I know there are such people, but they dared not appeal to the top echelon directly by bypassing the proper echelons.
—*Comments by Mao after reading a letter from Li Chung-yun, a vice director of the State Planning Commission, July 26, 1959.*

There were many things about which they did not consult with me. These things should have been discussed by the Central Committee and decisions taken on them. Teng Hsiao-ping never consulted with me. He had never consulted with me about anything since 1959.
—*Speech at a meeting, Oct. 24, 1966.*

You should not rely on your secretaries to do everything. You should mainly do things yourselves. Reliance on your secretaries for everything is a manifestation of your degeneration in revolutionary will.
—*A directive entitled "Sixty Work Methods," Feb. 19, 1958.*

At the present we are still without an atomic bomb. But we also had no airplanes and big guns in the past. We depended on millet plus rifles to defeat the Japanese aggressors and Chiang Kaishek. We have became fairly strong and we will be even stronger. The most reliable way is to keep military and government expenditures in proper proportion and to reduce military spending to 30 per cent of the state budget so that the expenditure for economic construction can be increased.

Do you genuinely want atomic bombs? Or do you want to lower the proportion of military expenditure and carry out more economic construction. Which is after all the better course? All you are requested to study the issue. This is a question of strategic policy.

—*From a circular entitled "0-10 Major Relationships," April 1956.*

Dear Comrade:

I have received your kind letter some time ago and am sorry to be so late in replying. As you wished, I have copied out on separate sheets all my classical poems that I can remember, and I enclose them. Please let me have your comments and criticism.

Up to now I have never wanted to make these things known in any formal way because they are written in the old style. I was afraid this might encourage a wrong trend and exercise a bad influence on young people. Besides, they are not much as poetry.

—*Letter to Editors of Shih Kan, Jan. 12, 1957.*

Lin Piao, Chou En'lai:

I have gone through this case. Things cannot go on in this way. Let the Central Committee issue an instruction against this. Next, write an editorial telling the workers and peasants not to interfere in the students' movement.

—*Instruction, Sept. 7, 1966.*

Attitude Toward the Masses

I have spent much time in the rural areas with the peasants and was deeply moved by the many things they knew. Their knowledge was rich. I was no match for them.

—*Talk with Mao Yüan-sin, February, 1966.*

At present some comrades fear mass discussion very much. They fear that the masses may put forward views different from the leading organs and leaders. When problems are discussed, they suppress the enthusiasm of the masses and forbid them to speak out. This attitude is extremely bad. Comrades, we are revolutionaries. If we have truly committed mistakes, we should solicit the views of the masses of the people and other comrades, and make self-examination ourselves.

—*Talk on the Question of Democratic Centralism,. Jan. 30, 1962.*

Tell the Ministry of Public Health that the Ministry works only for 50 percent of the nation's population, and that of this 50 percent mainly the lords are served.

The broad masses of peasants do not get medical treatment. The Ministry of Public

Health is not that of the people, and it is better to rename it as the Ministry of Urban Health or the Lord's Ministry, or the Health Ministry of the Urban Lords.

Medical education must be reformed. Basically there is no need to read so many books. How many years were spent by Hua or Li Shih-chen of the Ming dynasty in school? The important thing is to improve themselves through study in practice. The more books a person reads, the more stupid he becomes.

A vast amount of manpower and material has been diverted from mass work for carrying out research in diseases which are not easy to understand and difficult to cure—so-called principles of medicine. But no attention is paid to the prevention and improved treatment of common diseases.

—*Instruction on Health Work, June 26, 1965.*

Mao's Ideal Society

Comrade Lin Piao:

I acknowledge the receipt of the report from the General Logistics Department which you forwarded on May 6. I think this plan is quite good.

So long as there is no world war, the armed forces should be a great school, our army should learn politics, military affairs, and agriculture. They can also engage in agriculture, run some medium and small factories, and manufacture a number of products to meet their own needs. They should also do mass work and participate in the Cultural Revolution.

While the main task of the workers is in industry, they should also study military affairs, politics, and culture. Where conditions permit, they should also engage in agricultural production.

While the main task of the peasants is agriculture, they should at the same time study military affairs, politics, and culture. Were conditions permit, they should collectively run small plants.

This holds good for students too. While their main task is to study, they should in addition learn other things, that is, industrial work, farming, and military affairs.

—*Letter to Comrade Lin Piao, May 7, 1966, which now forms the basis for a series of May 7 cadre schools throughout China.*

On Education

Since ancient times, those who create new ideas and new academic schools of thought have always been young people without much learning.

It is reported that penicillin was invented by a launderer in a dyer's sop. Benjamin Franklin of America discovered electricity. Beginning as a newspaper boy, he subsequently became a biographer, politician and scientist.

Naturally one can learn something in school, and I do not mean to close down the schools. What I mean is that it is not absolutely necessary to go to school.

—*Speech at Chengtu Conference, March 22, 1958.*

The existing system of education won't do. The period of schooling should be shortened. There are too many courses of study at present. They are harmful to people and cause the students to lead a strange life everyday. Myopia has been on the increase.

Examinations at present are like tackling enemies. They are surprise attacks, full of catch questions and obscure questions. They are nothing but a method of testing official stereotyped writing. I disapprove of them and advocate wholesale transformation.

For example, if 20 questions are asked about "the Dream of the Red Chamber" and the students can answer 10 of them well—with original ideas—they may score 100 marks. But if their answers are unimaginative and contain no original ideas, even though they are able to give correct answers to all the 20 questions, they should be given 50 marks. The students should be allowed to whisper to each other in an examination or to sit for an examination under the names of other candidates. Since you have the correct answer, it is a good thing for me to copy it. We can try this.

The students should be allowed to doze off when lessons are taught by [bad] teachers.

—*Instructions given at the Spring Festival Concerning Educational Work, Feb. 13, 1964.*

On Bureaucracy

At the highest level there is very little knowledge. They do not understand the opinion of the masses.

They are very busy from morning until evening, but they do not examine people and they do not investigate matters.

Their bureaucratic manner is immense. They beat their gongs to blaze the way. They cause people to become afraid just by looking at them.

They are eight-sided and slippery eels.

Government offices grow bigger and bigger. There are more people than there are jobs. Documents are numerous; there is red tape; instructions proliferate.

—*Twenty Manifestations of Bureaucracy, undated but probably from 1966.*

On the Cultural Revolution

They really created a disturbance on the streets of Nanking. The more I saw, the happier I felt.

Do not be afraid to make trouble. The more trouble you make and the longer you make it last the better. Confusion and trouble are always noteworthy. It can clear things up. The more you are afraid of ghosts the more you will encounter them. However, do not fire your guns. It is never good to open fire.

—*Instructions, July 13, 1966.*

After returning to Peking I was most distressed. Some schools have quietly closed their doors; some have even suppressed the student movement. Who wants to suppress student movements? Only the warlords.

Some fear revolution. They want to patch things up and put the lid on. This is not permissible.

We should trust the masses and become students of the masses, then we can become teachers of the masses. The current great Cultural Revolution is a formidable situation. Can we or do we dare undergo the test of socialism?

The final test of whether or not socialism will make it will be decided by your putting politics in command and your going among the masses where together with them you will carry out the Great Proletarian Cultural Revolution.

—*From a talk to Central Committee leaders, believed to be in the summer of 1966.*

The revolution as been imposed on you people because you did not carry out the revolution yourselves.

During the session those comrades who have come to attend the conference should go to Peking University and the Broadcasting College to read the big-character posters. You cannot go today because there are documents to deal with. When you read the posters, tell them that you have come to learn from them and help them make revolution.

When you go there you should be surrounded by students. More than 100 people have been assaulted at the Broadcasting College. In this era of ours, it is a good thing to have the leftists assaulted by the rightists because the leftists are tempered in this way.

—*Address to Regional Secretaries and Members of the Cultural Revolution Group. July 22, 1966.*

The principal question is what politics we should adopt regarding the problem of disturbances in various areas. My views are as follows. I firmly believe that a few months of disturbances will be mostly for the good and that little bad will result from these disturbances.

If the students want to be in the streets, let them. What is wrong with their putting up big-character posters in the streets? Let the foreigners take pictures, they just want to show our backwardness.

—*Talk before the Central Committee Work Conference, Aug. 24, 1966.*

This meeting is more successful. At the last meeting we failed to penetrate things due to lack of experience. Nobody had thought, not even I, that a single big-character poster, the Red Guards, and the large-scale exchange of revolutionary experiences would lead to the demise of the various provincial and municipal committees.

—*Speech at a Report Meeting, Oct. 24, 1966.*

Comrade Chou En-lai:

Recently many revolutionary teachers and students and revolutionary masses have written to me asking whether it is considered armed struggle to make those in authority taking the capitalist road and freaks and monsters wear dunce caps, to paint their faces, and to parade them in the street. I think it is a form of armed struggle.

These methods cannot attain the goal of educating the people. I want to stress here that, when engaging in struggle, we definitely must hold to struggle by reason.

—*Letter to Chou En-lai, Feb. 1, 1967.*

34. EXCERPTS FROM RESOLUTION ON HISTORY OF MAO'S CONTRIBUTIONS AND MISTAKES

The New York Times, July 1, 1981

In 1927, regardless of the resolute opposition of the left wing of the Kuomintang with Soong Ching-ling as its outstanding representative, the Kuomintang controlled by Chiang Kai-shek and Wang Jing-wei betrayed the policies of Kuomintang-Communist cooperation and of anti-imperialists, massacred Communists and other revolutionaries. The party was still quite inexperienced and, moreover, was dominated by Chen Duxiu's right capitulationism, so that the revolution suffered a disastrous defeat under the surprise attack of a powerful enemy.

However, our party continued to fight tenaciously. Launched under the leadership of Zhou Enlai and several other comrades, the Nanchang uprising of 1927 fired the opening shot for armed resistance against the Kuomintang reactionaries.

The meeting of the Central Committee of the party held on Aug. 7, 1927, decided on the policy of carrying out agrarian revolution and organizing armed uprisings. Shortly afterwards, the autumn harvest and Canton uprisings and uprisings in many other areas were organized.

The First Division

Led by Comrade Mao Zedong, the autumn-harvest uprising in the Hunan-Jiangxi border area gave birth to the first division of the Chinese workers' and peasants' revolutionary army and to the first rural revolutionary base area in the Jinggang Mountains. The First, Second and Fourth Front Armies of the Workers' and Peasants' Red Army were also born, as were many other Red Army units.

In the agrarian revolutionary war, the First Front Army of the Red Army and the Central revolutionary base area under the direct leadership of Comrades Mao Zedong and Zhu De played the most important role. The Front Armies of the Red Army defeated in turn a number of "encirclement and suppression" campaigns launched by the Kuomintang troops. But because of Wang Ming's left adventurist leadership, the struggle against the Kuomintang's fifth "encirclement and suppression" campaign ended in failure.

The First Front Army was forced to embark on the Long March and made its way to northern Shaanxi to join forces with units of the Red Army, which had been persevering in struggles there and with its 25th Army, which had arrived earlier.

In January 1935, the Political Bureau of the Central Committee of the party convened a meeting in Zunyi during the Long March, which established the leading position of Comrade Mao Zedong in the Red Army and the Central Committee of the party, which were then in critical danger, and subsequently made it possible to defeat Zhang Guotao's splittism, bring the Long March to a triumphant conclusion and open up new vistas for the Chinese revolution. It was a

---

184

184

vital turning point in the history of the party.

At a time of national crisis of unparalleled gravity when the Japanese imperialists were intensifying their aggression against China, the Central Committee of the party headed by Comrade Mao Zedong decided on and carried out the correct policy of forming an anti-Japanese national united front.

During the war of resistance, the ruling clique of the Kuomintang continued to oppose the Communist Party and the people and was passive in resisting Japan. As a result, the Kuomintang suffered defeat after defeat in front operations against the Japanese invaders.

Eight Years of War

Our party persevered in the policy of maintaining its independence and initiative within the united front, closely relied on the masses of the people, conducted guerrilla warfare behind enemy lines and set up many anti-Japanese base areas. The Eighth Route Army and the new Fourth Army - the reorganized Red Army - grew rapidly and became the mainstay in the war of resistance.

Consequently, the Chinese people were able to hold out in the war for eight long years and win final victory in cooperation with the people of the Soviet Union and other countries in the anti-Fascist war.

After the conclusion of the war of resistance against Japan, the Chiang Kaishek Government, with the aid of U.S. imperialism, flagrantly launched an all-out civil war, disregarding the just demand of our party and the people of the whole country for peace and democracy. Our party led the People's Liberation Army in fighting the three-year war of liberation. The end result was the overthrow of the reactionary Kuomintang Government and the establishment of the great People's Republic of China. The Chinese people had stood up.

AFTER THE VICTORY OF 1949

From the inception of the People's Republic of China in October 1949 to 1956, our party led the whole people in gradually realizing the transition from new democracy to socialism, rapidly rehabilitating the country's economy, undertaking planned economic construction and in the main accomplishing the socialist transformation of the private ownership of the means of production in most of the country. The guidelines and basic policies defined by the party in this historical period were correct and led to brilliant successes.

After the basic completion of socialist transformation, our party led the entire people in shifting our work to all around, large-scale socialist construction. In the 10 years preceding the Cultural Revolution we achieved very big successes despite serious set-backs. By 1966, the value of fixed industrial assets, calculated on the basis of their original price, was four times that of 1956.

In the course of this decade, there were serious faults and errors in the guidelines of the party's work, which developed through twists and turns.

'Airing Views in a Big Way'

Nineteen fifty-seven was one of the years that saw best results in economic work after the founding of the People's Republic owing to the conscientious implementation of the correct line formulated at the 8th National Congress of the party. To start a rectification campaign throughout the party in that year and urge the masses to offer criticisms and suggestions were normal steps in developing socialist democracy. In the rectification campaign a handful of bourgeois rightists seized the opportunity to advocate what they called "speaking out and airing views in a big way" and to mount a wild attack against the party and the nascent socialist system in an attempt to replace the leadership of the Communist Party. It was therefore entirely correct ~n~ necessary to launch a resolute counterattack. But the scope of this struggle was made far too broad and a number of intellectuals, patriotic people and party cadres were unjustifiably labeled rightist, with unfortunate consequences.

All the successes in these 10 years were achieved under the collective leadership of the Central Committee of the party headed by Comrade Mao Zedong. Likewise, responsibility for errors committed in the work of this period rested with the same collective leadership. Although Comrade Mao Zedong must be held chiefly responsible, we cannot lay the blame on him alone for those errors. During this period, his theoretical and practical mistakes concerning class struggle in a socialist society became increasingly furious, his personal arbitrariness gradually undermined democratic centralism in party life, and the personality cult grew graver and graver. The Central Committee of the party failed to rectify these mistakes in good time. Careerists like Lin Biao, Jiang Qing and Kang Sheng, harboring ulterior motives, made use of these errors and inflated them. This led to the inauguration of the cultural revolution.

THE CULTURAL REVOLUTION

The Cultural Revolution, which lasted from May 1966 to October 1976, was responsible for the most severe setback and the heaviest losses suffered by the party, the state and the people since the founding of the People's Republic.

It was initiated and led by Comrade Mao Zedong. His principal theses were that many representatives of the bourgeoisie and counterrevolutionary revisionists had sneaked into the party, the Government, the army and cultural circles, and leadership in a fairly large majority of organizations and departments was no longer in the hands of Marxists and the people; that party persons in power taking the capitalist road had formed a bourgeois headquarters inside the Central Committee which pursued a revisionist political and organizational line and had agents in all provinces, municipalities and autonomous regions, as well as in all central departments; that since the forms of struggle adopted in the past had not been able to solve this problem, the power usurped by the capitalist-roaders could be recaptured only by carrying out a Great Cultural Revolution, by openly and fully mobilizing the broad masses from the bottom up to expose these sinister phenomena, and that the Cultural Revolution was in fact a great political revolution in which one class would overthrow another, a revolution that would have to be waged time and again.

These theses appeared mainly in the May 16 Circular, which served as the programmatic document of the Cultural Revolution, and in the political report to the 9th National Congress of the party in April 1969. They were incorporated into a general theory—the theory of continued revolution under the dictatorship of the proletariat—which then took an a specific meaning.

These erroneous left theses, upon which Comrade Mao Zedong based himself in initiating the Cultural Revolution, were obviously inconsistent with the system of Mao Zedong thought, which is the integration of the universal principles of Marxism-Leninism with the concrete practice of the Chinese revolution. These themes must be thoroughly distinguished from Mao Zedong thought.

As for Lin Biao, Jiang Qing and others, who were placed in important positions by Comrade Mao Zedong, the matter is of an entirely different nature. They rigged up two counter-revolutionary cliques in an attempt to seize supreme power and, taking advantage of Comrade Mao Zedong's errors, committed many crimes behind his back, bringing disaster to the country and the people.

Appraisal of the Situation

The history of the cultural Revolution has proved that comrade Mao Zedong's principal theses for initiating it conformed neither to Marxism-Leninism nor to Chinese reality. They represent an entirely erroneous appraisal of the prevailing class relations and political situation in the party and state.

The Cultural Revolution was defined as a struggle against the revisionist line or the capitalist road. There were no grounds at all for this definition. It led to the confusing of right and wrong on a series of important theories and policies. Many things denounced as revisionist or capitalist during the Cultural Revolution were actually Marxist and Socialist principles, many of which had been set forth or supported by Comrade Mao Zedong himself.

The Cultural Revolution negated many of the correct principles, policies and achievements of the 17 years after the founding of the People's Republic. In fact, it negated much of the work of the Central Committee of the party and the people's Government, including Comrade Mao Zedong's own contribution. It negated the arduous struggles the entire people had conducted in socialist construction.

No 'Great Order'

The confusing of right and wrong inevitably led to confusing the people with the enemy. The capitalist-roaders overthrown in the Cultural Revolution were leading cadres of party and Government organizations at all levels who formed the core force of the socialist cause. The so-called bourgeois headquarters inside the party headed by Liu Shaoqi and Deng Xiaoping simply did not exist.

Practice has shown that the Cultural Revolution did not in fact constitute a revolution or social progress in any sense, nor could it possibly have done so. It was we and not the enemy at all who were thrown into disorder by the Cultural Revolution. Therefore, from beginning to end, it did not turn "great disorder under heaven" into "great order under heaven," nor could it conceivably have done so.

History has shown that the Cultural Revolution, initiated by a leader laboring under a misapprehension and capitalized on by counterrevolutionary cliques, led to domestic turmoil and brought catastrophe to the party, the state and the whole people.

Nominally, the Cultural Revolution was conducted by directly relying on the masses. In fact, it was divorced both from the party organizations and from the masses. After the movement started, party organization at different levels were attacked and became partially or wholly para- lyzed, the party's leading cadres at various levels were subjected to criticism and struggle, and inner-party life came to a standstill and many activists and large numbers of the basic masses whom the- party has long relied on were rejected. At the beginning of the Cultural Revolution, the vast majority of participants in the movement acted out of their faith in Comrade Mao Zedong and the party.

Except for a handful of extremists, however, they did not approve of launching ruthless struggles against leading party cadres at all levels. With the lapse of time, following their own circuitous paths, they eventually attained a heightened political consciousness and began to adopt a skeptical or wait an-and-see attitude toward the Cultural Revolution, or even resisted and opposed it. Many people were assailed either more or less severely for this very reason. Such a state of affairs could not but provide openings to be exploited by opportunists, careerists and conspirators, not a few of them were escalated to high or even key positions.

In 1970-71 the counterrevolutionary Lin Biao clique plotted to capture supreme power and attempted an armed counterrevolutionary coup d'état. This was the outcome of the Cultural Revolution, which overturned a series of fundamental party principles. Objectively, it announced the failure of the theories and practices of the Cultural Revolution.

Comrades Mao Zedong and Zhou Enlai ingeniously thwarted the plotted coup. Supported by Comrade Mao Zedong, Comrade Zhou Enlai took charge of the day-to-day work of the Central Committee and things began to improve in all fields. During the criticism and repudia- tion of Lin Biao in 1972, he correctly proposed criticism of the ultraleft trend of thought. In fact, this was an extension of the correct proposals put forward around February 1967 by many lead- ing comrades of the Central Committee, who had called for the correction of the errors of the Cultural Revolution.

The Gang of Four

Comrade Mao Zedong, however, erroneously held that the task was still to oppose the ultraright. The 10th Congress of the party perpetuated the left errors of the 9th Congress and made Wang Hangwen a vice chairman of the party. Jiang Qing, Zhang Chunqiao, Yao Wenyuan and Wang Hangwen formed a Gang of Four inside the Political Bureau of the Central Committee, thus strengthening the influence of the counterrevolutionary Jiang Qing clique.

In 1975, when Comrade Zhou Enlai was seriously ill, Comrade Deng Xiaoping, with the support of Comrade Mao Zedong, took charge of the day-to-day work of the Central Committee. He convened an enlarged meeting of the Military Commission of the Central Committee and several other important meetings with a view to solving problems in industry, agriculture, trans- port and science and technology, and began to straighten out work in many fields so that the situ- ation took an obvious turn for the better.

However, Comrade Mao Zedong could not bear to accept systematic correction of the errors of the Cultural Revolution by Comrade Deng and counter the right deviationist trend to reverse correct verdicts, once again plunging the nation into turmoil. In January of that year, Comrade Zhou Enlai passed away. Comrade Zhou Enlai was utterly devoted to the party and the people and stuck to his post until his dying day. He found himself in an extremely difficult situation throughout the Cultural Revolution. He always kept the general interest in mind, bore the heavy burden of office without complaint, racking his brains and untiringly endeavoring to keep the normal work of the party and the state going, to minimize the damage caused by the Cultural Revolution and to protect many party and nonparty cadres.

35. Liang Heng and Judith Shapiro

AFTER THE NIGHTMARE

It was an early Spring Beijing evening, and the air was dry and windy. Bicycles flowed home from work through the walled streets like rivers through conduits, carrying anonymous figures with their heads swathed in gauzy scarves against the dust. The only pedestrians were gathered in dark clusters at the bus stops. Compared with the exposed street life of southern cities, the broad boulevards of the capital seemed oddly empty.

Judy and I walked along Changan Avenue, then turned up a side street into a tangled nest of *hutongs*, those mazelike, distinctively northern alleyways so evocative of old China. In the falling darkness, it was difficult to make out the square blue street numbers. We were looking for the home of a retired middle-school teacher named Jiang, for we had one last obligation to fulfill before our departure from China the following day.

Hundreds of years from now, it seemed to me, Chinese would still be asking each other to "help carry things" to their friends and relations, as if the postal service did not exist. Sometimes the little favors were so numerous as to daunt anyone contemplating a trip. Of course, there were good reasons why this was common practice in China: fear of the red-eye disease, the need to avoid tariffs, the difficulty of packaging hard-to-obtain delicacies such as fruit—but even my father's sister, who lived in comparatively modern Taiwan, used this ancient method. In New York, I often received phone calls from strangers bearing gifts from her, once from a pilot who said I had to meet him at the airport within the half hour, before he took off again.

This time, we were the messengers. Jiang was the younger brother of a historian who had left China before 1949 to study abroad and hadn't been back since. The professor had written me that my memoir of the Cultural Revolution had helped him understand what lay behind his brother's careful letters: I wrote a courtesy note back, mentioning that Judy and I would soon be returning to China for a visit. Another letter from the professor arrived, saying he was sending some medicine for us to take to his ailing brother. The mission was hard to refuse.

We finally found the address, in a narrow *hutong* lined with smooth, mud-plastered walls. It was an old-style, single-story dwelling of the type soon to be seen no more: Two old stone lions with chipped faces guarded the doorway, and inside there was a courtyard. Before the Cultural Revolution, this would probably have belonged to a single family; now, since the political upheavals and the population explosion (Chairman Mao encouraged us to reproduce, so that by sheer weight of numbers only we Chinese would survive a nuclear war), there would be many households living here. Jiang's doorway was in a corner, behind a scraggly attempt at horticulture in a large broken pot.

A man of about thirty-five with a broad, bony face and bristling haircut answered the door, and we assumed this must be old Jiang's son. He seemed immediately to know who we were. His uncle must have written that we were coming.

Inside, seated at a square table beneath a single dim light bulb, was an emaciated, stoop-shouldered gentleman dressed in a black padded jacket and woolen scarf. The deep, burnished wooden surface was set with a simple supper of meat buns and red bean porridge. Old Jiang made as if to stand to greet us, but he was obviously very weak, and the younger man urged him back into his chair, a standard institutional one of the borrowed type, with Such-and-Such Middle School painted on the back. Representing Old Jiang as host, the younger man began hastily to clear the food away, to our embarrassment, and to search in a cupboard for snacks with which to receive us. Only when we protested vehemently did he return to the table to take up his bowl and chopsticks to finish his meal.

We didn't intend to stay long, so we immediately took out the medications sent by the American professor: a box of packets of high blood pressure medicine; a large assortment of vitamin pills; penicillin; powdered ginseng as an old age tonic . . . it looked as if Old Jiang could use every bit of it.

He wasn't able to speak much, for he was prone to fits of coughing, during which his son would pat his back gently to help him spit. After a fit like this, he would breathe easier again for a few moments, only to begin coughing again if he tried to talk. His hands were pasty and trembling, and he had difficulty feeding himself, so as we spoke, the son tore the steamed buns into pieces with his chopsticks, and lifted them to the father's mouth, one small morsel at a time.

The room was damp and dark, serving as bedroom, kitchen, and sitting room all at once. The young man seemed concerned that we not make a troubling report to the professor about Old Jiang's living conditions, explaining there was some chance that the old man would be given one of the new apartments at the school, with central heating. Then he asked the inevitable hospitable questions about what cities we had visited, about how Judy had learned her Chinese, about the weather in Beijing as compared with where we lived. Old Jiang whispered a question of his own only once, and his son bent his head down to listen closer. "Oh," he said, with apparent reluctance. "His brother said in his letter that you've written a book about the Cultural Revolution?"

We told them that we wrote it because we believed that the tragedy should be recorded and discussed, not sloughed off like a bad dream.

The old man whispered, in a voice so faint that I could barely hear it, "We will always remember in our hearts."

Old Jiang's son seemed oddly uncomfortable about the turn the conversation was taking, and now began busily to pour warm water from a tin kettle into a metal basin, plunging a handtowel into it and wringing it out. "He mustn't get overtired," he explained apologetically, washing his father's face with practiced gentleness. "It's time for you to rest now," he said firmly into the old man's ear.

We stood up to leave, but the young man stopped us, saying, "I'll just put him to bed and go with you. It's easy to get lost in these hutongs." The custom of seeing people out was an unvarying one, and we feared he would feel he had been discourteous if we did not allow him this ritual. We sat down again to wait, watching him prepare his father for bed.

He unfolded the heavy cotton comforter, filled a heavy glass bottle from a hot water thermos, wiping it dry with a towel and placing it beneath the quilt to take off the chill. A medicine vial came from a wardrobe, from which he poured a dark liquid into a spoon for the old man to take obediently in his shrunken mouth. Supporting him by the elbow, he helped him sit on the bed, then gently removed his outermost jacket, pulling first at one thick black sleeve, then the other. He pulled off the shoes, old wool ones, and raised the limp legs onto the bed, unfastening the cotton pants and working them carefully off over the gray knit wool ones in which the old man slept. Then he smoothed the quilt over him, gently tucking it around his feet and neck. I envied the old man for this good son, regretting that my time to care for my own father had been so short.

The young man picked up a heavy coat. "Ready now," he said to us, and to his father, "Sleep well." As we stepped into the courtyard, he pulled the cord to turn out the light.

We walked a while in silence. The young man had pulled his hood up and didn't seem to want to talk. When we reached the first wide street, we told him it was unnecessary to see us out any further.

"It doesn't matter," he answered. "I'm going home anyway."

I was confused—I had thought he might live with his wife and children in another room off the same courtyard. It was unusual that a son let a man so feeble live alone. But perhaps he had no choice but to live at his work unit.

He was a bit of a queer fish, I decided, sometimes friendly and conversational, then suddenly almost sullen. I didn't want to press him. The three of us walked briskly, the young man buried in his thick hood, Judy with her scarf twisted around her head and neck. At last we came out onto Changan Avenue.

"You can find a taxi at that duck restaurant," said the young man pointing across the way to a neon sign in front of which were parked several imported tourist buses for foreigners.

We told him we planned to walk, since the night air was so fresh. Now the broad thoroughfare was very quiet, the dull lamps shining bright on pavement still wet from a passing night sweeper.

"I'll go with you a bit longer, then," he said. "I live over by Chaoyangmen."

"That's quite a distance you have to go to see your father," said Judy. "Do you have supper with him every night?"

The young man hesitated. This ordinary question seemed oddly tough to answer. Several bicycles, bells ringing, came from behind and saved him the necessity of reply. We walked a few more minutes in silence, until we could see Tiananmen Square in the distance. Suddenly he said, "Teacher Jiang isn't really my father, you know. I just call him that. My name is Hu Bo, and I used to be his student." He seemed relieved to have spoken it out at last. "In fact," he said to me, "although you and I are from different cities, we have a lot in common."

He seemed quite natural again. He told us that just now, when the subject of the Cultural Revolution came up, he had been very interested, but feared that the topic might cause Old Jiang to become overexcited. Even more important, he confessed, he lacked the face to discuss the events of the past in his teacher's presence. "You and I share the same past," he said. "But now you don't live in China anymore, and you don't have to deal with the people who lived through it with you. It's easy for you to say it should be remembered. But as for me, I usually want to bury it forever."

When the Cultural Revolution began, he told us, he was just graduating from upper middle school, and was preparing to take the examinations for Beijing University's Chinese literature department. He was from a workers' family—his father was at a steel plant, his mother manufactured textiles. If he was accepted, he would be the first in the history of his family to attend college.

He was interested in literature and had read a great many historical novels, poems, and traditional legends. When his special aptitude was discovered by his Chinese teacher, Old Jiang, he received special encouragement. Teacher Jiang was a devoted instructor. He often urged his students to become professors, engineers, scholars, and writers. "He used to say, 'The more famous you are, the prouder I will be.'" As Hu recalled this, his voice grew quiet and came close to breaking.

Although dedicated to all of his students, Teacher Jiang corrected Hu Bo's compositions particularly carefully, and once nominated him for an essay-writing contest open to Beijing's middle-school students. Young Hu won, and his parents brought a bottle of good liquor to Teacher Jiang's house to express their thanks. When Hu was reviewing for the examinations, Teacher Jiang invited him to his home after dinner for private coaching.

The teacher's daughter, also preparing for the exams, used to study together with him. The three of them spent hours in that room we had just visited, sitting around that same small square table. Young Hu found himself observing the girl secretly, her intelligent demeanor and pretty face, smelling her clean scent as they sat across from each other, learning the grammar of ancient times and looking quickly away when they accidentally met each other's eyes.

Then the Cultural Revolution broke out, and the hopes of Hu Bo's parents, of Teacher Jiang, of the daughter, and of Hu himself were dashed. The ambition to become a scholar became not only an impossibility but a crime. The universities were filled with cries of revolution; it would be a full ten years before students were once again enrolled in universities on the basis of ability.

But Hu Bo had another, even more glorious route open to him, because of his "good" working class background. His parents' lack of education was no longer a handicap to him but a source of pride. The battle lines were clear, with students of "bad" background and teachers on one side, the scions of the revolution on the other. Workers' and revolutionary cadres' children became masters of the middle school.

Considered the most dangerous "reactionary scholarly authority" of all was Teacher Jiang. His crimes were innumerable: he had encouraged students to become famous, so he was deliberately poisoning the revolutionary new generation with elitist ideas; he was from a landlord background, so his bourgeois capitalist attitudes were deeply ingrained; he had a younger brother in America, so he was an imperialist spy. Fully one-fourth of all the big character posters that covered the school walls denounced him; he was locked in a classroom between struggle sessions, only rarely permitted to see his family.

Hu Bo's hesitations were swept away by the mass revolutionary fervor and his desire to protect Chairman Mao. There was no middle ground. He had to become an activist or risk being accused of lagging behind, and his feeling for Mao quickly overcame his respect for Jiang. His parents had been saved by Mao from poverty, and their great, unquestioning reverence for Mao's authority had been instilled in him from childhood.

When the first Red Guard groups were organized in his school, he bacame a minor leader. By this time he was convinced that Teacher Jiang's encouragement of his studies had truly been intended to infect him with dangerous notions. It seemed quite natural, even glorious, to stand up in criticism sessions to repudiate Old Jiang, and to tell stories of the pernicious private tutoring sessions.

As Hu came to this part of his story, we arrived in Tiananmen Square, with its great, desolate expanse of concrete and stone. It was deserted, except for a few pairs of lovers, slowly pushing their bicycles as they walked side by side. The Martyrs' Monument looked large, lonely, and obscene. By unspoken agreement, we strolled toward it, memories linking me to Hu.

After several months, Hu recalled, Chairman Mao issued a new slogan, "If you don't attack what is reactionary, it will not fall down." Each day, the students promenaded their teachers in humiliation, making them clean bathrooms and sweep garbage, beating them publicly. One hot afternoon during a mass criticism session, an elderly physics instructor fainted from the heat. Teacher Jiang met the eyes of his old student, who was supervising the rally, and asked humbly that they be allowed to move into the shade. "I shall never forgive myself," said Hu Bo heavily. "I beat him. I took off my leather belt and beat him until my arm hurt."

Hu Bo sat down at the base of the Martyrs' Monument, the angles of his face illuminated hollowly from below by the surrounding ring of night lights. Judy and I joined him silently. We could feel how this sorrow weighed on his heart.

The relationship between Old Jiang and Hu Bo today was extraordinary, I thought. Most Chinese had little choice but to work sleeve by sleeve with the same people with whom they had lived through the Cultural Revolution, for China's workunit unit system determined that people often spent their entire lives with the same few coworkers. At my old college, middleaged teachers, who had once been on opposite sides in factional warfare, today prepared their lessons in the same small teaching groups; they attended assemblies in the same rooms that had once been used for criticism sessions. One woman I knew lived across the hall from the man responsible for the suicide of her father: she couldn't move away, so she had to suppress her anger and memories, chatting with her neighbor when they happened out on their balconies at the same time to hang their laundry, fetch a coal briquette, or water their plants.

At the *Hunan Daily,* when I was negotiating my father's return, I had been astonished to see how many people I recognized, childhood friends, "aunties" and "uncles," even an old teacher or two. My father attended a "tea and talk" party for retired cadres a few days after he moved in, and among the officials in charge of distributing candies and cigarettes to the old editors I noticed one of the very same radicals who had locked them up and stood guard at their humiliations. Now, the old victims had little choice but to accept his sweets, shake his hand, smile, and ask after his family. They all had to live together. But in their hearts, who knew what emotions raged? Surely few were capable of the kind of friendship that existed between Teacher Jiang and Hu Bo.

Hu Bo continued his story. In late 1968, he said, when the intellectuals were sent away from the cities to the countryside, the only teachers allowed to remain at the school were possible candidates for incarceration, people whose "questions" were not yet "made clear." Old Jiang was among them.

Then one day, Hu Bo escorted a group of teachers to the train station to make sure they departed as scheduled. By sheer chance, amid the huge crowd he spotted Jiang's wife and daughter. He found the girl as beautiful as ever, although her long braided hair had been chopped off into a short bowl. They were under the supervision of another group of Red Guards, probably from the wife's work unit. Apparently they too were being sent away.

All his secret feelings for the girl came back to him in a rush. But he couldn't bear to face her now. After the way he had treated her father she must surely despise him. He tried to hide himself in the crowd, to avoid those pretty brown eyes and intelligent gaze.

But the girl noticed him, and her face brightened as if at the sight of an old friend. She stood up and waved to summon him over. Then her mother nudged her and she sat down and looked the other way—they were being watched. In confusion, Hu Bo stood fast by his own group, and a few minutes later the platform entrance doors opened. As the girl passed through the gate, she turned and looked at him one more time, her eyes full of tears.

Later, Hu realized that her father must never have told his family about what was happening to him at school.

Old Jiang went to prison; Hu Bo became an increasingly influential political leader. Then he himself was sent to the countryside, as an "educated youth," to a rubber-producing area in far-away southwestern Yunnan. From the headiness of revolution, he was cast into a life of bitter loneliness and poverty. For the first time, he had a chance to think seriously about Old Jiang and his daughter, and what he had done to them. Many of the other ex-Red Guards sent to the border area with him tried to escape through the hills to Burma and thence to Thailand. Hu Bo had opportunities, but he was set on returning to Beijing.

When his father died in the mid-seventies, Hu Bo was given the chance to take a city job in his place, according to the policy of the time. After six long years of hard rural life, he was assigned a job as a ticket seller on an electrified tram line. Dull as it was, he threw himself into the work, trying to make something of his life again. He tried to forget, to repress his angry thoughts about the education he had lost that came flooding forth whenever the tram passed the universities in the northwest part of the city. At home, he cared for his aging mother as best he could.

Some months later, he learned from a classmate that Old Jiang's daughter had been sent to Heilongjiang, China's coldest province; there she had become desperately ill and died in an epidemic—she had been unable to get adequate medical treatment. Her mother died soon after. The classmate also told him that Teacher Jiang was now living alone in his old home and had been in failing health since his release from prison in 1971, during the slight liberalization following the Lin Biao Incident. "As soon as I heard, I wanted to go," said Hu Bo. "But I felt guilty. If I couldn't explain my actions to myself, how could I have faced him?"

Then one day, by sheer chance, Hu Bo had an errand to do in Old Jiang's district, and he ran into him on the street. His teacher looked so different, so much older and thinner, limping with a cane, that Hu was a few feet away before he realized who he was. He turned his head down and tried to pass without speaking, but it was too late: Old Jiang had recognized him. He called out to him, and Hu Bo had to stop. "To my great shame, he greeted me warmly," said Hu Bo with emotion. "He made me come with him to his room and gave me tea. When I tried to apologize for the past, he didn't even want to hear me: he said I had been only a child then, and could hardly be blamed for what had happened.

"From then on, my course became clear. I treated him like my own father." Hu Bo paused, and said simply, "You see, he has no one else."

I had never met anyone before who had chosen such a direct route for atoning for his crimes; few were prepared to confront their roles in the tragedy. Everywhere, you could meet victims, but few confessed that they had been victimizers as well. Still, I understood why Hu Bo could not speak of the past with Teacher Jiang. The scars were too deep to heal.

We had been sitting on the cold stone for so long that I had begun to shiver. We seemed to have attracted the attention of one of the green-coated military sentries on duty, and he walked by to take a curious look at us, staying at an unobtrusive distance. Hu Bo must have felt the time too, for he raised his hand to look at his watch, and exclaimed, "I have to hurry. My last bus leaves in a few minutes."

We walked him to his stop, past the Mao Mausoleum to Qianmen. Hu Bo grew reticent again, as if embarrassed to have spoken so much to strangers; at the same time, he seemed sorry to say goodbye. I was reluctant to let him go, too, for his story had evoked a flood of thoughts, and now there was no time to express them—the headlights of his bus were already flashing in the distance. "I'm glad to have met you," Hu Bo told us with sudden warmth, shaking hands before he boarded. "I hope we'll have other opportunities." Then he added, as if he had just remembered the occasion of our visit, "Tell Teacher Jiang's brother not to worry, he's being taken care of." He climbed in, the bus nearly empty at this late hour, and found a seat by the window. We stood and watched as his white hand, waving farewell, moved out of sight.

Perhaps because I hadn't shared my own memories, my mood was heavy. Judy and I walked slowly back through the square. Again we passed the Mao Mausoleum, the white marble edifice seeming unusually large and empty in the deserted concrete plain, like a vanity. Perhaps it appeared that way because it was still inhabited by a single man. I had no desire to linger nearby: Hu Bo's story was connected with Him too directly.

It was a sad and difficult paradox, I thought: our survival as a nation depended in many ways on whether the lessons of the Cultural Revolution could be transmitted to future generations. At the same time, Hu Bo and his teacher's relationship proved that it was essential that people do their best to forget, to put the anger behind them. Tragedies like that of Hu Bo and his teacher were common in many Chinese families, to different degrees. Why they had occurred was a question that Chinese of our century had to face.

To my mind, there was a long list of complex contributing factors: thousands of years of feudal tradition of obedience to authority; the Communist party's tight control of us; the many years of emphasis on political movements, which made us well-practiced machines for criticism/self-criticism; the special privileges and abuses of power by the new party elite, which elicited our envy and thirst for revenge; the lack of routes for expressing discontent and appealing injustices, which made us feel so bottled up inside; Mao's taste for categorizing people as members of ranked classes, exacerbating tensions . . . of course, the struggles within the party leadership over which road to socialism China should follow contributed to Mao's own paranoiac and desperate acts. But no matter which of these factors were most important, it seemed clear to me that as they flowed together tragedy was inevitable.

Even in my short lifetime, China had seen changes as extreme as those in any country I could think of. Looking toward the feeble light on the gate tower, I reflected that many of the actors in these changes had played their roles right here in Tiananmen Square, the very symbol of China's heart and soul.

In 1966 I had come here with thousands of others to stand in front of the portrait of Chairman Mao and swear my undying fealty. Here, I had joined a sea of Red Guards struggling for a glimpse of our Great Helmsman—perhaps Hu Bo too had been in the crowd. Here Mao had set the country on fire and forced nearly everyone into one of two roles: victim or victimizer.

Ten years later in 1976, also here in Tiananmen, tens of thousands of people who like me had lived through violence, struggle, family upheaval, hunger, and the insanity of leftist policies gathered in an illegal protest against the Cultural Revolution and the dictatorship of Mao. They all focused their attention on the speakers at the Martyrs' Monument where we three had just been sitting. The occasion was April 5, the traditional day of mourning for the dead, but the Gang of Four had decreed that there would be no ceremonies commemorating the recent death of Premier Zhou Enlai, who was known throughout China for his moderate views and protection of intellectuals and cultural relics. It is said that it took three days to wash away the blood spilled that day, but the sacrifice was well made: few doubt that it prepared the way for the events of that autumn, after Mao's death, when Tiananmen celebrated the fall of the Gang of Four. Now, nearly twenty years since the beginning of the Cultural Revolution, and ten since the death of Mao, a new revolution was under way, a modernization revolution. Not long ago, in yet another parade, a high-tech robot had been trundled through this great square as if to symbolize still more radical changes. As Judy and I had learned in recent months, the effects of these changes were being felt among all Chinese, from the poorest Hunan peasant to the dissident recently out of prison; from the most ordinary neighborhood noodle seller to the most thoughtful artist or intellectual.

Now the nightmare was over. Mao was truly dead, lying waxed and slowly shrinking not one hundred yards away. Most of the huge white statues and portraits of him were long gone, and his body would soon be joined in that hideous white mausoleum by other corpses whose lives had been less sinister in their effects. But in the excitement of earning money, modernizing, and enlivening the economy, I wondered how many people were like Hu Bo? After the long nightmare, how many were looking seriously at themselves, beginning with the basic question of their behavior toward other human beings? I knew that in China the clouds of the past would not dissipate, not for the next fifty years at least, for too many of us had been shaped during that terrible era, and our relationships with each other and our attitudes to the world around us had been affected too deeply.

Of course, anyone could see that the reforms, within the limitations of socialism, were putting China on a better course. But if you looked deeper, even in this golden time of growth and relaxation of controls, you would still discover just below the surface many of the familiar failings, habits, and distortions of reality that had brought the nightmare upon us in the first place. It was easy to fear that the seeds of new disasters lay amid the optimism, and that China's way into the modern world was still bound to be a troubled one.

A Note from the Authors:

Our collaboration is unusually complex and interdependent. Although we have chosen to write in the voice of Liang Heng, responsibility for this work is shared by both of us.

Liang Heng and Judith Shapiro

36. Deng Xiaoping

NEO-AUTHORITARIANISM

It is known that the controversial theory of neo-authoritarianism on the mainland has recently been noticed by CCP leader Deng Xiaoping. This 85-year-old statesman held that the modernization process in a backward country needs strongman politics with authority rather than Western-style democracy as a driving force.

According to sources concerned, since the debate on neo-authoritarianism developed in the mainland press last January, scholars have been continuously discussing this issue which has a bearing on the orientation of China's political structural reform. In late February, the influential Beijing Young Economists' Association and the China Economic Structural Reform Research Institute, when mentioning China's political reform, explicitly announced in the "Summary of the Symposium on the National Economic Situation" that "China needs an authoritative supreme leading group which can rally the social elite and the nation in this complicated environment to firmly and rhythmically advance this historic reform." Today, the debate has attracted attention from the top CPC leadership.

According to informed sources here, on March 6, when talking about work arrangements, Zhao Ziyang told Deng Xiaoping that there is a theory about neo-authoritarianism in foreign countries, and that domestic theoretical circles are now discussing this theory. The main point of this theory is that there should be a certain stage in the modernization process of a backward country wherein the driving force should come from strongman politics with authority and Western-style democracy should not be adopted.

Deng Xiaoping then said: This is also my idea. However, Deng Xiaoping had reservations about the term neo-authoritarianism. He said that the specific word for this notion can be reconsidered.

It is learned that the rumor about Deng Xiaoping's support for the theory of neo-authoritarianism has been quietly circulated among intellectuals in Beijing but it has not been officially confirmed. People here hold that the debate in mainland theoretical circles on neo-authoritarianism will not stop due to Deng Xiaoping expressing his attitude. The debate will continue in depth in connection with China's political realities.

Source: Zhongguo Tongxam She (China news organization) (Hong Kong) (April 7, 1989); FBIS, April 7, p. 15. Reprinted by permission of M.E. Sharpe, Inc., Armonk, New York 10504.

37. Fang Lizhi

CHINA NEEDS DEMOCRACY

In China, 1989 is the year of the snake. Though it is not certain that this snake will present any great temptations, the following is at least to be expected: The year will prompt the Chinese to examine their past more thoroughly and to take a more penetrating look at the present. The year will mark both the seventieth anniversary of the May 1919 Movement (an intellectual and political movement of prime importance against a background of nationalism and Western cultural influence) and the 40th anniversary of the founding of socialist China. These two anniversaries can serve as eloquent symbols of China's hope and despair.

These forty years of socialism have left the people in a state of dependence. In the fifties, watchwords such as "only socialism can save China" or "there is no New China without the Communist Party" were as readily accepted as laws of physics. Now a glance at the "New" China suggests that the naïve sincerity of those years and the people's enthusiasm have been betrayed.

Of course, the past forty years have not been entirely devoid of change or progress. However, the comparative criterion for measuring the failure or success of a society should be this: Has the distance between China and the world's most advanced societies increased or not? In light of this question, not only have the forty years of Maoist China been a failure but even the past ten "years of reform" have produced nothing to justify a chorus of praise.

The failure of the past forty years cannot be attributed—at least not entirely— to China's cultural tradition. The facts clearly show that almost all of the other nations proceeding from bases similar to China's have already joined, or are about to join, the ranks of the developed countries.

Nor can this failure be attributed to China's overpopulation. First, we must recognize that this overpopulation is itself one of the "political successes" of the Maoist years. It was Mao's policy in the 1950s to oppose birth control (regarded as a "bourgeois Malthusian doctrine") and to encourage rapid population growth. Furthermore, as everyone knows, one of the major factors retarding China's economic development has been the great succession of "class struggle" campaigns and large-scale political persecutions. Are we to believe that every overpopulated society necessarily produces such struggles and persecutions? Such a view is clearly illogical.

Logic leads to only one conclusion: the disappointments of the past forty years must be attributed to the social system itself. This is why in China today the pursuit of modernization has replaced faith in ideology. Socialism, in its Lenin-Stalin-Mao version, has been entirely discredited. At the same time, the May 4th Movement slogan "science and democracy" is being reintro-

Source: From *Libération* (Paris) (January 17, 1989): 5; FBIS, January 27, pp. 14-16. Reprinted by permission of M.E. Sharpe, Inc., Armonk, New York 10504.

duced and becoming a new source of hope for Chinese intellectuals.

The reforms of the past years, undertaken within the context of this ideological transition, have considerably changed China, which is no longer that of the Maoist period. We must regard these changes as positive. The emphasis now being placed on the economy in domestic policy and on ending "the exporting of the revolution" in foreign policy are two important instances of progress. Having said that, the banning of the "wall of democracy" nine years ago created the depressing feeling that when it comes to political reforms the authorities do not intend to do much.

Although the Chinese Constitution guarantees freedom of speech and other human rights, the Chinese Government has hitherto not always adhered to the UN human rights charter. In current practice, even a basic right such as the right to knowledge, which has little political impact, is frequently held in contempt. There are cases—some very recent—of natural science courses being banned for political reasons.

Chinese education, which for years suffered the ravages of Mao's anti-intellectual and anti-cultural political principles, has left China with a population in which the proportion of illiterates is the same as forty years ago. Nevertheless current education spending, as a proportion of China's GNP, is exactly the same as under Mao—30-50 percent lower than in countries on an economic par with China.

In recent years the authorities have stepped up their appeals for "stability" and "unity," especially since the emergence of signs of political unrest. Stability and unity seem to have been elevated to the status of supreme principles. However, when it comes to one of the prime causes of the instability in Chinese society— the state of civil war maintained with Taiwan—this supreme principle no longer applies. In its attempt to end the forty-year-old state of war, the Chinese Government has hitherto refused—at least in theory—to accept the principle of relinquishing the use of military force against Taiwan.

These various problems have created a constant conflict under the surface of Chinese society. The 1986 student demonstrations openly demanding freedom and democracy only brought these conflicts to the surface. In their efforts to minimize the impact of these demonstrations, the authorities were forced to resort to the following arguments: (1) Chinese culture lacks a democratic tradition and therefore cannot tolerate a democratic system. (2) Economic development does not necessarily require a democratic system. Indeed, a dictatorial system can be more efficient in this regard. What would suit China best is a dictatorial policy plus a free economy.

The brandishing of these arguments revives public awareness that what we have now is not a democracy but a dictatorship. If this is so, however, how can Marxism retain its place in China's orthodox ideology?

The first of these arguments could be called "the law of conservation of democracy." It implies that a society's "maximum level of democracy" can be fixed. If there is no democracy to start with there will be none subsequently either. Of course nobody has tried to prove this law because there are too many examples to the contrary. The argument cannot save the dictatorship in China but it can provide some comic relief.

The second argument does seem to be better corroborated by the facts. There really do seem to be some societies that have succeeded in combining political dictatorship with a free economy. However, there are also some examples of failure among them. It follows that the issue cannot be decided simply by listing precedents but must be treated specifically in China's own particular case. Can a free economy be compatible with the specifically Chinese form of dictatorial government? A glance at the China of 1988 proves that, broadly speaking, the answer is "no."

First, China differs from other countries in that its system of dictatorship cannot accept an entirely free economy. This is because the socialist dictatorship is entirely bound to a system of "collective ownership" (actually official ownership) and its ideology is fundamentally antithetical to the kind of rights of ownership required by a free economy. Furthermore, it has already been shown—twice, rather than once that China's dictatorial system lacks efficiency. It is enough to consider the corruption within the Communist Party itself to realize this. The ten years of "correction of party conduct" have in fact produced only an annual increase in the numbers of "unhealthy tendencies." Our minimum conclusion could be as follows: we need the public to be able to perform a greater role and we need a more independent judiciary. In practice this means more democracy.

China's hope for the present lies in the fact that more and more people have abandoned blind faith in the government. They have realized that the only way to social progress depends on the public's adopting a "supervisory" role. It should have the right to openly express criticisms of the authorities. The editor of a Canton journal recently wrote that his journal's role is to speak not on the Communist Party's behalf but on behalf of an emergent Cantonese middle class. The old idea that "you must not oppose your superiors" is losing ground. Democratic awareness is making headway. Democracy is more than a slogan; it is exerting its own pressure. The aim of this pressure is to force the authorities, gradually and by nonviolent means, to accept changes in the direction of political democracy and a free economy.

Since the period of the May 4th Movement in 1919, China's history (including the forty years since 1949) has proved this idea that democracy cannot be promulgated from above but that it is necessary to fight to gain it. We must not expect this to change in the decades ahead. However, it is precisely because democracy comes from below that, despite the many frustrations and disappointments of our present situation, I am still hopeful about the future.

38. A DOCUMENT CIRCULATED AMONG SENIOR PARTY AND GOVERNMENT OFFICIALS EARLIER THIS MONTH

APRIL 25, 1989

On the morning of April 25, 1989, (Prime Minister) Li Peng and (President) Yang Shangkun reported to Deng Xiaoping on the situation in Beijing. The Beijing Municipal Party Committee requested that the Central Committee give them the authority to broadly mobilize the masses to struggle with the opposing force, that is, the people behind the students.

Deng Xiaoping said, "This is not an ordinary student movement, but turmoil. So we must have a clear-cut stand and implement effective measures to quickly oppose and stop this unrest. We cannot let them have their way.

"Those people who have been influenced by the liberal elements of Yugoslavia, Poland, Hungary, and the Soviet Union have arisen to create turmoil. Their motive is to overthrow the leadership of the Communist Party and to forfeit the future of the country and the nation.

"We must move quickly to adopt preemptive measures in order to gain time. Shanghai's attitude was clear and they won time. We must not be afraid of people cursing us, of a bad reputation, or of international reaction. Only if China truly develops, and implements the four modernizations, can we have a real reputation.[1]

"The Four Basic Principles are indispensable. Comrade Yaobang was weak; and retreated; he did not truly carry through the campaign against bourgeois liberalization. At the end of 1986 [sic?], the purge against spiritual pollution petered out after only twenty-odd days.

"If we had effectively acted at that time, then the state of mind of the general public would not have developed into what exists today. It is impossible to avoid minor turmoil. That could have been handled separately, and would not have developed into what exists today. Now the Central Committee is forced to interfere and resolve the problem from the center.

"Among the Four Basic Principles, there is one—the people's democratic dictatorship. We need to use this one. Of course, we want to use it appropriately and minimize the crackdown.

"Now, we must be especially careful to prevent the unrest from spreading to middle schools. Maintaining stability in middle schools is very important. The workers are stable. Of course, there are some unstable factors. There is no problem with the peasants. We also must pay attention to the stability of other sectors of society. We must keep Beijing informed of this.

"This turmoil is entirely a planned conspiracy to transform a China with a bright future into a China without hope. The major harm is to negate the leadership of the Communist Party and to negate the socialist system. A dialogue can be held, but we cannot tolerate incorrect behavior. Pretending to overlook the problem will not solve it. That will only fan the names.

"We must do our best to avoid bloodshed, but we should foresee that it might not be pos-

Source: From *South China Morning Post* (Hong Kong) (May 31, 1989):12; FBIS, May 31, pp. 35-36. Reprinted by permission of M.E. Sharpe, Inc., Armonk, New York 10504.

sible to completely avoid bloodshed. In Georgia, the Soviet Union made a few concessions but failed to solve the problems. There was turmoil in Moscow, and the result was that they still have to arrest people. Other places in the Soviet Union could still erupt.

"The suggestions of the Beijing Municipal Party Committee is correct. The attitude of the Central Committee should be clear, and then the Beijing Municipal Party Committee's task would be easier. The turmoil this time is definitely national in scope, and we must not underestimate it. We must issue a forceful editorial and make use of the law.

"It is a shame that we have wasted time. They (the students) are using the rights of democracy and freedom in the Constitution to impose restrictions on us. Beijing has ten regulations concerning demonstrations—let's use these ten points to restrain them. We must prepare ourselves to enter into a nation-wide struggle, and resolutely crush the turmoil. Otherwise, there will be no peaceful days, indeed peace will be lost forever.

"I told (American President George) Bush, if China allows demonstrations with so many people in such a big country, how can we talk of stability? If there is no stability, nothing can be achieved.

"Now, there are some people doing the same old thing, just like the rebellion faction during the Cultural Revolution. They won't be satisfied until all is chaos. They would burst the bubble of China's hope, and prevent us from continuing economic development and the open door policy, thereby bringing immediate ruin.

"There are 60,000 students boycotting classes, but there are 100,000 who are not. We must protect and support the 100,000. We must lift the threat from their heads. Worker and peasant cadres support us. The democratic parties are good. We also have several million PLA [soldiers]. What are we afraid of? Of the 60,000 (students), many have been forced. The (student organized) monitors are illegal.

"Communist Party and Communist Youth League members should play an active role. The Communist Party organization should play an active role. We must reaffirm the discipline within the party. Party cells in factories, universities, middle schools, and state organs should hold meetings. If it is only students who stir up trouble, that is not a big deal. The main thing is not to let them stir up society as a whole.

"We need to strengthen the Public Security Ministry's work to maintain social order. Comrade Yaobang did make mistakes, but when someone has died, one should say good things about him. Indeed, he did many good things. For example, he supported reform and openness. But he was weak in the face of bourgeois liberalization. Nor was his attitude toward the economy correct. The high speed double digit approach will only produce greater inflation. Now the posthumous evaluation is too high.

"Some people struggle to evaluate him as a great Marxist, but he was not qualified enough. None of us are. After I die, I do not want to be given that title.

"Now the character of the student movement has changed. We need to quickly use a sharp knife to cut the tangled weeds in order to avoid even greater turmoil.

"Concessions in Poland led to further concession. The more they conceded, the more chaos. The opposition faction in Poland is very strong. They have two strong forces, religion and unions. China only has students. The other sectors are better. Your Standing Committee decisions are correct; you have a consensus. Only if you maintain a clear attitude and staunchly carry out measures and support the local leadership by allowing them to handle things, can we then stop this turmoil.

"We should not simply administer the economic environment, we should also administer the political environment. We may have more struggles like this in the future. We have said in the past that of the Four Basic Principles, we can talk less about implementing the people's democratic dictatorship, although we have said that we cannot do without it.

"But now don't you think we need it? In focusing against the Four Basic Principles, the students have grabbed the major point. Without the Four Basic Principles they will become unbridled and brazen, they will run wild.

"Both the Central Committee and the Standing Committee need two different groups—one to focus on construction, another to focus on turmoil. We need to focus our main energy on construction. We can't sink too many people into the other, although in the short term it is all right. Our action cannot be slow, otherwise it will involve more and more people."

In the document, Hu Qili added, "Normally, Xiaoping would revise his own words before putting it into a document, but because time is short, we will first circulate the spirit of his speech."

NOTES

1   The four modernizations are agriculture, industry, science and technology, and national defense—a development strategy advocated by Zhou Enlai in 1975 and subsequently promoted as central to Deng Xiaoping's program.

39. HUNGER STRIKE ANNOUNCEMENT

In this bright sunny month of May, we are on a hunger strike. In this best moment of our youth, we have no choice but to leave behind us everything beautiful about life. But how reluctant, how unwilling we are!

However, the country has come to this juncture: rampant inflation; widespread illegal business dealings by corrupt officials; the dominance of abusive power; the corruption of bureaucrats; the fleeing of a large number of good people to other countries; and the deterioration of law and order. Compatriots and all fellow countrymen with a conscience, at this critical moment of life and death of our people, please listen to our voice:

This country is our country,
The people are our people.
The government is our government.
Who will shout if we don't?
Who will act if we don't?

Although our shoulders are still tender, although death for us is still seemingly too harsh to bear, we have to part with life. When history demands us to do so, we have no choice but to die.

Our national sentiment at its purest and our loyalty at its best are labeled as "chaotic disturbance"; as "with an ulterior motive"; and as "manipulated by a small gang."

We request all honorable Chinese, every worker, peasant, soldier, ordinary citizen, intellectual, and renowned individuals, government officials, police and those who fabricated our crimes to put their hands over their hearts and examine their conscience: what crime have we committed? Are we creating chaotic disturbances? We walk out of classrooms, we march, we hunger strike, we hide. Yet our feelings are betrayed time after time. We bear the suffering of hunger to pursue the truth, and all we get is the beatings of the police. When we kneel down to beg for democracy, we are being ignored. Our request for dialogue on equal terms is met with delay after delay. Our student leaders encounter personal dangers.

What do we do?

Democracy is the most noble meaning of life; freedom is a basic human right. But the price of democracy and freedom is our life. Can the Chinese people be proud of this?

We have no other alternative but to hunger strike. We have to strike.

It is with the spirit of death that we fight for life.

But we are still children, we are still children! Mother China, please take a hard look at your children. Hunger is ruthlessly destroying their youth. Are you really not touched when death is approaching them?

We do not want to die. In fact, we wish to continue to live comfortably because we are in

Source: Originally printed at Tiananmen Square in *Xiwen daobao* (News express), May 12, 1989; reprinted in *Zhongguo Zhichun* (China spring) (New York) 75 (August 1989): 11-12. Reprinted by permission of M.E. Sharpe, Inc., Armonk, New York 10504.

the prime years of our lives. We do not wish to die; we want to be able to study properly. Our homeland is so poor. It seems irresponsible of us to desert our homeland to die. Death is definitely not our pursuit. But if the death of a single person or a number of persons would enable a larger number of people to live better, or if the death can make our homeland stronger and more prosperous, then we have no right to drag on an ignoble existence.

When we are suffering from hunger, moms and dads, please don't be sad. When we bid farewell to life, uncles and aunts, please don't be heart-broken. Our only hope is that the Chinese people will live better. We have only one request: please don't forget that we are definitely not after death. Democracy is not the private matter of a few individuals, and the enterprise of building democracy is definitely not to be accomplished in a single generation.

It is through death that we await a far-reaching and perpetual echo by others.

When a person is about to die, he speaks from his heart. When a horse is to die, its cries are sad.

Farewell comrades, take care, the same loyalty and faith bind the living and dead

Farewell loved ones, take care. I don't want to leave you, but I have to part with life.

Farewell moms and dads, please forgive us. Your children cannot have loyalty to our country and filial piety to you at the same time.

Farewell fellow countrymen, please permit us to repay our country in the only way left to us. The pledge that is delivered by death will one day clear the sky of our republic.

The reasons of our hunger strike are: first, to protest the cold and apathetic attitude of our government towards the students' strike; second, to protest the delay of our higher learning; and third, to protest the government's continuous distortions in its reporting of this patriotic and democratic movement of students and their labeling it as "chaotic disturbance."

The demands from the hunger strikers are: first, on an equal basis, the government should immediately conduct concrete and substantial dialogues with the delegation of Beijing institutes of higher learning. Second, the government should give this movement a correct name, a fair and unbiased assessment, and should affirm that this is a patriotic and democratic students' movement.

The date for the hunger strike is 2:00 P.M., May 13; location, Tiananmen Square.

This is not a chaotic disturbance. Its name should be immediately rectified. Immediate dialogue! No more delays! Hunger strike for the people! We have no choice. We appeal to world opinion to support us. We appeal to all democratic forces to support us.

Beijing, China

40. Zhao Ziyang and Li Peng

IMPORTANT NEWS:
ZHAO ZIYANG AND LI PENG VISIT FASTING STUDENTS AT TIANANMEN SQUARE

Announcer— Zhao Ziyang general secretary of the CCP Central Committee and Li Peng premier of the State Council at 4:45 this morning [19:45 GMT May 18] went to Tiananmen Square to see students who are on a hunger strike and to sincerely urge them to end their fast in order to protect their health.

Begin recording. Video report begins by showing Zhao Ziyang and Li Peng shaking hands with fasting students seated on a bus. Zhao and Li extend regards to the students.

Li Peng— Where do you go to school?
Unidentified student— I am from Teachers' University.
Li Peng— And you?
Second unidentified student— Teachers' University.
Li Peng— You are all students at Teachers' University.

Video shows one of the students maintaining order asking fellow students to make way for Zhao Ziyang and Li Peng to step off the bus.

Third unidentified student— Back up please.

Video shows a very tired Zhao Ziyang speaking through a small megaphone handed to him by a student.

Ziyang— I want to say a few words to the students. We have come too late.
Fourth unidentified student— You have finally come.
Ziyang— I am sorry fellow students. No matter how you have criticized us I think you have the right to do so. We do not come here to ask you to excuse us.

Source: Beijing Television Service, 23:30 GMT, May 18, 1989; FBIS, May 19, pp. 13-14. Reprinted by permission of M.E. Sharpe, Inc., Armonk, New York 10504.

All I want to say is that the fasting students are physically very weak now. Your fasting has entered its seventh day. This simply cannot go on. If the fasting lasts longer, the damage to the students' health will be irremediable, and their lives will be in danger. This is understood by everyone. The only thing—the most important thing—to do now is to immediately terminate this fasting.

I know your fasting is aimed at obtaining a very satisfactory answer to the issues you put forward to the government and the party. I think that a satisfactory answer is obtainable because the channel for our dialogue is still open. Some issues can be solved only through a process. Some issues—for example, the nature of your action—I feel can be eventually solved. We can reach a consensus. As you all know, many things involve complicated situations. It takes a process to solve them. You just cannot fast for six or seven days and adhere to the idea that your fast will not be terminated unless you receive a satisfactory answer, because if you end your fast only when you receive a satisfactory answer, it will be too late.

Your health will be irreparable. You are still young, fellow students. You still have ample time. You should live healthily and live to see the day when China completes the four modernizations. You are not like us, who are old. It is not easy for the state and your parents to nurture you and send you to college. How can you, at the age of only eighteen or nineteen, or in your twenties, sacrifice your lives like this? Just use your head and think. I am not here today to hold a dialogue with you. Today I just want you fellow students to use reason and try to understand what a serious situation is now facing us.

You all know the party and the state are now very worried. The entire society is [words indistinct]. All of Beijing is talking about your action. Moreover, as you all know, this situation in Beijing simply cannot go on anymore. This city of ours, the capital of China, is facing more and more grave situations every day. You comrades all have good intentions to do something good for the country, but this strike which has happened and is out of control, has affected everything—communications, transport, work, and the regular patients who want to see doctors.

In short, when you end your fast, the government will never close the door to dialogues, never. If you have questions, we will solve them. Despite what you say and the fact that we are a little late, we are getting closer to solving the problems. We are getting there step-by-step. That is all for now. My main purpose is to see the comrades here and express my feelings. I hope you comrades soberly think about this question. Those comrades who have organized the fast should also think soberly. Fasting is not something that can go on without reason.

We were once young, and we all had such a burst of energy. We also staged demonstrations and I know the situation at that time. We did not think of the consequences. You should soberly think of things in the future. The sixth day is gone and the seventh day is here. Will the fasting really go on for the eighth, ninth, and tenth days? I say many things can eventually be solved. If you want to wait for that day, the day you receive a satisfactory answer, then you should end the fast early. Thank you, comrades. I just wanted to see you all.

Video shows students surrounding Zhao Ziyang and asking for his autograph; Zhao is shown signing his name on a handkerchief, a notebook, and a piece of cloth handed to him by students. End recording.

Announcer—   Also visiting students at Tiananmen Square were Wen Jiabao alternate member of the Secretariat of the CPC Central Committee, and Luo Gan, secretary general of the State Council. The Tiananmen Square students' hunger strike has entered the seventh day. Many of the students are physically very feeble and weak. Yesterday evening and this early morning, many fasting students fainted and were rushed by medical personnel to hospitals for treatment.

41. Wu Ye

WHAT DOES THE STATUE OF THE *GODDESS OF DEMOCRACY* WHICH APPEARED IN TIANANMEN SQUARE INDICATE?

Some people erected a statue of the "Goddess of Democracy" without authorization in dignified Tiananmen Square and this evoked various comments among the people. According to the people's common sense, the erection of any monument in Tiananmen Square must first be approved by the government and must based on a relevant government decree.

In the square the Tiananmen rostrum, the flagpoles, the Monument to the People's Heroes, the memorial hall, the museum, and the Great Hall of the People are all built in good order and the layout is serious and solemn. The square is a site to hold grand ceremonies and major state activities and is an important place for domestic and foreign tourists to visit with reverence. It is the heart of the People's Republic and is the focus of the world's attention.

All citizens have the duty to cherish and protect Tiananmen Square. This is equal to cherishing and protecting our motherland and our nation and to cherishing and protecting our own rights. The square is sacred. No one has the power to add any permanent memorial or to remove anything from the square. Such things not be allowed to happen in China. Even in foreign countries, including some Western countries, similar things are not permitted.

The feelings of the young students who hope to promote the construction of democracy are understandable. Advancing socialist democratic politics is also the hope of all people throughout the country and the objective of the party and government's efforts. The positive demands raised by the young students play a role in promoting the realization of this objective. However, the erection of a statue of the "Goddess of Democracy" by some people in Tiananmen Square was not a positive action in seeking freedom and democracy; instead, it was a serious distortion of freedom and democracy and showed disrespect for other people's free and democratic rights. Freedom can only exist within the limits permitted by the law. When a citizen exercises his rights and uses his freedom he must not impair state, social, or collective interests and must not infringe upon other citizen's freedoms and rights. No one should be able to act as perversely as one likes.

Source: *Renmin ribao* (People's daily) (Beijing) (June 1, 1989): 1; FBIS, June 1, p. 28. Reprinted by permission of M.E. Sharpe, Inc., Armonk, New York 10504.

42. THE MAY 15 PETITION

On December 20, 1993, the United Nations General Assembly passed Resolution 48/126, proclaiming 1995 "The United Nations Year of Tolerance" in order to commemorate the fiftieth anniversary of the founding of the United Nations and to promote the basic spirit of the aim of the United Nations: tolerance. Our country is a founding member of the United Nations and is a permanent, veto-bearing member of the Security Council. Thus it should conscientiously implement this resolution and allow the spirit of tolerance, with which our country is relatively unfamiliar, to take root and flourish in areas like our country's politics, thought, region, culture, and education.

Tolerance is a mark of human civilization, and is the foundation and precondition of modern civilization. In the West, enlightened thinkers realized the responsibility of tolerance during the long battle fought against the autocracy of rule by divine right during the Middle Ages. Those who obtained political authority thereafter did not follow the old route of autocratic monarchy, but formed governments on the basis of respect for the rights and freedom of individual citizens. They did not insist upon ideological uniformity, but tolerated different ideas, beliefs, customs, and behaviors, allowing minorities of people the freedom to hold and publicize opinions (whether political, religious, scientific, cultural, or other types) that diverged from the majority. It was because of this spirit of tolerance that competing schools of thought developed in science and culture, which gave rise to a flourishing intellectual scene that has persisted throughout the years. The kind of thinking that viewed "heterodoxy" as a great scourge upon the people and led to the public burning of Bruno and the arrest and persecution of Galileo was abandoned, and this type of great historical tragedy was not repeated.

Turning our gaze to our own ancient culture, an intolerance of dissenting voices has gone on for thousands of years right down to the present day with no sign of weakening. In 1955, [the writer] Hu Feng and several of his companions were charged with the crime of "forming a counterrevolutionary clique" after they submitted a letter stating their view on literature and art. Over 2,000 others were soon implicated as well. In 1957 more than 11 percent of all the intellectuals in China (at least 550,000 people) who blindly responded to the [party's] call for a "rectification of work style and an airing of views" were labeled "rightists." The 10-year calamity begun in 1966, when a "revolution" in culture was staged, was an even greater national disaster during which dissent was completely wiped out. After 1978 the situation changed somewhat; false accusations were largely redressed, a more relaxed situation began to appear, and the economy began to develop rapidly. But a continued lack of tolerance, which is essential for modernization and "reform and opening up" in the true sense of those terms, resulted in the events of June 4, 1989—that human tragedy that shocked the world—as well as subsequent incidents in violation of citizens' basic rights.

To mark the United Nations Year of Tolerance, we should do our utmost to propagate this

The May 15 Petition, 1995, was drafted by physicist Xu Liangying and signed by 45 prominent academics. this version appeared in *Current History,* September, 1995, vol. 94, no. 593, pp. 264-5. Reprinted with permission of the translator, *Human Rights for China.*

tolerance, which is necessary to modern civilization, and strive for the true implementation in our country of the United Nations goal to "promote and encourage respect for the human rights and basic freedoms of all mankind" as stipulated in the United Nations Charter.

Accordingly, we hope the authorities will:

1) Treat all views in such areas as ideology, political thought, and religious belief with a spirit of tolerance, and never again regard individuals of independent thought and independent views as "hostile elements," submitting them to repressive attacks, surveillance, house arrest, or even detention.

2) Re-evaluate the June 4, 1989, incident according to the spirit of "seeking truth from facts," and release those people who remain in jail for their involvement in this event.

3) Release all those who have been imprisoned for their thoughts, religious beliefs, or acts of speech, and boldly end the ignominious tradition of literary inquisitions that has persisted in our country since ancient times.

At the same time, we also hope that all of society will, out of respect for others, cultivate a spirit of tolerance, adopt an attitude of reason and fairness when dealing with any form of discord or conflict, use peaceful means to achieve personal ideals and aspirations, avoid sentiments fostering extreme contradictions, and guard against violent behavior. Only in this way will it be possible for our country to move steadily along the path toward democracy and modernization.

Of course, advocating tolerance does not mean maintaining an all-encompassing unity at the expense of principle, or failing to distinguish between true and false, good and evil. Nor does it mean indulgence of moral degeneration or threats to society. Tolerance is inseparable from the concepts of modern democracy, freedom, human rights, rule of law, and so on; these are all complementary to one another. Tolerance is the essential meaning of democratic government and the condition for political democratization. Tolerance embodies a respect for human rights and freedom, yet is bounded by moral codes and law. Corruption has become a wind blowing through our country, and the trading of money for power, the embezzlement of public funds and other forms of corruption are found everywhere. We must do everything possible to remove and severely punish these thieves who are bringing disaster to the nation and its people. But it must be recognized that without the supervision of democracy, especially without the supervision provided by independent public opinion, corruption cannot be eliminated. The British historian Lord Acton pointed out as early as 108 years ago that: "Power corrupts, and absolute power corrupts absolutely." The 1789 French "Declaration of Human Rights" states even more clearly, "To ignore, overlook, or scorn human rights is the sole reason for human misfortune and corrupt government." This timeless truth should be commonly understood throughout our nation. To obtain tolerance, we must vigorously carry forward the current struggle against corruption that so deeply concerns our people.

The world needs tolerance; China needs tolerance. We hope that through the various events of the United Nations Year of Tolerance, the state of intolerance that has persisted in our country from ancient times through to the present will begin to change and that tolerance will gradually become the common spiritual wealth of our nation's people.